Bring Me H

SALTWATER AQUARIUMS make A GREAT HOBBY

Howell Book House™

SALTWATER AQUARIUMS make A GREAT HOBBY

John Tullock

Howell Book House
Published by Wiley Publishing, Inc., Hoboken, New Jersey

All color insert photos by Aaron Norman.

For general information on our other products and services or to obtain technical support please contact our Customer Care Department within the U.S. at (800) 762-2974, outside the U.S. at (317) 572-3993 or fax (317) 572-4002.

Wiley also publishes its books in a variety of electronic formats. Some content that appears in print may not be available in electronic books. For more information about Wiley products, please visit our web site at www.wiley.com.

Library of Congress Control Number: 2005024425

ISBN-13 978-0-7645-9659-9
ISBN-10 0-7645-9659-4

Printed in the United States of America

10 9 8 7 6 5 4 3 2 1

Book design by Melissa Auciello-Brogan
Cover design by Suzanne Sunwoo
Book production by Wiley Publishing, Inc. Composition Services

Table of Contents

Introduction

So you want to own a saltwater aquarium? Saltwater aquariums are extremely popular—but they're not for everyone. After reading this book, you'll understand a bit more about what it takes to own a saltwater aquarium and find out if there's one in your future. You'll learn the basics of saltwater aquarium ownership and what you need to do to find the right equipment and healthy fish. Unlike many guides that focus on simple saltwater aquarium ownership, I focus on how a saltwater aquarium will fit into *your* family and *your* life.

This book is intended for the first-time aquarium owner and also for the family looking to add an aquarium to their lives. Inside are checklists, tips, and questionnaires that will help you decide what to do when planning, setting up, and stocking your saltwater aquarium. These tools help you focus on what it takes to own a saltwater aquarium and help you assess your family's—and your saltwater aquarium's—particular situation. Expect to find:

- Worksheets that help you figure out if you're ready for a saltwater aquarium, assist you in finding the right saltwater aquarium, and give important questions to ask dealers.
- Checklists to help you find a suitable location in your house for your saltwater aquarium, figure out what equipment and supplies you need, and decide between a fish-only and a minireef saltwater aquarium
- Information on how to deal with problems, as well as guidelines for proper nutrition for your saltwater aquarium, and common saltwater aquarium mistakes and how to avoid them.
- Step-by-step instructions for setting up and stocking your saltwater aquarium

I hope you use this book as an interactive resource to turn to again and again to help with your decision-making and organization. Each chapter opens and closes with a bulleted list that guides you through the chapter at a glance.

At the back of the book is an appendix titled "Useful Resources." I encourage you to photocopy the forms, punch holes in them using a three-hole punch, and put them in a three-ring binder labeled "Aquarium Records," along with some sheet protectors where you can keep vital records and information about your saltwater aquarium handy at all times. I also include chore lists that you can post on the refrigerator and refer to at any time. As your saltwater aquarium becomes a part of your family, you'll find yourself constantly referring to the notebook. When was the last water change? How did things go with the tank sitter? Do you remember when the anemonefish laid eggs? All of these things and more make up your saltwater aquarium's life and should be written in your notebook. These will enhance your aquarium ownership experience.

With the tools and resources I provide for you, I hope you find the experience of owning a saltwater aquarium an enjoyable one.

Chapter 1

Are You Ready to Get a Saltwater Aquarium?

What's Inside . . .

- Learn how much time you need to devote to a saltwater aquarium.
- Learn how much money you'll spend on an aquarium.
- Learn what kind of knowledge you'll need to maintain an aquarium.
- Learn if an aquarium will make a good fit for you and your family.

Few places on earth captivate our senses as do coral reefs, the "rainforests" of the sea. In the last few decades keeping colorful reef fish and invertebrates in aquariums has become possible for home hobbyists. New technologies and techniques make it easier than ever before to re-create a reef ecosystem in miniature in your living room or den. But before you decide to embrace the saltwater aquarium hobby, you should give some serious thought to the undertaking. A saltwater aquarium requires investing a considerable amount of time and money as well as making the effort to learn about marine organisms and their biology. If you hope to achieve a deep sense of accomplishment watching the ocean's denizens behave in your den as they behave on an authentic reef, considering these factors first is a must.

Lifestyle Impacts

Just as getting a dog or a cat will change your daily routine, getting a saltwater aquarium will alter your life. For example, you'll need to make arrangements for care while you are away. Depending on the length of your stay, this can range from asking a friend to come in and feed the fish to hiring a professional maintenance service to cover an extended trip. On the other hand, fish don't need to be taken out for a walk, paper trained, or taken to the vet for shots. They don't bark at night or dig in your neighbor's flower beds. Some fish will learn to recognize your approach at feeding time, but they won't bounce around joyfully, obviously thrilled that you're home from work. Watching an aquarium can soothe jangled nerves and provide a sense of accomplishment not unlike that artists feel toward their creations, but if you are looking for companionship, you won't find it in an aquarium.

Time Commitment

I mention time commitment first because neglecting maintenance chores inevitably leads to problems. As a former aquarium store owner, I was called upon repeatedly for help in rescuing a saltwater tank from crisis. Almost invariably, the root cause of the difficulty was neglect. When water conditions deteriorate, so does the health of the tank's inhabitants. Water conditions usually do not decline precipitously overnight, nor are they due to being a couple of days late on a scheduled water change. Rather, small episodes of neglect or oversight lead to gradually declining water quality. Problems literally accumulate over time, until the fish become stressed in trying to cope physiologically. Then, bang! A weakened fish develops a parasite infestation. Within days, every fish in the tank is affected.

To keep your saltwater inhabitants healthy and happy, saltwater aquariums require regular and consistent maintenance. The time required to maintain your aquarium depends on the size of the tank. For example, if you have a 30-gallon tank, you'll need about an hour each week to perform routine maintenance, which includes testing and recording water conditions, feeding, cleaning algae off the glass, cleaning the exterior surfaces of the aquarium and its cabinet, and carrying out safety and performance checks on the equipment. In addition to weekly maintenance, about once a month, you need about 4 hours to remove some water and replace it with freshly prepared synthetic seawater. The time for weekly maintenance plus the monthly major water change equals a full workday. A larger tank will require more time. If you plan to make this an important family project, the family should decide if that much leisure time can be spared from other obligations.

If you and your family can manage a regular schedule of feeding and maintenance, an aquarium may be just the project you're looking for. Ask yourself, "Can we commit the time

Average Time Commitments

Following are the time commitments you need to make for small-, medium-, and large-size aquariums:

- For a 30-gallon tank, plan to spend 4 hours for weekly maintenance and 4 hours for monthly maintenance.
- For a 75-gallon tank, plan to spend 6 hours for weekly maintenance and 6 hours for monthly maintenance.
- For a 150-gallon tank, plan to spend 8 hours for weekly maintenance and 8 hours for monthly maintenance.

for this, and will we keep that commitment in the future?" If you answer yes, you greatly improve your odds of success.

With proper care, an established aquarium can provide enjoyment for many years. Some saltwater fish can live to be 20 years old, spending their entire adult lives in the confines of a tank. Others have natural life spans much shorter than this. Invertebrates, too, vary in longevity from a year or two in the case of some small shrimps, to virtual immortality in the case of a coral colony. You may replace several fish or other animals over the course of time, but the aquarium system itself can be perpetuated indefinitely when required maintenance is carried out on a timely schedule.

Financial Commitment

I have actually had saltwater aquarium owners complain to me that the cost of synthetic seawater prohibited them from carrying out a proper schedule of water changes. These individuals fail to take into account that the cost of replacing a tank of fish due to unhealthy water conditions greatly outweighs the cost of making water changes. As with any other aspect of life, there are both wise and foolish ways to save money (or spend it, for that matter) on a saltwater aquarium. Let's consider some of the wise ways.

Initial Costs

Initially, you can expect to spend around $1,000 for a basic saltwater aquarium that will look good, function properly, and enhance your living space. Larger, fancier systems cost considerably more. Consider the differences in initial cost between a 30-gallon basic saltwater system and a 75-gallon minireef system (see the following two tables).

30-Gallon Basic Saltwater System Initial Costs

Item	Cost
Tank	$70.99
36-inch stand (black pine):	$150.99
Lighting system (basic fluorescent strip light):	$32.99
30-watt lamp:	$11.99
Filter system and skimmer:	$59.99
100-watt heater:	$23.99
Seawater mix:	$7.50 (average price is $0.20 to $0.25 per gallon)
Substrate:	$30 (price per pound varies depending on the material, averaging about $1.00 per pound)

continued

30-Gallon Basic Saltwater System (continued)

Item	Cost
Live sand:	$37.50 (various brands and types average about $1.25 per pound)
Live rock:	$300 (various types range from $4.00 to $6.00 per pound)
Hydrometer:	$6.00
Thermometer:	$7 to $35
Test kits:	$50
Fish:	$50
Other critters:	$100
Total:	$938.94

The basic saltwater system would be a great choice if your primary goal is entertaining and inspiring the kids. Clownfish, for example, can live to be over 10 years old, and a single specimen could spend its entire life in your aquarium, along with a few hardy, interesting invertebrates. However, although clownfish make great pets, an aquarium intended to enhance the look of your living room or den needs to be larger than 30 gallons. The 75-gallon minireef system is large enough to provide a healthy environment for a variety of colorful and interesting sea life but is small enough to be manageable in an average home, both in terms of space and available time.

75-Gallon Minireef System Costs

Item	Cost
Tank (preinstalled with filter overflow connections):	$256.99
Overflow plumbing kit:	$51.99
Cabinet (black pine):	$219.99
Filter system and skimmer (plus all necessary fittings and hardware):	$350.00
Lighting system, including lamps: (two 150-watt metal halide lamps, two 96-watt compact fluorescent lamps, and three 1-watt LED lamps):	$939.99
Seawater mix:	$18.75
Substrate:	$75
Live sand:	$93.75
Live rock:	$750
Hydrometer:	$6

Item	Cost
Thermometer:	$7 (up to $35)
Test kits:	$50
Fish:	$150 (and up, depending on species)
Other critters:	$300 to $500 (or more, depending on species)
Total:	$3,269.46

Recurring Expenses

Certain items in your aquarium will require regular replacement. Recurring costs such as these can eventually add up to a greater expenditure than the aquarium itself. I've listed in the following tables items you'll regularly need to replace each year so you can get an idea of the yearly costs you'll face with your aquarium.

30-Gallon Saltwater System Yearly Upkeep Costs

Item	Cost	Frequency of Replacement (per year)	Total Cost Yearly
Seawater mix	$1.50	12 times	$18
Test kits	$50	1 time	$50
Food	$10	12 times	$120 (weekly live food treat, plus dry foods)
Medications	$10	1 time	$10
Parts	$20	1 time	$20

If you're considering a larger system, keep in mind that you'll also have more to replace (for instance, the bigger the tank, the more seawater mix you'll need). You can get an idea of the yearly costs from the following table.

75-Gallon Minireef System Yearly Upkeep Costs

Item	Cost	Frequency of Replacement (per year)	Total Cost Yearly
Seawater mix	$3.75	12 times	$45
Test kits	$50	1 time	$50
Food	$30	12 times	$360
Medications	$10	1 time	$10
Parts	$30	1 time	$30

Environmental Considerations

The majority of coral reef organisms seen in aquarium shops are collected from wild reefs, and when done appropriately, such collecting appears to have little impact on the reef community. In fact, aquarium harvesting likely does less damage than food fisheries do because a small amount of multiple species of fish are harvested as opposed to harvesting a large number of a single species. However, although it may have more of an impact on your wallet to purchase environmentally friendly items for your aquarium, you should keep the following environmental considerations in mind when deciding what to include in your aquarium:

- **Live rock:** Removing pieces of the reef structure itself has obvious implications. The amount of live rock harvested for the aquarium trade remains quite small in comparison to, say, the damage sustained by the reef during a hurricane. Nevertheless, many areas that formerly supplied live rock now prohibit its collection, and live rock "farms" have been created as a result. Buying live rock from farms has less environmental impact and usually costs no more than traditionally harvested rock.
- **Poisons:** The use of poisons, particularly sodium cyanide, to stun fish and make them easier to collect affects not only the coral reef environment, but also the health of the collector and the survivability of the fish collected. Cyanide also damages many other organisms besides the targeted fish, and the long-term impact of this on the reef could be significant. Bottom line: Avoid buying fish that may have been collected with cyanide. I will discuss how to do this in chapter 6. Buying marine fish that have not been collected with cyanide discourages this deplorable, destructive practice, although the same fish may cost twice as much.
- **Invertebrates:** For a truly natural-appearing aquarium habitat, invertebrates generally form part of the living community. Many more invertebrates come from wild reefs than from hatcheries, and in most cases, the impact of their removal is small. This alone has made the invertebrate tank attractive to many. Further, unlike the vast majority of marine fish, captive invertebrates often reproduce themselves, leading to a dynamic, naturalistic aquarium as unique as a work of art. The pros and cons of "minireef" aquariums (those emphasizing a variety of invertebrates) and "fish-only" aquariums (emphasizing fish, with invertebrates as a secondary, utilitarian component) will be discussed in detail in chapter 2. Buying captive-propagated invertebrates is often less expensive than purchasing the same species harvested from the sea.

Anyone contemplating a saltwater aquarium should be sensitive to the potential for environmental damage from unsustainable collecting of wild fish and invertebrates. Rest easy, though. You can avoid contributing to the problems by gaining a little understanding, using common sense, and enduring a little extra trouble and expense for the sake of the environment.

Learning Commitment

Reef biodiversity is part of the attraction of a saltwater aquarium, but the diversity of fish and invertebrates available often overwhelms beginners. Precisely because reef organisms come in great variety, you'll need some basic biological knowledge in order to sort them out and anticipate their needs. Because the chemical nature of the seawater surrounding these organisms is crucial to their survival, you'll need to know some basic chemistry, too. Books, hobbyist magazines, aquarium club meetings, online chats, conversations with the people at the pet shop, and the Internet all offer the resources you need. The information is out there, but you must be willing to seek it out and to interpret it in terms of your individual situation. Unless you learn about the saltwater creatures and their environment, you won't be happy with the results of your saltwater aquarium.

At this point, don't worry too much about the biology and chemistry. I intend to cover these areas as the need arises, with a minimum of technical jargon. (Any terms that might be unfamiliar are defined in the Glossary in appendix C.) In fact, deciding what you already know and don't know about these subjects—and filling in those gaps—is a fundamental part of creating your plan.

Is a Saltwater Aquarium Right for Your Family?

Use this worksheet to see if a saltwater aquarium is right for you and your family. If you answer yes to all of the following, you can expect years of enjoyment from your home aquarium. The movement and color of a coral reef will create excitement when friends drop by, not to mention enchanting your children, who universally seem to take a special delight in aquariums. With luck, you will create the inspiration for a child's career in marine biology, oceanography, or ecology. I've had the pleasure of seeing this happen repeatedly.

Questions to Ask Yourself and Your Family

Do you have a basic understanding of science, especially chemistry and biology, or at least a willingness to learn these topics?

____

____

continued

Are you willing to pay for an aquarium of suitable size and appropriate design to accommodate the creatures you favor?

____

____

Are you willing to incur the long-term maintenance costs?

____

____

Are you willing to commit 8 hours a month or more to caring for the aquarium?

____

____

Do you think paying more for environmentally sustainable products is getting good value for the money?

____

____

What You Now Know . . .

- You need to devote about 4 hours weekly and an additional 4 hours each month to maintaining your aquarium.
- The cost of an aquarium and its upkeep depends on the size you need or want—initial costs start at $1,000 and rise infinitely depending on size.
- Although you need to update your chemistry and biology knowledge to maintain your aquarium, filling in the gaps should be relatively painless.

Chapter 2

Designing Your Saltwater Aquarium

What's Inside . . .

- Learn how to create an aquarium plan.
- Learn the basic philosophy of natural aquarium keeping.
- Learn the difference between a minireef and a fish-only aquarium.
- Learn how to shop for equipment, supplies, and fish.
- Learn how to prepare your home for your new aquarium.

Designing a saltwater aquarium may sound like a huge undertaking, and it can be! However, with the proper planning and knowledge, you can put together a satisfying and exciting aquarium whether you plan to use it to satisfy your need for a hobby, to enhance your children's knowledge of science or awareness of the environment, or simply to add a dramatic element to your family's living space. Regardless of your motivation, you can find in this chapter the tools you'll need to plan properly for your aquarium as well as find a good dealer and good supplies.

Planning Basics

While no perfect home aquarium system exists, a key component of all successful home aquariums is the use of a plan. Working it all out on paper, long before the first trip to the aquarium shop, results in fewer mistakes and a healthier and more trouble-free completed system.

How to Plan

Please believe me when I say you will encounter conflicting recommendations in your search for saltwater aquarium information. Creating a basic plan helps you sort out all of this information. Here's the best way I have found to go about it.

1. Create a list of fish and/or invertebrate species that you think you might like to have in your proposed aquarium. Skip ahead to chapters 4 and 5 for more information about many of the critters you'll see in aquarium shops.
2. From your initial list, choose your favorite.
3. Find out what this "must-have" species needs to survive in a home aquarium. You can find the necessary information about some of the most popular species in chapters 4 and 5. For other species you may encounter, you can check sources such as the library, the Internet, or a hobbyist friend. For example, how big must the tank be? Tank capacity is the most important factor in the design, because cost, both initially and for long-term maintenance, is proportional to the size of the tank. A fish that grows to 2 feet in length obviously needs something larger than a 10-gallon tank.
4. Once you know the aquarium's dimensions, you can get quotes for a system of that size as well as quotes for the items you'll need to fill it (see the shopping list later in this chapter).
5. If the total price of the aquarium and its contents extend beyond your budget, decide how much money you can devote to the project. Then find out what fish can be accommodated in the tank that fits your budget.

Planning Points

Over the years, I have developed some simple planning guidelines. Keep these ideas in mind when developing the master plan for your saltwater aquarium.

Keep It Simple

Pay more attention to maintaining good water quality, providing proper nutrition, and carrying out proper maintenance, and less attention to installing the latest piece of high-tech equipment. Fancy equipment cannot substitute for proper maintenance. Start with a basic system and learn to maintain it properly. Then you will be better able to decide wisely if additional equipment will really help you to get more enjoyment out of the hobby. Some aquarium dealers are interested only in selling you more equipment, and their sales pitches are sometimes hard for the beginner to judge. If you think you are being pressured, you probably are. Find another dealer; there are plenty of good ones out there who deserve your business.

Keep It Roomy

Most likely, the size of the tank you choose will be determined by the needs of the fish you settle on for inhabitants. Saltwater fishes require ample space, depending on their mature size and, often, also upon the nature of their lifestyle. Even the largest aquarium is tiny when compared to the vast ocean around a coral reef. Choose species that are in proportion to the size of the miniature ecosystem you are designing. Resist the temptation to add "just one more fish", when common sense (not to mention the reference books) says the tank is at capacity. If your space and budget do not allow for a large tank, you may need to pare down your fish wish list to include only those you can properly accommodate.

Bigger Is Indeed Better

An old rule of thumb stated, "One gallon of tank capacity will support about 3 inches of fish." However, this merely considers the issue of filtration, that is, waste removal, without accommodating issues of territoriality, shelter, and swimming space. Given that the largest aquarium you might reasonably install will be tiny in comparison to the natural habitat that inspired it, the only generality I am comfortable with is: "Buy the largest saltwater aquarium your space and budget can manage." *In no event should your first saltwater aquarium be smaller than 30 gallons.*

Keep It Stable

The coral reef ranks among the most stable of all environments on Earth. Temperature, salinity, dissolved oxygen, and water clarity all remain relatively constant throughout the year. Even the length of the day varies little. Corals themselves, the basis for the existence of the reef ecosystem, only occur where water conditions satisfy their demands. Thus, reefs are only found in certain locations. Owing to the stability of their environment, reef fishes and invertebrates have not evolved adaptive strategies to cope with rapid fluctuations in environmental conditions. Maintaining stability in a saltwater aquarium requires reliable equipment, regular maintenance, and appropriate adjustments when conditions begin to deviate from optimal. I like to call this adjustment aspect of saltwater aquarium keeping the "test and tweak" routine. You test the water conditions and then tweak them back into line as required.

Keep It Clean

Aside from the issues of aesthetic appearance and basic hygiene, keeping the aquarium clean or, more precisely, "nutrient poor," is the single best way to avoid unwanted growths of algae. Aquarists spend far too much time and money trying various gimmicks and additives that are supposed to limit algae growth, when the basic problem is a failure to replicate in the aquarium the dynamic nutrient cycling process that occurs on natural reefs. There are some standard rules, of course: feed sparingly; remove dead organic matter promptly; siphon out debris regularly; carry out water changes as necessary. To control algae, however, do not allow dissolved nutrients to accumulate. Nutrients can be generated within the tank (compounds such as phosphate are released when food is metabolized by any organism), as well as from outside the tank (salt mix, improperly used additives, and especially tap water). Understanding the role nutrients play in your aquarium is where most of the chemistry comes in. Fear not, though, water testing the aquarium is much like testing a swimming pool or spa.

Beware of Microtanks

Saltwater aquariums as small as 1 gallon sometimes appear in shops. Often, these *microtanks* or *microreefs* come fully outfitted, that is, they are "plug and play." Self-contained, and small enough to fit on a desk or kitchen counter, these aquariums can be very tempting. I recommend, though, that you gain experience with a larger aquarium first. Tiny tanks are inherently unstable and provide no margin of error, or nearly none, when inevitable mistakes occur.

Keep It Natural

Try to duplicate to the fullest extent possible the conditions under which your aquarium's inhabitants were living while in the ocean. Thoroughly investigate the ecology of any species in which you are interested before you purchase a specimen. Your dealer or local library will have books on saltwater fish. Fish profiles in hobby magazines are also a good source for information on a particular species' lifestyle. While the majority of fish offered for sale in aquarium shops require essentially the same water conditions (remember what was said earlier about the narrow range of variation in the reef environment), they may differ quite significantly in size and temperament. Some are quite tolerant, others extremely finicky. Successful aquarium husbandry often depends on understanding such differences between species. Scientific knowledge about the ecology of any species always provides the most satisfactory guide to supplying its needs in a captive environment. This, by the way, is where most of the biology comes in. Learning what you need to know won't be difficult if you can tell the difference between a rose and a rhododendron. Good gardeners often make good aquarists.

Developing a Theme

Your saltwater aquarium design depends on why you want a saltwater aquarium. For example, children often lose interest in old pastimes and take up new ones and they grow and learn. A child's aquarium therefore should probably not involve too much expense, and need not be large or complicated. Potential inhabitants include mostly those that are durable enough to survive commonplace mistakes unscathed. On the other hand, an eye-catching focal point for your family room should be sized in proportion to the rest of the space, and the equipment needs to be relatively quiet and out of sight. Such an aquarium will exhibit a great diversity of fish and invertebrates. Stating a theme for your saltwater aquarium helps keep you on track when you actually choose equipment and livestock. Your aquarium's theme should be stated in a single sentence beginning with "Our saltwater aquarium will. . . ."

Philosophy of the Natural Aquarium

My approach to keeping saltwater organisms in captivity is really rather straightforward: Duplicate nature in as many details as possible with techniques as simple as possible. Providing a physical and chemical environment closely similar to that found in nature is essential. Bear in mind, though, that the dynamics of an ecosystem, even the small and relatively uncomplicated ecosystem of an aquarium, cannot be reduced to a table of numerical parameters. The aquarist who nods in satisfaction at a correct pH reading, yet fails to heed the message conveyed by a dying organism, is missing the point altogether. Beyond providing the correct water conditions, you must attempt to duplicate the *biological* environment found on a real coral reef. Begin by asking questions about the needs of the species that will occupy the tank, and then design an aquarium that provides for those needs, including such things as the need to be around other members of its kind, its preferences for a certain amount of territory, or a reluctance to eat anything but living foods.

One of the most useful techniques I have found for teaching people how to have a successful aquarium using the natural approach is to draw attention to the high degree of analogy between an aquarium and a landscaping project. Each is an artificial display that mimics a natural ecosystem. In both cases, the finished product develops slowly, as its living elements become acclimated to their captive surroundings and subsequently grow, mature, and reproduce themselves. In both cases, living organisms are the primary focus, but the overall result is a harmonious interplay of both living and nonliving components. Success in the husbandry of living creatures, be they flowers or fish, results from providing them with an adequate substitute for their natural environment.

Key Features of the Natural Method

Saltwater aquariums established by the methods outlined here are the most successful, easiest to maintain and most likely to provide what species need to complete their life cycles. The common features of such aquariums are:

1. Ample quantities of live rock and live sand
2. High-intensity, broad-spectrum lighting, and a natural photoperiod
3. Protein skimming to remove organic wastes rather than let them decompose
4. Husbandry focused on maintaining the temperature and chemistry of the water within narrow limits
5. Replication of the physical characteristics of a specific microhabitat in terms of substrate, currents, and structure (see the habitat examples in chapter 6)
6. Attention to the specific community and social relationships of the species housed together

If you succeed in providing an adequate substitute for the natural environment, the organisms displayed in the aquarium thrive, grow, and possibly reproduce themselves, living out a natural lifespan at least as long as that which they would survive in the sea. This book presents the distillation of 30 years of education and practical experience into an approach that will give desirable results, even for a beginner.

I will warn you that my approach relies so little on technical aids that aquarium dealers may tell you flatly that it will not work.

Minireef or Fish-Only?

Shopping for an aquarium for the first time, many would-be enthusiasts become so enamored with the minireef concept that nothing less will do. This is fine, as long as you understand the nature of the undertaking. Dealers will often say that a beginner should start with a fish-only tank and later graduate to a minireef. In my humble opinion, this has more to do with avoiding sticker shock on the first sale, and hopefully winding up with a customer with *two* tanks, than it does with the need for a "baby steps" approach for the beginner. If you want a reef tank, there is no reason to deny yourself, but be sure to consider the pros and cons (see the table later in this section).

Minireef Aquariums

A *minireef* is an aquarium that attempts to replicate a small portion of a real coral reef, including the physical, chemical, and biological interactions that occur there. A minireef differs from a fish-only aquarium in that the latter lacks many of the elements and interactions found in nature. A fish-only tank is merely an artificial display.

Fish are no more out of place in a minireef tank than they are in the environment of the reef itself, of course. Fish are the most obvious and colorful of the reef's fauna. The fish species available to aquarium hobbyists, however, represent only a small fraction of the reef's biodiversity. There are perhaps 4,000 species of fish found on reefs. Fewer than 5 percent of these constitute 90 percent of aquarium imports. On the other hand, the number of invertebrate species found on coral reefs is in the tens of thousands. Even though only a tiny fraction of these are imported regularly, the number of invertebrate varieties available to hobbyists far exceeds the number of fish species available. Sorting out this diversity can make the learning curve much steeper for a minireef than is the case with a fish-only tank. For example, corals can interact with one another in subtle ways that are not immediately apparent to beginners. Some release chemicals that may inhibit the growth of nearby competitors, a problem not readily apparent unless you have read about it, since chemical antagonism is not obvious from just looking at the tank. Creating a harmonious minireef community therefore requires you to sort out many more variables than is the case with a fish-only system. Many enthusiasts consider this part of the fun, though.

Fish-Only Aquariums

A fish-only aquarium need not be a representation of a specific type of habitat. The basic decorative elements of the tank may be chunks of plain rock rather than live rock, or coral skeletons rather than living corals. The various components of the display are not chosen to reflect a natural scene, but for their artistic or decorative effect alone. For example, one might pair a group of yellow fish with a group of blue fish for a pleasing color combination, without regard to whether these two species would ever be seen together in the ocean. Invertebrates are often included in fish-only tanks, but the selection is limited to those that won't become dinner for the fish, or that are themselves too predatory to be included in a minireef. While invertebrates are the star attraction of the minireef, they take only a supporting role in the fish-only system. Interestingly, the most popular invertebrates for minireefs are those that live fixed in one spot, such as corals, while fish-only tanks tend to include mobile invertebrates such as crabs or starfish.

Pros and Cons of Minireef and Fish-Only Aquariums

Fish-Only	Minireef
Minimum size: 30 gallons	Minimum size: 50 gallons
Ideal size: 50–75 gallons	Ideal size: 100 gallons or more
Lighting: Minimal, for viewing only	Lighting: Maximal, to support photosynthesis
Filtration system: Basic	Filtration system: Requires best available
Cost: ±$20 per gallon	Cost: ±$50 per gallon or more

Deciding If a Minireef or Saltwater Aquarium Is for You

To decide whether a minireef or saltwater aquarium fits your needs and wants, answer the following questions:

Do you have the money to afford the biggest tank possible? (If money isn't an issue, consider the minireef system, but if it is, stick with the fish-only aquarium.)

____

____

continued

Do you like the idea of mimicking a natural scene, or do purely aesthetic considerations appeal to you more than ecological accuracy. (Nature lovers may favor the minireef, while the artist will lean toward a fish-only aquarium.)

____

____

Do you prefer projects requiring a lot of attention to detail, or are you happier with a less-structured approach? (The diversity of life in a minireef poses more complex husbandry problems than the straightforward care required for a fish-only system.)

____

____

As a decorative element in your home, would you prefer a controlled, minimalist look to a more relaxed, comforting appearance? (Fish-only tanks lend themselves to the minimalist style; minireef tanks always appear "busier.")

____

____

Are behavior and movement more important than subtleties of form and coloration? (Minireefs tend to feature species that stay in one place, while fish are usually in constant motion.)

____

____

If you were making a garden instead of an aquarium, would you go with a formal, Italian design with evergreens, or an English cottage garden overflowing with flowers? (Fish-only aquariums are more like the former, minireefs more like the latter.)

____

____

Are you a fan of change? (Minireef aquariums grow and evolve continuously, but you may have the same four individuals in a fish-only tank for 10 years.)

____

____

What You'll Need

When you go out shopping for your new aquarium, arm yourself with a checklist so you don't leave out a crucial item of equipment or forget to ask about something important. Here's a checklist to use as a guide:

Tank

The fundamental tank specification is its holding capacity, which by now you will have decided on, based on your "must have" fish. Dealers generally like to sell an aquarium "combo" including the tank, a cover, lighting, and sometimes a stand or cabinet. Package deals like this can produce considerable cost savings and should always be considered. The downside may be that the lighting system offered is inadequate or that the cabinet finish does not match your décor. Better dealers know about these issues, and tailor their combo offerings accordingly. You will always be better off in the long run to purchase the right equipment separately, rather than to accept a less than perfect system for the design you have in mind, despite any cost savings.

Tanks are available in both glass and acrylic, and there are advantages and disadvantages associated with either material.

- Glass is more durable; acrylic scratches easily.
- Glass tanks cost less than equivalent acrylic ones.
- Acrylic tanks weigh far less than comparable glass tanks.
- Drilling acrylic for the installation of plumbing is a breeze and can be done with ordinary woodworking tools. Drilling glass should be left to professionals.
- Acrylic tanks usually have cross bracing at the top, which restricts the size of the opening, making it difficult to add large pieces of coral or other decorations. The cross braces also get in the way of nets, hoses, and other equipment during maintenance. Glass tanks smaller than 4 feet in length usually do not need cross bracing, and larger tanks up to 6 feet long have only a single narrow brace in the center.
- From the standpoint of interior design, glass looks more traditional while acrylic tends to appear more contemporary.
- The variety of tank shapes possible with glass is limited, while acrylic can be formed into almost any shape imaginable.
- Acrylic can also be used to construct the cabinet, in any color. Glass obviously cannot be used for that purpose.

Consider a glass tank if you are concerned primarily with minimal cost and maximum durability. Consider acrylic if aesthetic design is of prime importance.

Filtration System

This may be one or several components, depending on the size and complexity of the aquarium design. Old-fashioned undergravel filters operated by air or small water pumps called

Saltwater Aquarium Shopping List

Fish-Only System:

Tank: Plain tank with no installed plumbing connections
Filtration system and skimmer: Combination unit that hangs on the back of the tank
Cabinet: Many choices of materials and colors
Lighting system and lamps: simple fluorescent strip light is sufficient
Cover: Most people use a plain hinged cover with a strip light

Minireef:

Tank: Predrilled tank with installed overflow, prefilter, and plumbing connections
Filtration system and skimmer: Combination unit located underneath the tank, providing a refugium and space to access the skimmer
Cabinet: Many choices of materials and colors
Lighting system and lamps: multiple fluorescent lamps up to 50 gallons, metal halide supplemented with fluorescent lamps for larger systems, blue LED night lights optional
Cover: May use a plain hinged glass cover or a completely enclosed hood, depending on lighting system design.

For Either System:

To determine the cost of either dead or live sand, allow 1 pound of sand per gallon
To determine the cost of either dead or live rock, allow 2 pounds of rock per gallon
Synthetic seawater mix: Enough for initial fill plus one 50 percent water change
Heater: Allow 5 watts per gallon
Thermometer: Select for accuracy and ease of use
Salinity measurement: Hydrometer or refractometer
Test kits: pH, ammonia, nitrite, nitrate, alkalinity

Each of the items on the list requires separate consideration of the pros and cons of available designs.

powerheads remain available and are sometimes touted for filtering a small, simple aquarium. They can be used, but require considerable maintenance to operate optimally. Their location, underneath the substrate at the bottom of the tank, with all the decorations sitting on top, means that repair or major maintenance requires tearing down the whole tank to get at the filter. My advice: pass. Choose instead a pump-driven filter that either hangs on the back of the tank, or is installed underneath. Study the information on filtration capacity in chapter 3 for an understanding of the important points of filtration design. Proper water conditions can only be maintained via adequate filtration, so scrimping on this crucial part of the system is a fool's choice. Regardless of the design, filtration system capacity should be correctly sized for the tank capacity, with plenty of room to spare.

One filtration component often misunderstood is the *foam fractionator*, often called a *protein skimmer*. This device is an essential piece of equipment for minireef aquariums, but it bestows great benefits on a fish-only system as well. The basic design for all foam fractionators involves pumping a stream of fine bubbles through a column of aquarium water in such a way that certain dissolved organic pollutants become sequestered in thick foam that is collected for disposal. In principle, this works like making meringue out of egg whites. The introduction of a large amount of air causes bubbles to form, surrounded by the albumin protein in the eggs. The protein stabilizes the bubbles (like soap does for a child's bubble-blowing toy) resulting in a stiff foam. As the foam rises higher and higher above the surface of the water column, it spills over the top and into the collection cup of the fractionator. Foam fractionation is the only available method for isolating organic pollutants away from the tank water and should be included in every aquarium design.

Support Furniture

Far too many hobbyists fail to choose quality support furniture for their aquariums. They thus end up with something that looks totally out of place in their home, or worse, is poorly designed from a practical standpoint. In recent years, manufacturers have awakened to the need for quality, stylish aquarium support furniture. If innovative designs have not yet made it to the dealer near you, think about either a mail-order or custom-built cabinet. Especially if the aquarium will be a feature of your living area, settling for flimsy construction or a style inconsistent with the rest of the room will lead to dissatisfaction. Let the person who usually makes décor decisions in your household choose the color and finish for the cabinet. Then make sure it provides adequate support for the weight of the tank and access to the equipment you'll need to install underneath. The cabinet should also be designed to afford protection to nearby surfaces and the floor in the event of a spill. The inside of the cabinet should be coated with a water-resistant finish, and its floor should provide a slight lip all around to temporarily contain spills.

Light Fixtures

A fish-only aquarium needs lighting that shows off the colors of the fish, but need not necessarily be extremely bright. For smaller tanks, say under 4 feet in length, a single fluorescent lamp running the length of the tank should suffice, although more light than this is fine and will only enhance the beauty of the fish. Saltwater invertebrates that rely on photosynthesis for the bulk of their nutrition (see chapter 5) need more light than this—a lot more. For tanks in the 30- to 50-gallon range, at least two, and preferably four, fluorescent lamps across the entire length of the tank should provide the minimal acceptable light intensity. Bright illumination is a hallmark of the minireef design. Larger aquariums, especially those with a depth exceeding 15 inches, require the high intensity lighting provided by metal halide, high output (HO) or very high output (VHO) fluorescent lamps, or a combination.

Cover

Whether part of a combo or purchased separately, you really only need a cover if there is a possibility of something jumping out or something jumping, or more likely falling, in. Tightly covering the top inhibits crucial gas exchange at the water surface, and can diminish the light fixture's effective output by half. Many manufacturers offer lighting fixtures that enclose the entire top of the tank. Often this fixture is called a *hood*. In this case, the lamps underneath the hood should be protected by a glass or plastic panel, but the glass cover intended to sit on a flange molded around the aquarium top should be omitted. The hood supports the lamps a few inches above the water surface, and on the outside encloses the top of the tank with a strip of material matching the cabinet underneath. This not only gives a finished appearance to the whole display, it hides unsightly wiring and other paraphernalia, and gives the aquarium a custom-built look.

Synthetic Seawater

Very few aquarists will have access to natural seawater of sufficient cleanliness for aquarium use. Inshore, natural seawater may be lower than normal salinity owing to freshwater influx from estuaries. Regrettably, it may also contain harmful pollutants and pathogenic microorganisms. Collecting natural seawater for the home aquarium may therefore require boating or other troublesome ventures, and is seldom worth it. If you live beside the sea on a pristine bay, good for you; go ahead and collect your own seawater. No perfect synthetic substitute exists. The rest of us, however, can do quite well with the synthetic mixes, and they are certainly more convenient to use and store. Seawater mix is *not* dehydrated seawater, and the sea salt sold in the grocery market will not produce seawater when reconstituted with water. This phenomenon results from chemical behavior that we need not consider in detail. Just remember that all synthetic mixes are formulated from separate chemical components, not produced from natural seawater. All are supplied in plastic bags in quantities suitable for 5, 10, or more gallons of finished product.

I am often asked to recommend a brand of synthetic seawater mix, as several vie for the market and all make effusive claims about being the best at duplicating natural seawater. This is advertising hype. Over 90 percent of what's in the bag is sodium chloride, common table salt. It's the other components that make the product "seawater" and the choices from among available industrial chemicals for creating a suitable formulation are rather limited. Some mixes may be too low or too high in their minor components, but all approximate seawater quite well in terms of their major components. (Interestingly, much advertising copy is devoted to those minor components, thus carefully avoiding mention that most of the bag consists of exactly the same things as the competing brand.)

I have used every major national brand of seawater mix over the years and find little difference among them. Private or limited distribution brands range from quite good to something better suited for driveway de-icing. My best advice: Choose one of the national brands available in your area and stick with it consistently.

Water-Testing Supply Checklist

For any saltwater aquarium, your water testing "laboratory" should be equipped with:

- ☐ A thermometer
- ☐ A hydrometer, a refractometer, or a conductivity meter for measuring salinity
- ☐ A pH meter or chemical pH test kit
- ☐ A test kit for alkalinity
- ☐ Test kits for ammonia, nitrate, and nitrite

For a minireef, your lab should also include:

- ☐ A test kit for calcium

For troubleshooting, you may also need:

- ☐ A test kit for phosphate
- ☐ A test kit for copper

Test Equipment

As you will soon realize, water testing is the key to maintaining proper water conditions in your saltwater aquarium. Purchasing your testing equipment wisely means knowing what to look for in terms of cost versus value. Cheap toys often marketed for aquarium testing are unsatisfactory. Cheapness almost always translates into inaccuracy. On the other hand, you do not need ultra-precise, analytical-grade equipment costing thousands of dollars. The middle ground contains devices and tests that score high on accuracy and low on precision, and are consequently priced in a range affordable to most hobbyists.

For example, if it's freezing outside, an accurate thermometer should read pretty close to 32 degrees F (0 degrees C). A variation, or inaccuracy, in the range of 1 or 2 degrees is acceptable. A thermometer capable of telling you that the current temperature is 31.679 degrees F while more precise is no more accurate, in a practical sense, than one that reads 32 degrees F because all you really need to know is if the weather is at or around the freezing point.

Thermometer for Temperature Measurement

Get yourself a good thermometer. Accurately taking your tank's temperature seldom presents a problem, and although coral reef fish and invertebrates experience a range of temperature in the wild (roughly 68 degrees F to 82 degrees F) sudden, dramatic fluctuations in temperature are stressful and should be avoided. Maintaining a home aquarium at 75 degrees F is recommended. Avoid keeping the tank constantly at the upper extreme of the temperature range. Alas, most aquarium shop thermometers fare poorly in comparison to liquid-in-glass thermometers made for a variety of purposes and the various digital thermometers available from greenhouse, pool, and spa suppliers. Constant monitoring of the temperature, though ideal, is not necessary, but you should be able to note the temperature at a glance whenever you are near the tank. This usually means continuous immersion of the thermometer or digital probe. Make sure the one you choose is up to the task, sealed against leakage and incapable of being corroded by seawater.

Hydrometer, Refractometer, or Conductivity Meter for Salinity Measurement

Hydrometers measure specific gravity. Knowing this value together with the temperature allows you to estimate salinity, the single most important normal condition of seawater. Salinity is awesomely constant over vast stretches of ocean. Around coral reefs, salinities of 35 to 36 parts per thousand (ppt) prevail. This means the seawater bathing the reef contains 35 to 36 grams of dissolved salts per kilogram of water. Since weighing out a kilo of seawater, evaporating it, and reweighing the remaining salts is impractical, salinity is seldom measured directly. The hydrometer provides an indirect measure of salinity when used with a pair of conversion tables (see chapter 8 for more on calculating this value).

Hydrometers are popular with aquarium hobbyists because they are inexpensive. Two types exist. One floats, and the specific gravity is read from a scale printed on the neck of the device. The other, known as a *dip-and-read* type, is filled with tank water, and the specific gravity is noted from the position of a floating needle. Either one works well if calibrated and properly used.

A *refractometer* estimates the salinity of a water sample by measuring its refractive index. You place a drop of water in the sample chamber and peer through the instrument like a nineteenth-century boat captain peering through a telescope. You read the salinity directly from the scale. An individual instrument is designed to operate at a certain temperature, which will be specified on the refractometer or the literature that comes with it. Make sure the one you choose is designed to give an accurate reading at 75 degrees F.

If you'd rather avoid conversion tables and so forth, choose a digital conductivity meter. You stick the probe in the water and read the salinity directly. Depending on the design, temperature correction is handled automatically by a sensor in the probe, or manually by adjusting a temperature setting to match the tank. All of the calculations take place in the meter's microprocessor. The downside of such digital luxury, of course, is the considerable additional cost.

A pH Meter or Chemical pH Test Kit for pH Measurement

After salinity, pH is the most important parameter of the saltwater environment. It affects everything from the respiration of fishes to skeleton construction in corals. Natural seawater has a pH of 8.3, with scarcely any variation except when influenced by incoming freshwater

runoff. If you remember high school chemistry, you know that the pH of pure water is 7.0. Anything lower than 7.0 on the pH scale is said to be acidic, while anything above 7.0 is alkaline. Aquarium pH is easily measured in much the same way as a swimming pool or hot tub, with a chemical kit, a dip-and-read test strip, or a digital meter. Good digital pH meters are expensive, and the probe requires a lot of babying to give accurate readings over a long life span. Meters typically measure pH to two decimal places, which is more precise than you really need. On the other hand, dip-and-read tests, though accurate and inexpensive, may not offer enough precision. Most give only the nearest whole pH unit, but for the aquarium a tenth of a pH unit is needed. Thus, the best choice is a "wet" test that involves placing a measured water sample in a vial and adding a test reagent that changes color in response to the pH of the sample. The color of the sample is then compared with a printed chart or read electronically (at much greater expense, of course) and the corresponding pH determined. Electronic reading of this and other color change tests requires an instrument known as a *spectrophotometer*. Hobbyist-grade spectrophotometers are on the market, but they tend to be expensive. Your eyes will do the reading almost as well.

Test Kit for Alkalinity Measurement

Alkalinity refers to the ability of a solution (in this case, seawater) to remain at a constant pH as acid is added. The higher the alkalinity, the greater the amount of acid needed to change the pH. The alkalinity (sometimes known as *carbonate hardness* or *KH*) of seawater is about 7 milliequivalents per liter (meq/L). Saltwater aquariums should maintain similar levels. The most useful alkalinity test for home applications involves mixing the water sample with a small amount of pH indicator, then adding a standard acid solution until the pH "breaks" or changes suddenly, evidenced by the abrupt color change of the indicator. Each drop of acid corresponds to a unit of alkalinity. Alkalinity is expressed in different ways, so you may need the conversion factors to derive milliequivalents per liter from the kit you select.

Alkalinity Conversion Factors

Alkalinity is expressed in milliequivalents per liter (meq/L). Other terms you may encounter are:

Carbonate hardness expressed in parts per million (ppm); 50 ppm = 1 meq/L
Alkalai reserve expressed in grains per gallon (gr/gal); 2.92 gr/gal = 1 meq/L
German hardness (KH) expressed in degrees (dKH); 2.8 dKH = 1 meq/L

Depending on the brand of test kit you purchase, you may need to convert your readings to alkalinity, using the conversion factors above.

Test Kit for Measurement of Nitrate, Nitrite, and Ammonia

Proteins, found in every kind of food that might be eaten by a fish or an invertebrate, contain nitrogen compounds. These eventually wind up in one of two places: in the proteins of the animal that consumes the food or in the water, as excreted ammonia. As you might expect, fish and invertebrates do not thrive if forced to live in their own excreta. Fortunately, nitrifying bacteria can be cultivated in the aquarium. These bacteria convert ammonia first into nitrite and then into nitrate. Tests for ammonia and nitrite are used to determine if this process is proceeding correctly. Tests for these two compounds should always be zero. Nitrate, the end product of biological filtration, is tolerated by most saltwater organisms. However, nitrate accumulation often parallels that of other waste compounds that may be responsible for harmful effects. Thus, nitrate levels can be used as a rough indicator of the overall condition of the aquarium. It does little harm, in my view, to think of nitrate itself as undesirable, even though this is not strictly correct. The point is that the condition of aquarium water changes over time, that these changes are generally undesirable, and that they can be alleviated through maintenance. Nitrate is an easily measured indicator of the extent of these changes. For details of the important role played by nitrogen compounds in the life of your saltwater aquarium, see chapter 3.

What You May Want

The equipment just described constitutes the basics. Several other items could be included on your shopping list. Some automate routine tasks; others serve specific needs that not everyone will share, and some are just plain nice to have. Although you don't absolutely need the following, you may want them.

- **Timers:** A timer to control the lighting sits at the head of my list of desirable optional equipment. If you plan to use one, be sure to buy a compatible lighting system. Some fluorescent fixtures may not work with a timer, and retrofitting may be difficult. Set the timer to provide 12 hours of light. More elaborate lighting systems featuring fluorescent and metal halide lighting in combination often will accept two timers. One timer controls the fluorescent lamps, turning them on about an hour before the metal halide lamps, and off about an hour after. A second one controls the metal halides. This produces a "dawn-midday-dusk" lighting pattern that mimics natural diurnal fluctuations. Lighting this fancy usually only appeals to the owners of large minireef tanks, but any saltwater aquarium will benefit from bright, natural-looking lighting.
- **Seawater containers:** For preparing and storing synthetic seawater, several kinds of containers come in handy. Seawater mix cakes and becomes difficult to measure accurately if exposed to humidity. Once you open the bag, it keeps better if stored in an airtight food container. Depending on the amount you want to have on hand, you might consider 5-gallon plastic buckets with lids. Food products such as jelly and frosting come packed in them. Ask at your local bakery or deli. As a general rule, anything suitable for food storage accommodates seawater equally well. Not only do jelly buckets

work for storing dry mix, the ones with a tight-sealing lid hold prepared seawater for easy storage. Five gallons is all the water you will want to hoist or tote at one time. If your seawater needs go beyond a few buckets, you may want to invest in a seawater mixing tank. You can order one from an aquarium supplier, or make your own from a plastic garbage can, some plastic hose, and an inexpensive aquarium pump. Plans for this and other equipment you can make yourself can often be found in hobbyist magazines or online.

Costs for Nice, but Not Necessary, Additions

Item	Cost
Timer/s	$10–20
Seawater containers	$5 each
Siphon	$5
Copper medication	$5
Copper test kit	$10–30
Net	$3–5 each
Catch cup	$3
Purification system	$50 up

- **Siphon:** To carry out partial water changes, some people like to buy a specially made aquarium siphon with an intake that makes accidentally siphoning out a fish or shrimp less likely. These sometimes come with a hand pump for the hobbyist squeamish about getting a mouthful of tank water when starting the siphon. For the ultimate in convenience, upscale filtration systems may provide a drain controlled by a valve. Run a hose to the nearest sink or bathtub drain, open the valve, and draw off as much water as desired, effortlessly.
- **Copper medication and test kit:** Sooner or later, you'll be confronted with a fish infected with parasites. The most common fish parasites can be effectively treated by exposing the fish to an excess of copper ions. It's worth having a copper medication and a copper test kit on hand, so you won't need to rush out for one when the need arises.
- **Net and catch cup:** Sometimes moving a fish or other critter becomes necessary. Since critters rarely see the advantages of this, they seldom cooperate. You will need a net or two, and a clear, square plastic box aquarium dealers call a *catch cup*. Though they for some unknown reason seldom offer them for sale, most dealers use catch cups when catching fish for customers. The cup has a bend at the top that conveniently allows it to hang on the top edge of the aquarium. Don't make the common mistake of using the net to capture a shrimp or fish. Many sea creatures have spiny parts that can become hopelessly entangled. Extricating them from the net often leads to injury. Use the net instead to goad a fish out of hiding behind a rock, or to steer one into the catch cup. A net facilitates retrieving objects other than living creatures from the water. You'll want one if only for this. Make sure the handle is longer than the tank is deep.

- **Purification system:** Algae may grow excessively if the water supply contains an abundance of certain compounds, particularly phosphate. Installing a purification system may be the only answer to persistent problems with undesirable types of algae. Along with this equipment, you will need additional test kits. We will return to this issue in the discussion of water supplies in chapter 7.

Where to Find Equipment and Supplies

Saltwater aquarium enthusiasts have a plethora of choices, from specialty dealers to big-box pet retail chains to mail-order suppliers. If you live in or near a reasonably large city, I suggest you start by looking for a store that sells only saltwater aquariums. Such a store can be expected to have a better selection, more knowledgeable personnel, and possibly better prices than a store in which saltwater species are only a sideline. My second choice would be a shop that specializes in both freshwater and saltwater aquariums, and my third choice would be a full-line pet shop. Of course, there are good saltwater departments in stores that sell other kinds of pets, but stores that specialize in fish are usually better.

Specialty Dealers

As with anything else in life, there are good aquarium shops and bad ones. First and foremost, you should look for a store with a large saltwater dry goods section and a varied inventory of healthy fish living in well-maintained holding tanks. A dirty, unkempt, poorly lighted store should be an immediate signal to look elsewhere. Dusty inventory indicates that turnover is slow. Ergo, the store probably lacks regular customers. This should tell you something about the satisfaction level of previous visitors.

Expect that attempts will be made to sell you products or specimens. After all, the store *is* in business to make money. However, a sales pitch should not be the sole communication you have with the staff. Professional retailers know that the key to their business success is having successful hobbyists for customers. You should be able to discern a sincere interest in your success as an aquarist from the conversations you may have in the store. This would include such things as, for example, steering you away from fish that would be inappropriate for your tank because of size or compatibility problems, or, if you describe yourself as a beginner, your level of expertise. Remember, though, that most dealers will sell you anything you want if you insist.

One guide to dealer selection is membership in the American Marinelife Dealers Association (AMDA). I founded this organization to promote best management standards of practice in the retail saltwater aquarium industry. Dealers who are members of AMDA pledge to provide proper care for the fish and invertebrates they stock and to supply accurate information about them to customers. The AMDA membership directory is available by visiting their Web site at: www.amdareef.com.

Questions to Ask Specialty Dealers

To identify whether a specialty dealer runs a good shop, you should ask the salesperson, manager, and/or owner these questions. One good sign to watch for: if someone does not know the answer to your question, they take the time to look it up in a book. Good shops always answer your question or refer to well-used reference books behind the counter.

How often do you receive shipments of fish? (If the answer is "weekly" this shop does a brisk saltwater business and probably has plenty of repeat customers.)

____

____

How long do you guarantee your fish? (Stores with confidence in the quality of their livestock will offer some sort of guarantee. A week is reasonable.)

____

____

What are the terms of your guarantee on livestock? (Reasonable requirements are a store receipt, return of the corpse in question, and a request for a water sample to test. Most shops void the guarantee if the water tests show the tank is in bad shape.)

____

____

Can I buy all the fish at once, or should I spread my purchases out? (Good shops will advise spreading out your purchases.)

____

____

How can I make sure my fish never get sick? (The answer should offer no ironclad promise, but should stress proper care and feeding.)

____

____

continued

Point to a fish mentioned in chapter 4 and ask for details about its size, care, and compatibility. (The answer should approximate the information given in the book.)

____

____

Mention that this will be your first aquarium. Ask if you can have a seahorse. (The dealer should suggest you gain experience before trying a seahorse.)

____

____

Let's say that the dealer seems knowledgeable, your conversation goes well, and you feel that this may be the store that you are looking for. The next step is to evaluate the specimens themselves, and there are several things that you should consider.

Full-Line Pet Shops

I particularly dislike seeing saltwater aquariums being marketed by shops that carry other types of pets, such as gerbils, reptiles, or puppies. Unless the store provides a separate area, ideally a separate room altogether, for its fish displays, health problems can crop up due to several factors. Most dangerous is airborne ammonia from pet litter (I'll have much more to say about ammonia in chapter 3). If you enter a pet shop and smell ammonia, chances are the fish are swimming in it, too. Other sources of fish stress may be the noise and vibration generated during the care of larger, terrestrial animals. There's also the real possibility of neglected maintenance by a staff stretched thin from wearing too many husbandry hats.

Big-box retailers seldom offer high-quality saltwater fish and invertebrates for the same reasons smaller pet shops fail in this area, but their discount pricing policies may make them a good source for equipment and supplies. Check out all the ones in your area.

Mail-Order Suppliers

What about mail order? I'll be completely honest. I helped to start one of the major mail-order suppliers of saltwater fish and invertebrates, and I am proud to say that during 10 years in business, the quality of stock supplied by this company was very high. I will say this about mail-order suppliers in general: The good ones are better than many local shops. Otherwise, how would they have managed to stay in business when customers must pay freight costs and have no opportunity to see the fish that they are buying? Shop owners often complain about mail-order livestock suppliers, but the fact is that the customers would not buy live specimens by mail order if they were not frustrated with their local dealer.

The Importance of Prior Research

Always carefully study the characteristics of any fish or invertebrate you are considering before you go shopping. Spending an hour doing prior research can save a lot of headaches in the long run. Don't buy fish on impulse. Aquarium shops sell fish that grow much too large for the home aquarium. They sell fish that cannot be enticed to eat in captivity. They sell fish that will devour everything else in your tank. They sell fish that may bite or sting you. I've been tough on dealers in this chapter, but remember that the ultimate responsibility for your aquarium lies with you. If you purchase on impulse, suffering the consequences later is your fault, not the dealer's.

After several years selling saltwater invertebrates, fish, and supplies via mail order, I can recommend this avenue to anyone for whom the local merchants fall short, but with a cautionary note. You can sometimes save a lot of money by ordering online or on the phone. You can often find rare and unusual livestock, as well. On the other hand, equipment that arrives unassembled may challenge your skills, and the distant supplier may not be able to offer help via phone or e-mail. Livestock, of course, can arrive in poor condition, even dead. Getting a replacement or refund may be problematic. My advice is to stick close to home, unless you find a great deal on a brand name product you already use or a critter you simply cannot resist. If you are going to buy livestock, order *only* from reputable sources. The best way to zero in on good mail-order dealers is by talking to other aquarists. Meet them in your local shop, join your community's aquarium club, or chat online. When you travel, try to visit livestock suppliers that do mail order. Many of them also have a retail store. Use the same criteria you would use to evaluate a shop in your home town. If the company passes muster, consider placing an order.

How to Recognize Quality Saltwater Fish

In many cases, a major factor in achieving success with a saltwater aquarium is the state of health of the fish and invertebrates when you buy them. Stress and starvation resulting from poor holding and handling by collectors and exporters may have more to do with mortality of ornamental saltwater fish than chemicals used in collection, or any inherent weakness in the fish's constitution. Therefore, care in purchasing may be the most important aspect of managing your aquarium. Here are some suggestions for making wise decisions.

- **Choose species that routinely come from good sources.** Several popular aquarium fish come largely or exclusively from Hawaii, where aquarium collecting is well-regulated. In addition, shipping from Hawaii to the mainland is relatively inexpensive and does not involve red tape, since it is interstate commerce. I have noted few problems with Florida or Caribbean specimens over the years as well, provided they are given proper care by the retailer and subsequently by the hobbyist. Good Hawaiian fish include:

- Yellow tang (*Zebrasoma flavescens*)
- Potter's angelfish (*Centropyge potteri*)
- Vanderbilt's chromis (*Chromis vanderbilti*)
- Several desirable butterflyfishes, such as the raccoon (*Chaetodon lunula*), threadfin (*C. auriga*), and longnosed (*Forcipiger flavissimus*)

Good Florida fish include:

- French angelfish (*Pomacanthus paru*)
- Yellowhead jawfish (*Opisthognathus aurifrons*)

Typical Caribbean imports that usually arrive on our shores in excellent shape include:

- Royal gramma (*Gramma loreto*)
- Black capped basslet (*G. melacara*)

If none of these species is on your want list, just ask the dealer if they have fish from Hawaii or Florida.

- **Choose captive-propagated fish.** Captive-propagated fish are among the best possible choices, especially for the beginning aquarium hobbyist. Many species of anemonefishes are available from hatcheries, along with several kinds of gobies and dottybacks. Dealers usually advertise that they have captive-propagated stock, but always inquire. Captive-bred specimens may be smaller than wild-caught counterparts, but will, of course, grow to the size typical for their species. In all cases, captive-bred fish acclimate better to aquarium conditions and have fewer problems than do similar specimens harvested from the wild.
- **Become familiar with the signs of poor health that fish may exhibit.** Watch out for:
  - Rapid movement of the gill covers ("panting" or "gasping"). This could indicate that the fish is infested with parasites.
  - Ragged fins, and the presence of lesions, open wounds, or similar abnormalities. Fish can lose a bit of fin tissue or a scale or two without serious consequences, but any damage should appear to be healing.
  - Apparent bloodiness or cottony fungal growth.
  - A fish that hides excessively. Unless the behavior is characteristic for the species, this is a sign that the fish is in some kind of distress.
  - Hollow belly or thinning of the musculature behind the head. These are signs of poor nourishment.

Four Rules for Buying Saltwater Fish

1. Know your dealer.
2. Know which fish come from which area of the world.
3. Learn to recognize the signs of poor health.
4. Don't shop only for price.

- **Know what healthy fish look like.**
  - Their colors are bright.
  - They search actively for food.
  - Their fins are held erect.
  - When viewed head on, the fish should be convex in outline, not concave.
- **Find out how long the retailer holds new arrivals.** The retailer should hold all new arrivals for at least a week before releasing them; 2 weeks in holding would be better. If this is not the routine at the store you select, they should at least be willing to hold a fish for you if you agree to buy the fish after the holding period is up. Saltwater fish have a harrowing journey from the reef to the retailer. They require a period of rest and adjustment before they are sent home with a hobbyist. A few days, or just until the fish has had its first meal, is not enough time for recovery.
- **Recognize the difference of cost versus value.** If you take away one lesson from this section it should be this: *cheap saltwater fish are almost never a bargain*. Once you find a dealer that consistently provides you with good quality fish, your best bet is to support that dealer with your business, even if a particular specimen is a few dollars less across town.

Getting Ready

By now you should have a fairly complete aquarium design. You know what equipment you need; perhaps you have already ordered the tank and stand. You also have a clear idea of the fish and other sea life you will be placing in the aquarium. You developed a timetable for acquiring those specimens and adding them to your aquarium (see chapter 6). The next step in realizing your dream of a thriving saltwater aquarium is to ready the area of your home where the aquarium will be installed.

Location, Location, Location

Finalize your choice of location. Avoid locating the tank in front of a window. Although filtered sunlight may benefit corals or seaweeds, temperature fluctuations near a window may be too great. Consider also the effects of ventilation. A stuffy room gets much warmer than a well-ventilated one. Similarly, if the tank is subjected to drafts, or is too close to a floor or wall vent, excessive heating and/or cooling of the water may occur. The kitchen or family room may be routinely warmer, for example, than a seldom-used spare bedroom. Of course, aquarists living in Georgia may have different temperature control problems than those living in North Dakota. A simple way to tell if the aquarium will remain close to the desired temperature is to fill a 30-gallon plastic trash can with tap water and place it in the approximate location of the planned aquarium. After 24 hours, check the temperature. If it is at 75 degrees F or less, perfect.

Also take into account the pattern of foot traffic near the aquarium. Vibration from a busy area of your home may constantly keep the fish agitated. It's best not to locate the tank where children routinely play or near a frequently used doorway. Opening the door repeatedly creates vibration and blasts the tank with cold air during the wintertime. And kids, of course, are kids.

And don't forget about the floor. If you've ever spilled a whole pitcher of tea, you'll know for certain that you don't want 30 gallons of saltwater on the floor. Avoiding a tank disaster merely requires a quick determination of the weight of the aquarium and its equipment compared to the load-bearing capabilities of the house or apartment.

The weight of the water is of primary concern. Seawater weighs 8.5 pounds per gallon. That means a 30-gallon tank holds 255 pounds of water. For a home aquarium, every precaution must be taken to ensure that the floor and the aquarium support furniture will carry this much weight. Fortunately, structural failure in the commercially available aquarium stands and cabinets rarely occurs, so this consideration takes on more importance in a built-in or custom design. The floor is another matter. Novice aquarists often assume that aquariums come only in sizes and shapes that can safely be accommodated in any home. This, however, is not the case. Because saltwater aquariums need to be relatively large, your floor may need shoring up before you install the tank.

A check of the building codes in your area will likely reveal that the floor in your house can support about 100 pounds per square foot. (Codes differ, but this is a typical specification.) The 30-gallon tank in our example is 12 × 36 inches, or 3 square feet. It will hold 255 pounds of water, and the tank and equipment will add more pounds, for a total of say 300 pounds in all. Three hundred pounds divided by 3 square feet yields 100 pounds per square foot, within the capabilities of the floor, although just barely. If you have any doubts as to the ability of your home to structurally accommodate your aquarium, you should check with a licensed contractor. A contractor can also recommend appropriate remedies for any problems that are discovered.

Here's a worksheet for calculating the gallon capacity and floor load produced by an aquarium of any dimensions:

Aquarium Floor Load Worksheet

Length of tank ______________________ inches, multiplied by width of tank ______________________ inches, equals the base area in square inches: ______________________.

Dividing the base area in inches __________ by 144 gives the base area in square feet: ________________.

Multiplying the base area in inches ________ by the height of the tank in inches ____________________ gives the capacity of the tank in cubic inches: ____________________.

Dividing the tank capacity in cubic inches by 251 gives the capacity in gallons: ____________________.

Multiplying the capacity in gallons by 8.5 pounds yields the weight of the water: ________________ pounds.

Multiply the weight of the water by 1.2 to give the estimated weight of the entire system: ___________.

Note: If the aquarium will have a sump or refugium tank, its weight must also be included. Calculate the capacity of the sump by the method just described, add that to the main tank weight, and multiply the total by 1.2 to arrive at the weight of the entire system.

Divide the system weight by the base area in square feet to give the load: ____________________________.

The load should be less than 100 pounds per square foot, or whatever you determine to be the load-bearing capacity of the floor.

Load capacity problems occur mostly with floors supported on wooden joists. A simple remedy is to install jack posts, available at any do-it-yourself store, to support the joists directly underneath the aquarium. For maximum support, the long axis of the aquarium tank should be perpendicular to the way the joists run. Since joists are usually spaced 16 to 24 inches apart, this will mean that the tank will be supported by two or more joists. Since the tank will usually be located against a wall, it will be sitting near the end of the joists, where their capacity is greatest. Orienting it in the opposite direction, parallel to the joists, may mean that the tank is sitting along the length of a single joist, or worse, merely resting on the plywood subfloor between two joists. Either situation can cause the floor to sag several inches, which is likely to split hardwood, stretch vinyl or carpet, or crack tile.

On a concrete slab floor, such as in a basement room, weight will be of less concern. In an apartment building, discussing the load numbers with the building superintendent may be a good idea. You don't want the tank winding up in the downstairs neighbors' living room!

Protecting Nearby Finishes

Saltwater aquariums have a habit of flinging small amounts of salt spray all over the place. Water movement created by the filtration system, splatters that occur during maintenance, and even the occasional movement of a fish at the surface can cause water to leave the tank and wind up where it is unwanted. If this goes unnoticed, significant, sometimes irreversible, damage can be done. I once made the mistake of hanging a large print (an underwater scene, naturally) in a mirrored frame on the wall above my 75-gallon aquarium. In less than a month, enough seawater found its way out of the tank to permanently damage the mirror on the lower edge of the frame.

Saltwater is extremely corrosive. The silver on my mirrored frame turned jet black. Saltwater will quickly rust ferrous metals, create a white crystalline bloom of corrosion on aluminum or galvanized surfaces, and produce greenish-blue excrescences on copper and brass. Metals, therefore, are to be avoided in the area immediately adjacent to the aquarium.

Various wood finishes are quickly broken down by saltwater, too. Painted wood surfaces should be repainted with an exterior-grade paint mixed to match the original finish. Natural wood finishes should be protected with a coat of clear marine-grade spar varnish, as is often used for boat decks. Even with these precautions, wipe up spills and splashes as soon as they are noticed, or damage may still occur. Remember that it is much easier to take such precautions now, before the tank is in place, than to repair and refinish damage after the aquarium has been set up. Not only do you have the hassle, but also you must take care not to contaminate the aquarium with varnish, paint, and thinners, and their fumes.

Typical indoor surface materials that are unaffected by seawater include glazed ceramic or quarry tile, laminated and synthetic stone countertops, fiberglass, and plastics of all types.

Obviously, any materials that you would normally not use in an area where water could get at them, such as fabrics, paper products, water-based paints, and so forth, should never be used near the aquarium.

Electricity and Water Supplies

Give some thought to the convenient availability of electricity and water in the vicinity of the aquarium. There are important safety, as well as practical, considerations involved.

Electricity

All the equipment needed for a functional aquarium system requires electricity. As you are creating your plan, count up the number of electrical cords that will eventually lead from the tank to a power source. There will be at least one for the filtration system, one or two for lighting, one for temperature control, etc. Now look at the area where you plan to put the tank. If the electrical supply consists of a single duplex outlet 10 feet away, you may be in trouble.

If you are installing a small system, say up to 75 gallons, you may be able to get by with one of those power strips nearly everyone uses to hook up their home computer. If you envision a larger system, or a built-in one, or if you just like to have things done right, you may want to consider modifying the existing wiring, or even installing a new circuit just for the aquarium. This will require the assistance of a licensed electrician, unless you are entirely confident in doing the wiring yourself. Before you call for an estimate, take a few moments to assess the power requirements of your system so you can tell the electrician what your needs are. Over the years I have discovered that electricians are seldom familiar with the power requirements of aquarium systems unless of course they are hobbyists themselves.

Use the worksheet below to calculate the power requirements for your aquarium system. Specifications for individual pieces of equipment, such as a pump, can be found on the housing. Engraved into the plastic on the bottom of the electric pencil sharpener on my desk, for example, are the words "120V 60Hz 2.0 amps". This translates to 120 volts, 60 hertz (cycles per second), and 2.0 amperes. You'll need to convert everything to amperes. Some items, like fluorescent lamps, may be rated only in watts. To determine the number of amperes such devices require, divide the wattage by the operating voltage. For example, a 40-watt fluorescent lamp operated at 120 volts draws 40/120, or 0.34, amperes.

Aquarium System Power Requirements Worksheet

Enter the wattage for each component of the system. Assume your house power is 120 volts if calculating watts from amperes.

Lighting system:

_____ fluorescent lamps at _____ watts = __________ watts

_____ metal halide lamps at _____ watts each = __________ watts

_____ LED lamps at _____ watts each = __________ watts

Heater: __________ watts

Filtration pump: __________ watts

Skimmer pump: __________ watts

Powerheads: _____ at _____ watts each = __________ watts

Other accessory: __________ watts

Other accessory: __________ watts

Total System Wattage **(sum of above column)** __________ **watts**

Each electrical circuit in your house is designed to carry a certain number of amperes, determined by the power rating of the breaker controlling that circuit. Your refrigerator, for example, is usually on its own 30-amp circuit, while your water heater may be supplied from a 60-amp or larger circuit. This is done to prevent devices that use a lot of electricity from overtaxing the circuit and starting a fire. Convenience outlets are usually 20 or 30 ampere circuits. If you are simply plugging the aquarium equipment into a wall outlet, you want to make sure its electrical demand does not cause the breaker to trip.

Even if you find it unnecessary to install new wiring to supply electricity to your aquarium, you should modify the existing outlet or breaker with a special ground fault circuit interrupter (GFCI) outlet or breaker. These devices are inexpensive and are required by most electrical codes for circuits serving wet areas, such as your bathroom. The GFCI device monitors the line and shuts off power to the outlet if abnormal electrical flow to the ground is detected. This prevents serious injury or death, should a conductor come into contact with water. Since seawater is an excellent conductor of electricity, GFCI protection is absolutely essential for all electrical components of the system.

By calculating the power requirements of your aquarium and making sure they are adequately met from the outset, you avoid not only safety hazards but also the possibility that the system will shut down because of an overload. Should that happen while you are away for the weekend, the result for your tank could be disaster.

Water

The ideal home aquarium would have a drain and a water tap available underneath the tank. In the average home, of course, this is unlikely to be the case, and other arrangements have to be made to facilitate water changes. Give some thought to this in the planning stages, so you won't end up neglecting maintenance because lugging water back and forth becomes a chore.

First, consider your needs in terms of the tank's capacity. As a rule, you will be changing about 20 percent of the tank each month. The simplest way to accomplish this is to use a hose to siphon water out of the tank into a 5-gallon bucket, dump the bucket and repeat. To refill, previously prepared seawater from a storage vessel is siphoned into the bucket and then poured into the aquarium. If you have a 100 gallon system, you'll be moving four buckets, each weighing around 45 pounds, between the tank and the nearest sink. If this prospect seems daunting, other options are available.

A nifty device, known as a *drain-fill siphon* is available in aquarium shops. (I actually first became acquainted with this gadget in a water bed store, but water beds seem scarcer in recent years than they once were.) Shaped like a T lying on its side, it creates suction by means of an aspirator. The force of water flowing through the vertical part pulls water in through the side arm. You thread the device onto a spigot, and attach a length of garden hose to the side arm. The other end of the hose is placed in the tank. When you turn the water on (full blast, which produces the strongest suction) tank water is pulled through the hose and drains into the sink. Although it wastes a bit of tap water, this seems a small price to pay for the work done, and it is far less messy than toting buckets down the hall.

The ideal arrangement, of course, is to have water and a drain available immediately adjacent to the aquarium. Usually, this is only practical for a large, built-in system. You'll need the help of a plumber for this kind of customization. If you are planning to go this route, also consider installing a utility sink in the service area for the aquarium.

Water Purification

Call your utility company and request information about the chemical composition of your tap water. Most of the time, you'll get a lot more information than you really need. If the pH is neutral or nearly so and the hardness is high, the tap water will make good synthetic seawater. Your main worry concerns phosphate. Phosphate finds its way into our drinking water as a result of fertilizer runoff. While not harmful to drink, the additional phosphate can often be a major factor in the development of excessive algae growth in your minireef. If the utility company says the phosphate content of your tap water is near 1.0 ppm or more, consider purification of your tap water before using it in your minireef.

If your water needs are comparatively small, say you have a 30-gallon tank, you can probably use distilled water from the grocery store, which will have no phosphate at all. Buying and transporting all those jugs of distilled water will become a chore if your water needs are anything but modest. For most home aquarium hobbyists, purifying their tap water with a reverse osmosis unit offers a more practical alternative.

Reverse osmosis (RO) units work by using the water pressure in the pipe to force tap water through a special membrane that excludes almost everything but water itself. Impurities are discharged in a wastewater stream, and purified water escapes, drop by drop, from another outlet. Because production is slow, you'll need a plastic container of some sort to catch and store the RO water. Most units produce about 3 gallons of wastewater for every gallon of product. The wastewater can be used for watering the garden. You can buy a reverse osmosis unit at most do-it-yourself stores and aquarium shops. Some are designed for use with municipal tap water, others for well water. Make sure you get the correct one for your application. Usually the units have an activated carbon filter that removes chlorine and a mud and sand filter to take out particulate matter. These prefilters help preserve the life of the RO membrane. Both prefilters should be changed about once or twice a year. Membrane life is hard to predict, because it depends on the chemistry of the tap water, but most units will produce hundreds of gallons before the membrane requires replacement.

To accurately determine when the activated carbon prefilter needs replacement, perform a chlorine test on the wastewater periodically. You can buy a chlorine test at most aquarium shops, or from a pool and spa supplier. The effectiveness of the RO membrane can be checked periodically with a hardness test. In this case, check the product water. Normally, its hardness will be extremely low or zero. If the hardness starts to climb, it's time for a new RO membrane.

Storage

You will need space and suitable containers to store a supply of prepared synthetic seawater. How much room of course depends on the size of the aquarium. For a 100-gallon system, you need at least 20 gallons for a routine water change. It is always helpful to have a bit more than the minimum supply, though, because in an emergency you may need to change more than 20 percent of the water. For example, if a contaminant finds its way into the tank, a massive water change may avert disaster. Also, about once or twice a year, you will want to do a major cleaning, changing about half the water or more. I recommend you have enough seawater on hand to carry out at least a 50 percent water change, and 100 percent would be even better.

Having a cabinet near the aquarium makes it easy to keep useful accessories, food, tank additives, and so forth close at hand. If you use a kitchen cabinet or other wood furniture, make sure to protect the inside from saltwater, either with a coat of water-resistant paint, or by using plastic tubs or baskets to organize your tank accessories inside the cabinet. Don't make the mistake of trying to store everything under the aquarium. Stuff will always be in the way when you need access to the pump. Also, aquarium cabinets tend to get dusty, because they are usually open in the back to allow heat to escape. Thus, your stored items will quickly get dusty and spotted with salt splatters.

Planning ahead for adequate storage and protecting the areas adjacent to the aquarium from potential damage will make maintenance simpler (and therefore more likely to be done on a regular basis). You will also find the aquarium experience more rewarding if you are not constantly concerned about damage to furniture, wallpaper, or whatever. Recognize the potential for problems and take appropriate action to avoid them.

What You Now Know . . .

- A fish-only aquarium may be easier to plan and less expensive to equip than a minireef, but a minireef may be more interesting in terms of the variety of sea life you can include.
- Choosing a good dealer may be the most important decision you make in regard to your aquarium project.
- Selecting quality saltwater fish involves knowing the dealer, knowing which fish come from where, recognizing the signs of poor health in fish, and a willingness to pay more for top-quality specimens.
- Preparing your home for your aquarium involves checking the load-bearing capacity of the floor, protecting finishes, and providing for water, electricity, and storage near the aquarium.

Chapter 3

Understanding How a Saltwater Aquarium Works

What's Inside . . .

- Understand the physical and chemical cycles governing the changes that occur in your aquarium over time.
- Recognize the key characteristics of the coral reef environment that must be duplicated in the aquarium.
- Learn to manage your aquarium by working with Mother Nature, not against her.

Marine aquariums develop into miniature ecosystems that can mimic the ocean to a remarkable degree. In the marine aquarium as well as in the sea, dynamic, cyclical processes affect water chemistry. Managing your aquarium's ecosystem is critical to the survival of your fish.

Physical and Chemical Cycles

Characteristic of all natural ecosystems, physical and chemical cycles also occur in the artificial ecosystem of the aquarium. Understanding these dynamic processes is the key to understanding how your aquarium works on a day-to-day basis, allowing you to anticipate problems before they endanger your fish. Four major cycles involve most of the activity within the aquarium. They are the nitrogen cycle, the diurnal light cycle, the carbon cycle, and the phosphorus cycle.

The Nitrogen Cycle

By far the most important chemical cycle that occurs in the saltwater aquarium is the nitrogen cycle. Here's how it works: Fish and invertebrates produce ammonia, which poses a significant threat to aquarium inhabitants. Because ammonia poses the greatest threat to your aquarium, the level of ammonia in your aquarium should not be allowed to rise above about 0.1 mg/L. (See chapter 8 for more on how to detect and treat high levels of ammonia.)

Microorganisms: The Base of the Ecosystem

A tank of seawater becomes an aquarium when you add living organisms. Among the first of these to arrive are bacteria, algae, fungi, and other single-celled organisms that may be wafted in on a current of air. They are abundantly present in and on the live sand and live rock often used to "seed" the new aquarium. Within a few weeks, microscopic life coats every available surface. These organisms play a crucial role in the development of the artificial ecosystem that a functioning saltwater aquarium eventually becomes. Any organism placed within the closed system of an aquarium immediately begins to change the chemistry of the water.

Ammonia is converted first to nitrite and then to nitrate by beneficial bacteria (nitrifying bacteria). Nitrate thus accumulates in the aquarium. Because nitrate accumulation reflects the level of biological activity going on in the aquarium, the amount of nitrate should remain constant over time as long as conditions do not change. Thus, measuring nitrate accumulation allows you to spot sudden fluctuations that may be a sign of trouble.

Nitrate is not considered toxic to marine organisms, but you should maintain low levels of nitrate, usually around 20 mg/L NO_3—N or less, because nitrate concentrations around natural reefs are quite low. For the aquarist using simple test kits, this number is effectively zero. In most aquariums, achieving such low levels of nitrate is impossible. Nevertheless, nitrate monitoring offers a convenient way to observe the *nitrogen equilibrium* of the system. An aquarium is in nitrogen equilibrium if the amount of nitrate detectable in the water remains constant with time.

The Diurnal Light Cycle

Diurnal light cycle means the change from day to night that occurs every 24 hours. Maintaining a constant pattern encourages normal growth and activity from the aquarium's inhabitants. Photosynthetic organisms such as seaweeds are the most obvious beneficiaries of the aquarium lighting, but the fish also need a change from day to night and back again to regulate their metabolism. Like humans, most fish sleep at night. Nocturnal fish, those that are active at night, sleep during the day, usually in a dark place such as a cave or in the shade of a rock ledge. Sleep is apparently just as important for fish as it is for us, judging from the elaborate precautions some species take to allow for a rest period each day. Many wrasses, for example, bury themselves in the sand at night, while parrotfishes (not a very good choice for the home aquarium, by the way) cover themselves with a mucus cocoon for slumber. Many fish adopt a strikingly different color pattern at night; this is often referred to as *sleep coloration*.

As far as the fish are concerned, as long as there is a period of darkness alternating with a period of light, the intensity of the light falling on the aquarium is of little consequence. Not

Getting Your Nitrifying Bacteria on Board

When you initially set up your aquarium you'll lack the nitrifying bacteria needed to convert ammonia to nitrate. Nitrifying bacteria will work their chemical "magic" with no additional encouragement from the aquarist, but first you have to get the bacteria into your aquarium. Here's how you go about that:

- Add one or two hardy "starter" fish by themselves. (This is the oldest method used by hobbyists. The small numbers of nitrifying bacteria on the fish's body slowly multiply, feeding on the ammonia excreted by the fish.)
- Add a cup of substrate material from an established aquarium along with a small, hardy fish. (This modification was added when people learned that the larger initial introduction of nitrifying bacteria in the gravel gave faster results than the small numbers introduced with the starter fish.)
- Add a cup of substrate material from an established aquarium along with ammonia in chemical form. (Adding ammonia as a chemical avoids risking the loss of the starter fish, or finding that a suitable starter fish is incompatible with the planned inhabitants of the tank.)
- Add the recommended amounts of live rock and live sand as described in chapter 5 along with one or two hardy fish. (Live rock and live sand in these amounts will bring along sufficient nitrifying bacteria to establish a functional system instantly.)
- Add a commercially produced culture of nitrifying bacteria and one or two hardy fish. (This method offers advantages especially for a fish-only system that does not rely on live rock.)

In each case, the bacteria feed on ammonia, either added as a chemical or from the addition of a fish or two. Small, hardy fish are chosen both because they can tolerate transient water quality problems and because they are inexpensive.

so with seaweeds and the symbiotic algae of various invertebrates. For these photosynthesizers, bright light is absolutely essential. Even though the best aquarium lighting is puny in comparison to the illumination produced by the sun, photosynthetic saltwater organisms not only grow but reproduce themselves at light levels recommended in chapter 2 for minireef tanks (that is, multiple fluorescent lamps or combinations of fluorescent and metal halide lamps). Organisms that depend on photosynthesis also need a day-night cycle to help regulate their metabolic processes. In some corals, for example, spawning behavior is influenced by the light cycle.

Photosynthesis takes place only during the daylight hours and alters the pH of the aquarium by removing carbon dioxide from the water. As a result, the measured pH of the aquarium water will vary depending on the time of day. In order for comparisons to be made from one time to the next, the pH should be checked at the same time of day each time you perform the test. It normally will be highest just before the lights go out in the evening, and lowest just before "dawn" occurs.

The Carbon Cycle

Carbon tends to move through the aquarium system in much the same way nitrogen does. When a fish ingests food, some of the carbon contained in the food, in the form of a variety of organic compounds, is utilized by the fish for its energy needs or as building blocks for growth. The rest is excreted. Fish feces and uneaten food are attacked by small invertebrates and microorganisms, each seeking its share of the carbon (and other raw materials) remaining. When these organisms in their turn become part of the food chain, the cycle is closed. At some point, however, the food will have given up all the useful materials composing it, and the remainder will be organic compounds that are broken down very slowly. These compounds become dissolved organic carbon (DOC) in the aquarium water. Because DOC tends to color the water yellowish, German aquarists refer to it as *gelbstoff*, or "yellow matter." Like nitrate, *gelbstoff* accumulates continuously in the aquarium but is rare in the waters of a real coral reef. Unlike nitrate, this mixture of compounds has definite harmful effects that experienced aquarists can observe. Little research has been done to link specific compounds to specific problems, but the positive effects of DOC removal are widely agreed upon. Removal of DOC is best accomplished via foam fractionation, mentioned in chapter 2.

The Phosphorus Cycle

Like carbon and nitrogen, phosphorus flows through the aquarium ecosystem from consumer to decomposer to producer and back again to consumer. In the aquarium water, most phosphorus will be in the form of phosphate. Phosphate accumulation parallels that of nitrate and DOC. The total amount increases continuously in the absence of water changes or other means of removal. Excess phosphate likely does no harm, but like nitrate it is rare in the reef environment. Levels that develop in the closed system of the aquarium are therefore unnaturally high. The usual consequence of phosphate accumulation is an algal bloom. Various kinds of seaweeds and filamentous algae that normally grow in moderation suddenly become the stuff of B-movie horror, covering any available surface and engulfing everything in their path like some extraterrestrial blob. Ubiquitous in nature, phosphate almost always enters the aquarium in excess via the water supply. This may mean water purification is necessary in your area. The options for dealing with this issue are covered in chapter 2.

Overview of the Coral Reef Environment

The oceans teem with life, but nowhere in such colorful diversity as on the coral reef. The peculiar conditions needed by reef-building corals result in the confinement of reefs to limited areas. Reefs only form in tropical waters. Fringing reefs skirt shorelines on the continental shelf. Continuous walls of coral reef occur along the coast in some areas. This pattern of development results in a barrier reef. In the open sea, fringing reefs may form around small islands; sea level fluctuations and land subsidence can cause the nurturing island to disappear underwater, leaving a donut-shaped reef or atoll. Barrier reefs are found on the eastern side of the land mass, a phenomenon thought to be the result of prevailing currents and tidal flow patterns that help keep the water free of sediment and therefore crystal clear most of the time. Reefs achieve their highest level of development in the barrier form. The largest structure on earth built by living creatures is the Great Barrier Reef of Australia, stretching some 3,200 miles (2,000 kilometers) along that country's eastern coastline.

Nearly every type of living organism occurs in some form on the reef. An abundance of microhabitats, food, and a stable underwater "climate" receive credit for this astonishing level of diversity. Different species have evolved specialized lifestyles to exploit every conceivable niche. Often, specialization results in a loss of adaptability. The degree of adaptability, or lack thereof, plays a crucial role in determining whether a particular species can be accommodated successfully in an aquarium.

Specialization among reef organisms involves a complex interaction among factors such as the chemistry of the surrounding water, physical parameters such as depth and turbulence, and biological factors such as the presence of suitable food, predators, and potentially disease-causing organisms. Each of these must be taken into account when stocking a saltwater aquarium with its living components.

The Physical Environment—Light, Shelter, and Water Movement

Coral reefs develop only under specific conditions. Light, in particular, must reach the coral organisms because all hermatypic (reef-building) corals harbor photosynthetic, symbiotic algae, known to biologists as *zooxanthellae*. Thus, reefs form only where water clarity is sufficient to allow adequate light penetration. Sediment, usually transported from the coastline by rivers, reduces light penetration and can smother corals. Clear, sediment-free water is the primary physical requirement for the development of a coral reef. Temperature, water movement, and underwater topography all play a role, as well.

Reefs develop primarily in areas where the water temperature averages in the mid-seventies. Inshore shallows and lagoons may become much warmer than this during the day, and then cool off again at night. Consequently, organisms from the lagoon may be more tolerant of temperature fluctuations than those from the outer reef, washed by the open sea. Similarly, the water in the lagoon is much less turbulent than on the outer face of the reef. Corals that require heavy wave action are seldom found growing alongside those accustomed to the quiet waters of the lagoon. Substrate conditions can further subdivide a habitat. Organisms that attach themselves to a solid surface will be found in areas of the lagoon with a hard bottom of fossil coral. Other species are adapted to sitting upon, or burrowing within, sandy substrates. Currents determine the location of accumulations of sand, mud, or clean-scoured rocks, providing another example of the influence of water movement on the ecosystem.

Aquariums designed for exhibiting coral reef fishes and invertebrates must therefore be amply large, brightly illuminated, and temperature-controlled, and provide adequate water movement and appropriate substrates.

Interactions: The Biological Environment

Understanding that a complex web of ecological interactions exists on the reef explains why specific conditions have to be met in the aquarium before reef species will survive. For the vast majority of species available to saltwater aquarium hobbyists, a single, basic set of water conditions, easily achieved with simple techniques, is sufficient for survival, growth, and often reproduction. Some species demand more than others do, however. Merely having the correct amount of light or a low level of nitrate may not be enough. Among fish, the mandarin dragonet feeds only on tiny living crustaceans that it plucks from among rocks. It frequently starves rather than accepts alternative foods. I like to call a finicky species like this the *pivotal species* in the aquarium. When conditions are suitable for the pivotal species, it is a safe bet that less demanding tank mates will also be accommodated.

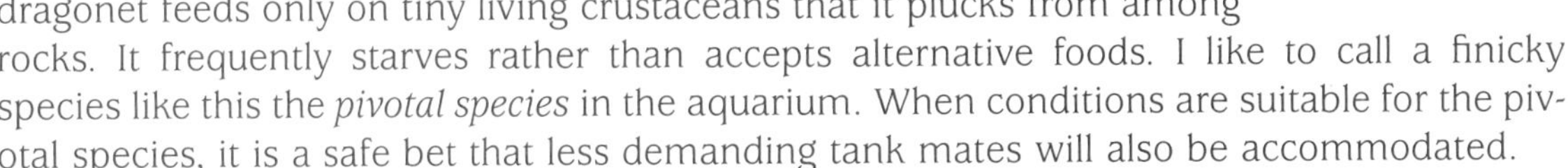

Identifying a pivotal species in your aquarium stocking plan will simplify other aspects of designing the system.

Let Nature Take Its Course

Your saltwater aquarium becomes a dynamic ecosystem from the moment you add any living thing. The natural cycles that characterize real ecosystems will establish themselves in the aquarium with no effort on your part, perhaps in spite of the mistakes you make. If you want to succeed with the saltwater aquarium hobby, your best bet is to understand these processes, work with them, and avoid attempts to thwart them. Like death and taxes, physical, chemical, and biological cycles come with the territory.

What You Now Know . . .

- Aquariums exhibit physical and chemical cycles not unlike those found in natural habitats.
- The important cycles in the aquarium are the nitrogen cycle, the carbon cycle, the phosphorus cycle, and the diurnal light cycle. Each must be considered in terms of its effects in the aquarium.
- Physical space, water chemistry, light availability, water movement, and substrate type must be manipulated to suit the needs of the aquarium's most finicky inhabitants.

Chapter 4

Stocking Your Tank I: Fish

What's Inside . . .

- Learn the characteristics of fish suitable for the home saltwater aquarium.
- Learn about the various families of saltwater fish and their needs in the aquarium.
- Learn which species will live peacefully together and which ones may fight.
- Learn which fish are the best choices for fish-only aquariums, minireefs, or both.
- Learn which saltwater fish should be avoided by the home aquarist.

Now that you understand how saltwater aquariums behave, and you have a basic plan in mind, it's time to think about fish and/or invertebrates in more detail. Unless you plan to feature only a single species, you will end up creating a miniature ecosystem, complete with plants, consumers, and decomposers. This will not happen overnight, but as the tank matures and you add additional inhabitants, the interactions begin to resemble more and more what happens on a natural reef.

The Best Home Aquarium Fish

Hundreds of species of saltwater fish are collected for the aquarium trade. Their suitability for the home aquarium varies over a wide range. The best fish species for the typical hobbyist are those that share some or all of the following traits:

- **Remains small in size, preferably no more than 3 or 4 inches at adulthood.** Some suitable species reach 6 inches in length or more, but these are the exception. Larger fish simply need more room than can be provided in a home tank.
- **Accepts a range of readily available foods.** Some fish species will greedily consume almost anything tossed into the tank; others will starve before accepting aquarium foods. Both kinds are likely to be found in pet shops, so it behooves you to know something about the fish's feeding habits before you buy.
- **Exhibits no unusual level of aggressive behavior.** Species that are tolerant of tank mates are often called *community fish*. While some communities remain peaceful only because their citizens cannot swallow each other, the best aquarium species are docile unless threatened. Unusually aggressive species need a tank to themselves.

- **Possesses bright coloration, interesting behavior, or both.** The clown anemonefish (*Amphiprion ocellaris*) provides a good example of a species that is both colorful and charming, especially when paired with a host anemone. Most of the popular species are so because they are brilliantly colored, but some, such as anglerfishes, appeal to aquarists because of their remarkable behavior, despite being somewhat on the dowdy side when it comes to coloration.
- **Has been legally and sustainably collected.** Since most saltwater aquarium fish are taken from wild populations, aquarists everywhere have an obligation not to encourage, through their purchasing patterns, unsustainable collecting techniques.

Getting to Know Fish

When you go shopping for aquarium fish, it is helpful to quickly distinguish the various families that will be displayed together in the dealer's tanks. The number and arrangement of the fins, body shape, and coloration are the most useful characteristics for identifications of this sort.

Parts of the Fish Body

Before getting into a consideration of some specific species, you need to learn your way around the body of a fish, so you'll understand my description of each species. Besides, when you go fish shopping, it helps to know the lingo.

Here are the basic areas of the fish's body:

- The front end, or anterior, bears the head.
- The most prominent features are the mouth and the eyes. Mouth structure can tell you a lot about the fish's feeding habits. An elongated, forceps-like mouth is suited to picking small organisms from rocks or seaweeds. A large mouth studded with sharp teeth usually marks a predatory species, and so forth.
- The eyes of many reef fishes are camouflaged by bars, stripes, or other optical illusion techniques. Some fish have false eyes on the opposite end, to fool predators into biting at a less vital area of the body.
- The gill covers, or opercula (singular operculum) mark the point at which the head ends and the body begins.
- Toward the read end, or posterior, fish possess a tail, or caudal fin, attached to the body by a short, fleshy stalk, the caudal peduncle.
- The dorsal area, or back, bears the dorsal fin. Some fish have two dorsal fins, others only one.
- The ventral area, or belly, bears the pelvic fins, which usually lie just anterior to the anus.
- On each side, behind the gill covers, are the pectoral fins.

Coloration

The body of the fish is covered with skin, which not only secretes a mucus coating that protects the fish from pathogens and reduces drag while swimming, but also generates the scales. Both skin and scales can contribute to the overall body coloration. Scales, because they contain crystals of a substance called *guanine*, often contribute to iridescence in the color pattern. Horizontal bands or lines of color are called *stripes*, to distinguish them from *bars*, which run vertically. Color also appears in dots, circles, squiggles, and virtually any other pattern you might envision. One of the primary attractions of reef fishes is their gaudy coloration; some almost appear to have been made from painted porcelain.

Color plays many roles in the ecology of reef fishes. For example, it may provide a marker allowing members of the same species to recognize each other at breeding time. Often, color provides camouflage against the typical background over which the fish swims. Color may also serve to distract a predator.

Who Lives with Whom?

Selecting an appropriate community for your saltwater aquarium is, unfortunately, not simply a matter of selecting several specimens that appeal to you and tossing them into the same tank. While the different species of fishes and invertebrates that you see in aquarium shops may well live together in apparent harmony on the reef, once confined in the aquarium their interactions can range from benign indifference to vicious hostility. Therefore, it is important to take into account the lifestyles of each of the potential inhabitants of your tank.

Three major considerations apply in the selection of a compatible community of saltwater fishes: size, social needs, and disposition. Dealing with these concerns first simplifies the process of creating a list of potential tank mates, since one generally cannot manipulate the aquarium environment to get around these constraints.

Housing Invertebrates

The first question you should answer regarding the species that will live in your captive sea is "Do I want invertebrates in the tank?" While an invertebrate aquarium can be interesting and relatively simple to maintain, combining invertebrates and fishes must be done with care, lest some inhabitants become food for others. On the reef, invertebrates such as crustaceans and mollusks are important food sources for many kinds of fishes. Obviously, trying to keep predators and prey together won't work. Chapter 5 will discuss invertebrates in more depth.

How Big Will It Get?

It should be immediately apparent that choosing a fish that will outgrow its quarters is asking for trouble, although this error is frequently committed by the novice aquarist. I've heard all sorts of excuses: plans for a bigger tank never materialized, no one realized the fish would grow so quickly. I've also heard repeated the curious fallacy that the size of the aquarium can somehow restrict the growth of its occupants. I've heard stories like this while standing across the counter from a hobbyist looking for a home for an overgrown pet. Unfortunately, few shops are willing, or even able, to accept specimens that have become too large to be accommodated by their owners. For one thing, shops must allocate their holding space parsimoniously—there may simply be no room this week for an unanticipated guest, especially a sizable one. For another, shopkeepers are often concerned that returned specimens may harbor disease problems that might spread to the other inventory. And only the most generous shop owner would welcome a specimen that was not purchased there initially, although this is a request that I have personally received many times.

If the shop can't take your overgrown fish, other options may be limited. Public aquariums seldom accept such donations, for example. The only choices may be buying another tank, or euthanasia. Better to avoid this problem altogether, and find out the maximum anticipated size of any fish you are considering to be sure your tank can accommodate it.

Always listen to your dealer's recommendations concerning the range of sizes that are suitable for your aquarium. Above all, use common sense. A fish that will reach 12 inches in length is a completely impractical choice for a 36-inch tank. Unless you plan to set up a rather large tank as a first effort, say over 100 gallons (usually such a tank will be 6 feet long), it is best to limit yourself to fish that grow no larger than about 3 to 6 inches, with the upper portion of this size range reserved for tanks that are at least 4 feet long. Doing so will not limit your choices all that much; there are scores of species from which to select. Remember that choosing specimens of suitable size for your tank will mean that their chances of living out a normal life span under your care will be greatly enhanced.

Social Needs

Having made a list of potential inhabitants that will not outgrow your aquarium, you next must consider the typical social needs of species within the families you have selected. Coral reef fish exhibit a range of behaviors because natural selection has favored those behaviors leading to survival and reproductive success. You can do little, therefore, to alter these innate patterns. You can, however, choose species whose typical behavior will not create conflicts in the captive community.

- **Prefers to not live with others of their own kind:** Families in which this behavior is common (with occasional exceptions) include dottybacks, dragonets, hawkfishes, groupers, triggerfishes, large angelfishes, and wrasses. The rules, however, are not absolute. Often, the gender of the fish determines whether it will tolerate others.

Size Guidelines

Here are some rough guidelines for choosing the right-size fish for your tank:

- For tanks 3 feet in length or smaller, choose from the following families: basslets, dottybacks, anemonefishes, some damselfishes, dwarf angelfishes, some hawkfishes, dragonets, blennies, gobies, jawfishes, and cardinalfishes.
- For tanks from 3 to 6 feet in length, the choices expand to include wrasses, butterflyfishes, and tangs, along with anthias and comet groupers, and some lionfishes, eels, rabbitfishes, puffers, triggerfishes, and boxfishes.
- Tanks over 6 feet in length could hold a larger community of any of these, and are essential for large angelfishes, groupers, and triggerfishes, or any species that reaches over 1 foot in length, eels excepted.

Typically, male dragonets, wrasses, and both dwarf and large angelfishes will not allow another male within sight, but all these males accept female companionship. In these families, females will usually, but not always, remain peaceful with each other.

- **Prefers group living:** Fish deprived of group living may not fare well. Certain species of anthias are good examples. They normally live in shoals, and should be kept in groups of at least three individuals, preferably five or more, in the aquarium. To understand why this arrangement is so important, we need to know more about the social behavior of anthias. Each shoal is dominated by a mature male, and consists of females and juvenile males that swim below him in the water column. The fish feed on plankton in open water, fully exposed to predators. The hierarchy of the shoal apparently serves as protection. When something happens to the dominant male, one of the younger males takes his place. That sounds simple enough, but the way it occurs is intertwined with the development of sexual maturity. It is not merely a behavioral change, but an irreversible physiological one, that maintains the dominance hierarchy. Anthias begin life as females and develop into males as they mature, a characteristic found in several types of saltwater fishes and known as *protogynous hermaphroditism*. The juvenile males—actually females approaching maturity—resemble younger females in coloration and fin development. When the dominant male dies, the changes that occur in the appearance of the juvenile male who succeeds in taking his place can be quite dramatic. Within days, his fins develop the characteristic luxuriance of the mature male, and his color pattern changes entirely. Along with these changes in appearance come all the changes in behavior associated with being the top dog, rather than an underling. Nature often goes to such extraordinary lengths to maintain a successful lifestyle on the coral reef. If they are deprived of the security of the shoal, anthias often fail to eat and slowly starve.

- **Prefers shoals (a large school fish):** Similarly, most species of surgeonfishes, also known as *tangs*, are shoaling fishes. While unlike anthias surgeonfish gender apparently does not determine dominance, tangs nevertheless exhibit a social hierarchy, or *pecking order*. The implications for aquarium care are straightforward: Keeping two fish together will result in one individual being constantly harassed by the other. This will eventually cause the poor subordinate to die of starvation or disease. Keeping a group of tangs together, mimicking the natural pattern, spreads the aggression among several fish and no one specimen takes all the heat. A warning, though: Some species of tangs are so aggressive that they are intolerant of others unless the group consists of a great many individuals. Keeping a large shoal of such species is usually impossible for the typical hobbyist, so the answer is to restrict yourself to a single specimen. The powder blue tang (*Acanthurus leucosternon*) provides a good example of a species that must be kept singly, although it occurs in huge shoals in the Indian Ocean. Tangs in general are suitable only for larger aquariums. Their frequent confinement in tanks of less than 6 feet in length may be the main reason why this family of herbivorous grazers is widely regarded as especially susceptible to parasitic infestations and disease in captivity.
- **Prefers female companionship:** Harem formation can be important to a fish's well-being. Dwarf angelfishes (*Centropyge*) are similar to anthias in that the younger specimens are all females that eventually mature into males. One male typically has a harem of several females within his territory and excludes all other males. Duplicating this social structure in the aquarium not only leads to a peaceable community, it generally rewards the aquarist with the opportunity to watch the spawning behavior, which may occur at dusk almost every day.
- **Prefers monogamy—either mated or unmated:** Some fish need to be paired with a single mate to thrive. Most butterflyfishes, for example, travel only in pairs. These may not be reproductive pairings, however, as two males or two females may form a bond. This behavior probably evolved to provide security as the fish forage along the reef. Two heads, as we know, are better than one. Exceptions exist, of course. The copperbanded butterflyfish (*Chelmon rostratus*) will not permit another of its species to live in the same aquarium. Conversely, pennant butterflyfish (*Heniochus*) species form shoals. They do better in captivity if a group shares the same tank. Like tangs, the butterflyfish family has a reputation for being difficult to keep. However, the need for a large territory, usually lacking in the aquarium, may be a significant source of stress. Stressed-out fish are always less likely to adapt successfully.
- **Prefers monogamy—the mated kind:** Some kinds of fish, such as the signal goby (*Signigobius biocellatus*), are virtually always found as mated pairs. They do poorly in the aquarium if kept without a mate.

Aggressive Dispositions

Some fish are so aggressive that they may pose a threat to any tank mate that is not similarly robust. In this category are big predators—lionfishes, groupers, eels, and triggerfishes—along with the small but spunky damselfishes.

- Lionfishes, groupers, and eels usually express their aggressive tendencies only toward potential food items or members of their own kind. Many of them eat other fishes. Others specialize in certain kinds of invertebrates, usually mollusks or crustaceans. Do not make the mistake of relying on specialized feeding habits to permit you to "get away with" keeping these specimens with inappropriate companions. Some eels feed largely on cephalopods, such as octopus, for example, but will adapt the menu to include their neighbors if necessity demands it.
- Triggerfishes can be aggressive just for the heck of it. Some individuals may be so intolerant of any companionship that keeping them in solitary confinement is the only option. These fish may also rearrange the tank decorations to suit themselves. While they can be amusing pets that demonstrate remarkable intelligence, triggerfish should be included in a community aquarium only with great caution. There are a few species, such as the bluethroat triggerfish (*Xanthichthys auromarginatus*) that are not so temperamental and can be kept in a community tank. Others, such as the undulated triggerfish (*Balistapus undulatus*) may attack anything that moves, including your fingers. Do your homework before succumbing to the temptation to purchase these fish, despite their undeniable beauty.
- For achieving maximum aggressiveness for their body size, no saltwater fish can match certain members of the damselfish family. This large group of generally hardy species exhibits a variety of lifestyles. However, several commonly available ones are quite territorial. For example, the domino damselfish (*Dascyllus trimaculatus*) occupies a single coral head and will defend this territory to the death, even attacking fishes much larger than itself should they stray too close. Too many dealers recommend starting out with a damselfish or two. After the damselfish has occupied the aquarium alone for a month it comes to regard the entire tank as its exclusive domain, with disastrous consequences for any newcomer that the aquarist might subsequently introduce.

Saltwater Fish Families

Each of the species mentioned can successfully be maintained for the duration of its normal life span in an aquarium of 30 gallons established and maintained by the methods described in this book. The sole exception is the Hawaiian turkeyfish, which will eventually require a 50-gallon tank. While two or more of the smaller species, gobies, for example, might be combined within the same 30-gallon tank, having a community of more than two or three fish will require a bigger aquarium. For each species in the list, its adult size, food preferences, habitat preferences, and other pertinent information are summarized in tables.

Understanding Scientific Names

Do you find scientific names daunting? Gardeners use terms like *Chrysanthemum*, *Rhododendron*, and *Philodendron* without hesitation. These are scientific names. Why are the scientific names for plants easy for the average person to use, but not the scientific names for aquarium fishes and invertebrates? Possibly, nonscientists are afraid of appearing foolish through mispronunciation. Fear not. Even professionals may pronounce the same name slightly differently. As long as everyone can agree on which animal the name refers to, etymological concerns should take a backseat.

Scientific names make our communications about saltwater organisms more precise. The species that I refer to as *palette surgeonfish* may be called *regal tang* by someone else, but the scientific name *Paracanthurus hepatus* is unambiguous. That's the beauty of scientific names; every organism that has been formally described has but one scientific name used throughout the world to refer to that particular organism. So, whether one is in Brooklyn or Berlin, *Clibanarius tricolor* refers to the same animal. *Blue-legged hermit crab* could refer to a different critter, depending on local usage.

The importance of having a precise understanding about just which organism is being discussed can hardly be overestimated. Many times a species that is easy to keep has a relative that is similar in appearance but is very difficult to keep. Confusion can easily arise when only common names are used.

Apart from the elimination of confusion, scientific names can supply valuable information about the organisms to which they refer. Most scientific names mean something. Consider *Zoanthus sociatus*. Loosely translated this means *flower animal that lives in colonies*, an apt description of the animal. How about *Cirrhilabrus rubriventralis*, or *bristle-lipped fish with a red belly*? Isn't this fun?

A scientific name consists of two parts. The first identifies the *genus* (plural, *genera*) or group, to which the organism belongs. Thus, *Amphiprion ocellaris* and *Amphiprion percula* are two species within the same genus. The second part of the name identifies the species. *Forcipiger longirostris* is *the long-snouted forceps-carrier*. Sure enough, the snout of this butterflyfish is much longer than that of the *longnosed butterflyfish*, *Forcipiger flavissimus*. See how confusing common names can be? *Forcipiger flavissimus* means *the most yellow forceps-carrier* obviously distinct from the long-snouted. Taken together, the two parts of the scientific name uniquely identify a specific organism.

Fishes for Fish-Only Aquariums

	Food	Size	Found In
Angelfishes, Pomacanthidae			
Centropyge argi, Atlantic pygmy angelfish	Algae	2½ inches	Florida and Caribbean
Centropyge loriculus, flame angelfish	Omnivorous	3 inches	Hawaii, elsewhere in Pacific
Centropyge potteri, Potter's dwarf angelfish	Algae	2–3 inches	Hawaii
Butterflyfishes, Chaetodontidae			
Chaetodon auriga, threadfin butterflyfish	Varied diet several times daily	9 inches	Hawaii
Chaetodon kleini, Klein's butterflyfish	Small pieces of seafood several times daily	6 inches	Hawaii, Indo-Pacific
Chaetodon semilarvatus, golden butterflyfish	Small pieces of seafood several times daily	9 inches	Red Sea
Forcipiger flavissimus, yellow longnosed butterflyfish	Small pieces of seafood several times daily	8 inches	Hawaii, elsewhere in the Indo-Pacific
Goatfishes, Parupeneidae			
Parupeneus multifasciatus, multibarred goatfish	Varied diet 3–4 times daily	12 inches	Indo-Pacific
Groupers, Cephalopholidae			
Cephalopholis miniata, coral grouper	Carnivorous	15 inches	Indo-Pacific
Chromileptes altivelis, panther grouper	Carnivorous	30 inches	Indo-Pacific
Hawkfishes, Cirrhitidae			
Amblycirrhitus pinos, red spotted hawkfish	Varied diet of seafood	4 inches	Florida and Caribbean
Neocirrhites armatus, flame hawkfish	Varied diet of seafood	4 inches	South Pacific
Oxycirrhites typus, longnosed hawkfish	Varied diet of seafood	5 inches	Hawaii, Indo-Pacific
Lionfishes, Scorpaenidae			
Dendrochirus brachypterus, fuzzy dwarf lionfish	Living shrimp and/or feeder fish several times a week	6 inches	Indo-Pacific
Dendrochirus zebra, dwarf lionfish	Living shrimp and/or feeder fish several times a week	7 inches	Indo-Pacific
Pterois volitans, common lionfish	Living shrimp and/or feeder fish several times a week	15 inches	Indo-Pacific

continued

Fishes for Fish-Only Aquariums (continued)

	Food	Size	Found In
Sea Basses, Serranidae			
Serranus tigrinus, harlequin bass	Any seafood of appropriate size	4 inches	Western Atlantic
Snappers, Lutjanidae			
Lutjanus kasmira, bluelined snapper	Aggressive carnivore of crustaceans and fishes	12 inches	Indo-Pacific
Surgeonfishes (Tangs), Acanthuridae			
Acanthurus coeruleus, Atlantic blue tang	Algae	9 inches	Florida and Caribbean
Naso lituratus, naso tang	Mixture of vegetable and seafood daily	18 inches	Indo-Pacific
Paracanthurus hepatus, regal tang	Seafood chopped in small pieces	6–12 inches	Indo-Pacific
Zebrasoma flavescens, yellow tang	Algae, feed several times daily	6 inches	Hawaii, Indo-Pacific
Triggerfishes, Balistidae			
Balistoides conspicillum, clown triggerfish	Anything of appropriate size	8–10 inches	Indo-Pacific
Balistapus undulatus, undulate triggerfish	Anything of appropriate size	10–12 inches	Indo-Pacific
Rhinecanthus aculeatus, Picasso triggerfish	Anything of appropriate size	10 inches	Hawaii
Wrasses, Labridae			
Choerodon fasciatus, harlequin tuskfish	Varied diet of seafood	8–10 inches	Australia, Indo-Pacific
Thalassoma bivittatum, bluehead wrasse	Varied diet of seafood	5 inches	Florida and Caribbean
Thalassoma lucasanum, paddlefin wrasse	Varied diet of seafood	6 inches	Eastern Pacific

Fishes for Minireef Aquariums

	Food	Size	Found In
Anthias, Anthiidae			
Pseudanthias bicolor, bicolor anthias	Plankton substitute several times daily	5 inches	Indo-Pacific
Pseudanthias ventralis hawaiiensis, Hawaiian longfin anthias	Plankton substitute several times daily	3 inches	Hawaii
Serranocirrhitus latus, sunburst anthias	Plankton substitute several times daily	4 inches	Indo-Pacific

	Food	Size	Found In
Blennies, Blenniidae			
Acanthemblemaria sp., sailfin blennies	Small pieces of seafood daily	2–3 inches	Eastern Pacific
Escenius bicolor, bicolor blenny	Filamentous algae	4 inches	Indo-Pacific
Meiacanthus atrodorsalis ovaluensis, canary blenny	Small pieces of seafood daily	4 inches	Indo-Pacific
Cardinalfishes, Apogonidae			
Pterapogon kauderni, Banggai cardinalfish	Varied diet of seafood	4 inches	Indonesia
Damselfishes, Pomacanthidae			
Chromis vanderbilti, Vanderbilt's chromis	Plankton substitutes several times daily	3 inches	Hawaii, Indo-Pacific
Chromis viridis, green chromis	Plankton substitutes several times daily	4 inches	Indo-Pacific
Chrysiptera cyanea, orange-tailed blue damselfish	Small pieces of seafood daily, filamentous algae	4 inches	Indo-Pacific
Dascyllus aruanus, the three-striped humbug	Small pieces of seafood daily, filamentous algae	4 inches	Hawaii
Dascyllus melanurus, black-tailed humbug	Small pieces of seafood daily, filamentous algae	4 inches	Hawaii, Indo-Pacific
Dascyllus trimaculatus, three spot humbug	Small pieces of seafood daily, filamentous algae	4 inches	Indo-Pacific
Anemonefishes			
Amphiprion clarkii, Clark's anemonefish	Small pieces of seafood daily, filamentous algae	4–5 inches	Indo-Pacific
Amphiprion frenatus, tomato anemonefish	Small pieces of seafood daily, filamentous algae	6 inches	Indo-Pacific
Amphiprion ocellaris, common clown anemonefish	Small pieces of seafood daily, filamentous algae	4 inches	Indo-Pacific
Amphiprion percula, percula clown anemonefish	Small pieces of seafood daily, filamentous algae	4 inches	Indo-Pacific
Premnas biaculeatus, maroon anemonefish	Small pieces of seafood daily, filamentous algae	6+ inches	Indo-Pacific
Dartfishes, Microdesmidae			
Nemateleotris magnifica, common fire goby	Plankton substitute several times daily	4 inches	Hawaii, Indo-Pacific
Pterelotris heteroptera, blue gudgeon	Plankton substitute several times daily	5 inches	Indo-Pacific

continued

Fishes for Minireef Aquariums (continued)

	Food	Size	Found In
Dottybacks, Pseudochromidae			
Pseudochromis aldebarensis, neon dottyback	Small pieces of seafood daily	<4 inches	Arabian Sea
Pseudochromis fridmani, orchid dottyback	Small pieces of seafood daily	<3 inches	Red Sea
Pseudochromis springeri, Springer's dottyback	Small pieces of seafood daily	<2 inches	Red Sea
Dragonets, Callionymidae			
Pterosynchiropus splendidus, mandarin	Tiny, living invertebrates	5 inches	Indo-Pacific
Synchiropus picturatus, psychedelic fish	Tiny, living invertebrates	3 inches	Indo-Pacific
Fairy Basslets, Grammidae			
Gramma loreto, royal gramma	Small pieces of seafood daily	4 inches	Florida and Caribbean
Gramma melacara, black-capped basslet	Small pieces of seafood daily	3 inches	Florida and Caribbean
Gobies, Gobiidae			
Amblygobius rainfordi, Rainford's goby	Small pieces of seafood and filamentous algae daily	3 inches	West-central Pacific
Cryptocentrus cinctus, yellow watchman goby	Small pieces of seafood daily	4 inches	Indo-Pacific
Gobiodon okinawae, yellow clown goby	Small pieces of seafood daily	1½ inches	Indo-Pacific
Gobiodon rivulatus, banded coral goby	Small pieces of seafood daily	1½ inches	Indo-Pacific
Gobiosoma multifasciatum, green-banded goby	Small pieces of seafood daily	1½ inches	Eastern Pacific
Gobiosoma oceanops, neon goby	Small pieces of seafood daily	1½ inches	Florida and Caribbean
Gobiosoma puncticulatus, redheaded goby	Small pieces of seafood daily	1½ inches	Eastern Pacific
Signigobius biocellatus, signal goby	Small pieces of seafood daily	<4 inches	Indo-Pacific
Jawfishes, Opistognathidae			
Opisthognathus aurifrons, yellowheaded jawfish	Small pieces of seafood daily	4–5 inches	Florida and Caribbean

Popular Species for Fish-Only Tanks

This group includes species that may feed on fish smaller than themselves, or on desirable invertebrate tank mates, as well as those simply too rowdy for a minireef aquarium. It is worth noting that some of the species mentioned in this section may also fit into the minireef community, provided certain tank mates are avoided (see the section later in this chapter).

Angelfishes (Pomacanthidae)

If you want to create a saltwater aquarium that truly reflects the natural reef habitat, it's hard to ignore the angel- and butterflyfishes. These fish, once placed in a single family because of their similarities, are now assigned to families Pomacanthidae and Chaetodontidae, respectively. Most of the large, spectacular species in both these families are incompatible with invertebrates, however, because the invertebrates constitute their natural diet. Because they are difficult to catch, angelfishes usually command higher prices than similar sized fishes from other families.

The lovely angelfishes come in two basic kinds. Dwarf angels rarely exceed 4 inches in length. They are placed in the genus *Centropyge*. Larger angelfishes, in several genera including *Pomacanthus*, *Holacanthus*, and others, grow impressively large and require an aquarium of at least 100 gallons. Though often extremely beautiful, large angelfishes are usually a challenge for the beginning hobbyist.

Not so with the *Centropyge* angels. This group includes some of the best aquarium fishes. A couple of them are even at home in a minireef tank. Most, however, have rather catholic tastes and will feed on a variety of invertebrates. For this reason, I have chosen to discuss them in this section. Consider any of the species listed in the tables on pages 55 through 58, with one caveat: the male of a given species may not tolerate any other angel in the tank and will certainly never allow another male in his territory. On the other hand, the normal social pattern for *Centropyge* is harem formation (one male with several females sharing his territory). In *Centropyge* the larger individuals are always male, whose role at this stage of life consists in making the territory safe for his harem. Not only does his behavior ensure that the area of the reef used by him and his mates for grazing algae remains free of other fish that might raid the larder, it also certifies his sole breeding rights. Thus, male dwarf angels who are successful in territorial defense pass along their (presumably superior) genes to offspring that will carry on this tradition at the proper time in their own life spans. Since males grow larger than females, you can often duplicate this arrangement if the tank is sufficiently spacious. Simply select one larger and several smaller individuals. Although dwarf angels live in harems, the male spawns at any given time with only one female. By some criteria imprinted in his genetic makeup, the male selects a candidate female and proceeds to dazzle her with a courtship display. The two finally dart toward the surface, where eggs and sperm are released. Spawning is crepuscular, that is, typically occurring at sunset, and has been observed with regularity in the aquarium. The tiny pelagic larvae hatch in only 24

Dwarf Angelfishes at a Glance

- Hobbyists who want to keep a mated pair of dwarf angelfishes should start with one large and two or three smaller individuals. The larger fish is, or will become, male, while the smaller ones will be female.
- Feed dwarf angelfishes flake foods, along with brine shrimp, worms, frozen chopped seafood products, and especially algae. The diet should contain about 75 percent plant matter.
- Don't try to keep more than one species of dwarf angelfish per tank, as there will almost certainly be territorial squabbles.
- Successful aquarium spawnings of dwarf angelfishes are commonplace. However, no one has successfully raised the fry to maturity. It is suspected that the main problem is providing a suitable food. As the fry grow, their feeding preferences may change, complicating matters further.
- The best environment for dwarf angelfishes is a reef tank with abundant live rock and a natural population of filamentous algae and small invertebrates on which the fish can graze constantly.
- Provide a single dwarf angelfish with a tank of at least 30 gallons. A mature male and two or three female specimens should have at least a 75-gallon tank.
- Dwarf angelfishes are sensitive to copper medications. Proper care is essential. Once the fish develops a parasitic infestation, treatment can be extremely difficult, and may in itself cause the fish to die if copper is used.

hours and remain planktonic for around a month. Spawning in captivity is quite common for dwarf angels, but the young have proven exceedingly difficult to rear to maturity. Eventually, though, someone will crack the secret; these fish will not only be more widely available, but the price should drop a bit. Although intolerant of less than optimal conditions, dwarf angelfish are nevertheless adaptable and highly desirable aquarium specimens.

Many *Centropyge* have been imported for aquariums over the years. Some of the more familiar ones are the lemonpeel angelfish, *C. flavissimus*; keyhole angelfish, *C. tibicen*; bicolor angelfish, *C. bicolor*; false lemonpeel, *C. heraldi*; and the coral beauty, *C. bispinosus*. Over the years, three species have become my personal favorites because they are readily available, inexpensive, and adapt easily to the aquarium if their needs are met. These are pygmy angelfish, *C. argi*; flame angelfish, *C. loriculus*; and Potter's angelfish, *C. potteri*.

Centropyge argi (cherub angelfish, Atlantic pygmy angelfish)

Found in Florida and the Caribbean, this is the smallest of the angelfishes, rarely reaching 3 inches. Much of its diet consists of algae, which it crops from rocks and other surfaces almost continuously during the daylight hours. It also feeds on small invertebrates, such as shrimps, but it won't bother corals and can be maintained without concern in a minireef aquarium. Occasionally, an individual fish will take a fancy to coral polyps or the mantle of a tridacnid clam, but unless the behavior is persistent, little damage is likely. Dark blue, with an orange face and a bright blue circle around the eye, this is a feisty species. The male will fight to the death with another male, and may not even accept a female if he is already established and the aquarium is too small. Only keep a pair together if your tank is larger than 50 gallons and both are introduced at the same time.

Centropyge loriculus (flame angelfish)

Although it is found in other parts of the world, this fish should hail from Hawaii if you plan to keep one. The shorter travel time and more carefully regulated collection practices mean you are more likely to get a specimen in good health. The flame angelfish lives in deeper water. Down there, you take what you can get, and this fish feeds on a variety of small invertebrates and algae. It therefore adapts readily to captivity. This species has a reputation for durability, and its brilliant red coloration highlighted with black bars and bright blue markings on the fins make it one of the most striking fish in the tank. With justification, it is quite popular with hobbyists. It may become territorial, and may also nip at minireef invertebrates, such as soft corals. Like many other angels, it may attack members of its own kind, other angelfish species, and other fishes similar to it in coloration, shape, or behavior. Therefore, it is probably at its best in a medium-size community tank with other species that fulfill none of these criteria.

Centropyge potteri (Potter's dwarf angelfish)

This dwarf angel is endemic to Hawaii, meaning it occurs nowhere else. Regularly imported, its brilliant orange coloration highlighted with glowing blue squiggles makes it hard to resist. Somewhat less adaptable than others in its genus, it needs a tank with plenty of hiding places, an abundant growth of filamentous algae, and a good crop of tiny invertebrates. Wait until the aquarium has been established for a while before trying this species. If it cannot nibble it may refuse to feed and starve. Despite its apparent shyness, it can become aggressive toward other angelfishes and any tank mate that poses a threat. Usually, the latter behavior indicates the tank is too crowded. Moving to a larger tank or reducing the number of fishes in the smaller tank are the only remedies for this problem.

Butterflyfishes (Chaetodontidae)

Among the most beautiful and graceful creatures on the reef, butterflyfishes have a reputation for being delicate. Some, admittedly, are impossible to maintain in captivity because of their insistence on a specific type of invertebrate food, often the polyps of only one or a few species of corals. Providing a constant supply of living corals would challenge even a public aquarium not located next to a coral reef. On the other hand, several butterflyfishes adapt readily to captive diets. Butterflyfishes are basically disk-shaped, often with a slightly or greatly protruding mouth used for plucking small prey from the substrate. The dorsal and anal fins often extend the entire length of back and belly, frequently terminating in an elongated "trailer." This gives the fish a resemblance to an arrowhead. Because they feed largely on invertebrates, the majority of butterflyfishes are unsuited to the minireef, which they will regard as a buffet. Often somewhat timid, they should not be placed in a community of aggressive species.

Chaetodon auriga (threadfin butterflyfish, auriga butterflyfish)

This species can reach 9 inches in length, although aquarium specimens seldom achieve such size. The anterior two-thirds of the body is pearly white; the rest of the body and the tail are golden yellow. There is a black eye spot on the outer edge of the dorsal fin above the tail, while the actual eye is camouflaged by a black bar. Although it needs a roomy tank over 4 feet in length, this is one of the best butterflyfish species for the aquarium. Never finicky, it should receive a varied diet of seafood several times a day. This fish is definitely not for a minireef; it will nibble most kinds of desirable invertebrates. It can sometimes be aggressive toward species that resemble it in coloration and seldom tolerates another of its kind in the same tank.

Chaetodon kleini (Klein's butterflyfish, corallicola butterflyfish, blacklip butterflyfish)

Considered by many to be the most aquarium-adaptable butterflyfish, this Hawaii/Indo-Pacific species reaches about 6 inches in length. It is golden brown, with a black eye bar and black lips. The face is pearly white. Like other butterflyfishes, it should be fed several times a day with a variety of seafood. A good community fish, it should be introduced before its tank mates, thus affording it an opportunity to establish a territory before it must deal with more aggressive neighbors. This species can even be maintained successfully in a minireef as it does not feed on a wide variety of corals, but it is probably safest in a fish-only aquarium.

Chaetodon semilarvatus (golden butterflyfish)

Stunning and unfortunately quite expensive this species from the Red Sea reaches about 9 inches. Younger specimens adapt readily to the aquarium and should be fed several times daily with a variety of seafood. Sometimes it is unwilling to begin feeding in captivity, often requiring the temptation of living foods. If possible, only purchase specimens that feed in the dealer's tank. Since the fish can command several hundred dollars in price, the dealer should be willing to hold onto it for a while if you place a deposit. That way, a specimen will have the opportunity to settle in, begin feeding, and recover from the trauma of capture and shipment before being uprooted again and whisked away to your tank. More or less round in shape and a beautiful golden yellow all over, its flanks are highlighted by 10 to 12 orange-brown bars. The eye is camouflaged by a blue-gray patch. Unlike many butterflyfishes, it tolerates its own kind well and can easily be kept in pairs or a small group if you are willing to make that much of an investment.

Forcipiger flavissimus (yellow longnosed butterflyfish)

Reaching about 8 inches in length, this fish has been popular with saltwater hobbyists for a long time. Among the butterflyfish clan, it is surely the most durable, largely because of its hearty appetite. These fish begin feeding almost immediately, and will take a wide variety of easily obtained foods. Feed them several times a day. Keep only one per tank, or there may be a spat. Squarish, flattened from side to side like most of its kin, the greatly elongated snout resembling forceps is this fish's most characteristic feature. The body is bright yellow, except

for the head, which is black above and pearly below, the line of demarcation bisecting the eye and effectively camouflaging it. The tail fin is colorless, but the yellow caudal peduncle sports a black false eye edged with pale blue. This butterflyfish has long, thick dorsal fin spines. These will be pointed aggressively at anything the fish perceives as a danger.

Reef-Compatible Butterflyfishes

Minireef enthusiasts often shy away from including butterflyfishes. The misperception that all members of this family will feed on invertebrates and destroy the tank is responsible for this attitude. However, a few members of the butterflyfish clan are indeed reef compatible. I include them here, rather than in the next section, to avoid two separate discussions of the same family.

Heniochus diphreutes (schooling bannerfish)

Found in the Indo-Pacific region from South Africa and the Persian Gulf all the way to Hawaii, this one is by far the best choice among the chaetodontids for a minireef. It is closely related to the longfin bannerfish, *H. acuminatus*, and requires careful examination to distinguish it. Make certain of the ID, however, because *H. acuminatus* can be destructive in a tank full of sessile invertebrates. *H. diphreutes* has a less protruding snout, longer pelvic fins, and a shorter anal fin than does *H. acuminatus*. The color patterns, unfortunately, are virtually identical. The white body is decorated with three black bands, one extending only from the forehead to the eye, the second across the gill cover and onto the pelvic fins, and the third reaching from the rear margin of the dorsal fin to the rear margin of the anal fin. In both species, the posterior portion of the dorsal fin and the caudal fin are bright yellow. Both species also have a greatly elongated "banner" extending from the anterior dorsal fin nearly the entire body length. *H. acuminatus* does not usually form schools, being solitary when a juvenile and pairing as an adult. The absence of schooling behavior may be the most reliable way for aquarists to separate these two species, unless the retailer has resolved this

Butterflyfish at a Glance

- Frequent feeding with a variety of foods seems to be the most important factor in the care of butterflyfishes.
- Only place the recommended species in a minireef tank. The others will feed on corals and other sessile invertebrates.
- Some butterflyfishes are good at ridding your tank of pesky *Aiptasia* anemones.
- Being residents only of coral reefs, butterflyfishes demand excellent water quality.
- The normal pattern for most butterflyfishes is to travel in pairs, but many will not tolerate their own kind in the confines of an aquarium.
- Please see the information on page 95 concerning butterflyfishes that feed exclusively on corals and that should not be purchased by aquarium hobbyists.

issue for you. Planktivorous, *H. diphreutes* should be fed frequently on a variety of finely chopped seafood, such as brine shrimp, mysids, shellfish, and frozen preparations. The fish also needs some plant matter in its diet and will occasionally feed on filamentous algae plucked from rocks. It seldom bothers sessile invertebrates. Besides its need for good water quality, usually not an issue in a thriving reef tank, the greatest challenge facing the aquarist in maintaining the schooling bannerfish is providing frequent small feedings throughout the day. It also needs a roomy tank, roughly 100 gallons for a school of five individuals. All these should be added simultaneously because, as with numerous other school-formers, a dominance hierarchy is established. Placing a single fish alone may lead to aggression problems when additional specimens are subsequently added. Smaller individuals are also easily intimidated by bolder tank mates of other species, and thus should be introduced to the aquarium before other kinds of fish are added. The best source for *H. diphreutes* is Hawaii. Check with your dealer.

Chelmon rostratus (copperband butterflyfish)

Perhaps the showiest species of reef-compatible butterflyfishes, it also has a reputation for being less than hardy in the aquarium. Some individuals adapt readily, while others simply refuse to eat and starve. It is possible this has to do with the treatment they receive prior to arriving in your dealer's tank. The often repeated advice to make sure the fish is feeding well before you buy applies doubly to *C. rostratus*. It is difficult to resist. Pearly white with bright orange vertical bars and an elongated snout, it seldom feeds on sessile invertebrates unless it is not kept well fed. It is often aggressive toward other members of its species and should be maintained singly in the aquarium. Both this and *Forcipiger* are good at eliminating *Aiptasia* anemones from the aquarium. Excellent, though costly, specimens of *C. rostratus* can be obtained from Australia.

Goatfishes (Parupeneidae)

Goatfishes get their name from the paired barbels protruding from each corner of the mouth, resembling a goat's whiskers. These they employ to grub in the bottom for worms and other invertebrates. As a rule, they are nervous, highly active, and require a large tank that affords plenty of swimming room.

Goatfishes at a Glance

- Although goatfishes search out food on the bottom by using their barbels, they will accept a variety of aquarium foods.
- Goatfishes are nervous, active fish that need plenty of swimming room, so they do poorly in small tanks.
- Goatfishes are nonaggressive toward anything not of interest as food, and may be harassed by more robust species.

Parupeneus multifasciatus (multibarred goatfish)

Typical of the family, this species should be fed three or four times daily or it may lose weight. It reaches a foot in length. Russet colored, with darker red-brown bars on the rear flanks, it feeds not only by grubbing in the substrate, but also by swallowing smaller fishes whole. Despite its size, it may be picked on by aggressive tank mates.

Groupers (Cephalopholidae)

If you have a large aquarium and want hardy, undemanding fish, one of the grouper clan may be for you. All groupers are sit-and-wait predators, spending most of the day hoping for a fish small enough to swallow whole to swim by.

Cephalopholis miniata (coral hind, miniata grouper, coral grouper)

An Indo-Pacific species that adapts readily to captivity, its coloration can only be described as flamboyant, golden yellow overall with blotches of brilliant red, and covered from head to tail with fluorescent blue spots. It reaches about 15 inches in length, and so needs a roomy tank. Long-lived in captivity, it will greedily accept any sort of meaty seafood, and it grows rapidly. Usually only aggressive if its favored lair is invaded, it will swallow whole any fish or crustacean of appropriate size.

Chromileptes altivelis (panther grouper)

Reaching nearly 30 inches, this fish will require a tank of about 200 gallons to live out its normal life span in captivity. The entire body is creamy white, decorated with dark brown polka dots. This color pattern, combined with its amusing swimming behavior, make it among the most popular species in the trade. It is seldom aggressive and ignores any fish too large to swallow. Don't be tempted to buy a young specimen for a small tank unless you are prepared to provide much larger accommodations later, because they grow very rapidly. If the adult size does not pose a problem in your situation, this fish can be a member of the household for up to 20 years, and often learns to recognize its owner.

Groupers at a Glance

- Groupers all grow to a large size and need a correspondingly large aquarium.
- Groupers are sit-and-wait predators who spend most of their time waiting in ambush for prey.
- Groupers feed on crustaceans, other invertebrates, and fish. They will swallow anything edible of appropriate size.
- Groupers live long in captivity with appropriate care and feeding.

Hawkfishes at a Glance

- Lacking a swim bladder, hawkfishes spend more time sitting than they do swimming.
- Hawkfishes are predatory and will feed on most types of ocean-derived foods.
- Hawkfishes ignore most invertebrates, but are not to be trusted with small shrimps or diminutive fish species.
- Generally hardy, hawkfishes are a good choice for the beginning aquarist.

Hawkfishes (Cirrhitidae)

Here's a family suited to almost any aquarium situation, although they all will eat small ornamental shrimps and smaller fishes. Adult size ranges from about 4 to about 6 inches. Hawkfishes lack a swim bladder, and therefore cannot easily control their buoyancy. They prefer to spend time perched on a rock or coral head rather than hovering in midwater. Only two hawkfish species should be considered for the minireef aquarium, although both are quite desirable. The flame hawkfish (*Neocirrhites armatus*) is perhaps a better selection than the longnosed hawkfish (*Oxycirrhites typus*) only because the latter has a larger mouth and bigger appetite. Neither gets very large. Both perch in coral heads in a delightful way that suggests they are supervising all events taking place within the tank. The red-spotted hawkfish (*Amblycirrhites pinos*) is better suited to a fish-only aquarium.

Amblycirrhitus pinos (red spotted hawkfish)

This hawkfish hails from the Atlantic. The body is cream-colored with vertical dark brown bars. The tail and paired fins are red, and the head is decorated with bright red dots. Its hardiness is legendary, and if fed regularly with a varied selection of seafood will live for many years in captivity.

Neocirrhites armatus (flame hawkfish)

Bright red all over with a black circle around the eye and a black stripe at the base of the dorsal fin, the flame hawkfish enjoys enormous popularity. In part because of this, it tends to be pricey. Although sometimes aggressive toward other bottom-dwelling fishes, it usually behaves if the aquarium is spacious. I recommend a tank of 50 gallons, despite the relatively small adult size of 4 inches. Collected in the South Pacific, it eats almost anything of appropriate size to swallow, and is especially fond of snails.

Oxycirrhites typus (longnosed hawkfish)

Imagine a fish decorated like a red-and-white checkered tablecloth! The body is elongate, with a prominent snout. Despite its appearance the mouth is quite large, and this hawkfish poses a threat to small fishes and shrimps. Hardy and undemanding, the longnosed hawkfish is collected in the Hawaii/Indo-Pacific region.

Lionfishes (Scorpaenidae)

My first saltwater aquarium fish was a lionfish. Also known as *scorpionfishes*, this family contains some of the most durable fish to be found in the reef environment. They are equally at home in a fish-only tank or a minireef, although don't trust them with ornamental shrimps. Even the larger lionfishes are seldom aggressive toward anything too large to be of interest as food. The term *scorpionfish* refers to the venomous spines of the dorsal and pectoral fins. The fish rarely uses its spines offensively, but inadvertent contact will result in an extremely painful sting that may require medical attention. For this reason, I don't recommend them to households with small children. Another drawback is their requirement for living foods, at least until they become accustomed to life in an aquarium. After weaning to nonliving foods, a lionfish can be successfully maintained for 10 years or more. All the lionfishes described are similar in coloration. The body is pale, overlain with red-orange to dark brown bars. The fins are elaborate, and are what make the fish so appealing. The enormous pectoral fins are sometimes used to herd the small fishes or shrimps that constitute most of the lionfish's diet. Once the prey is driven into a cul-de-sac, the lionfish picks them off at its leisure.

Dendrochirus brachypterus (fuzzy dwarf lionfish)

This is a nocturnal fish, active mostly at night. Eventually, aquarium specimens learn to come out during the day like everyone else, but it may starve if not fed after dark during its initial days and weeks in the tank. This lionfish may never learn to eat anything but living foods, and this should be carefully considered before you purchase one. Enhancing its appearance, numerous appendages and flaps of skin decorate the fins, leading to its common name. These "decorations" probably make the lionfish look like an algae-covered rock when it is resting, fooling both potential prey and cruising predators. If a predator attacks anyway, the dorsal spines will deliver a sting to the inside of the predator's mouth, and the lionfish will be spit out to swim another day. It grows to about 6 inches.

Lionfishes at a Glance

- All lionfishes possess venomous spines capable of inflicting a painful sting that sometimes requires medical attention. They are not recommended for households with small children.
- Dwarf lionfishes are nocturnal, feeding only at night, and may need the temptation of living fish or shrimp to begin eating in captivity.
- Larger lionfishes, such as *Pterois volitans*, are long-lived and durable aquarium subjects that demonstrate considerable intelligence.
- Never trust a lionfish to ignore any tank mate that it is capable of swallowing.
- Because they eventually reach 6 inches or more in length, lionfishes should be considered only if the aquarium is sufficiently large.
- Dwarf lionfishes should always be provided with hiding places into which they can retire during the daytime.

Dendrochirus zebra (dwarf lionfish)

Almost identical to the preceding species in terms of size and dietary needs, this lionfish is also nocturnal and needs a place to retire during the daylight hours. This little fellow is widely available and is an ideal fish for the beginning hobbyist. It requires plenty of caves, overhangs, and similar hiding places. It will learn to be active during the day, but only after becoming accustomed to aquarium life. It is not as finicky as *D. brachypterus* and quickly learns to eat aquarium foods. Feed about every other day with frozen fish or shrimp. Initially, it may be tempted with live guppies or grass shrimp, either of which is usually available from your dealer. It grows to about 7 inches in length.

Pterois volitans (common lionfish)

This was my first saltwater fish, and remains my favorite to this day. It is a highly satisfactory species for either a fish-only tank or a minireef. Its sole drawback is a propensity to eat ornamental shrimps and any fish small enough to fit into its capacious mouth. Reaching 15 inches in length, *P. volitans* needs a large tank to feel at home. It is naturally quite long-lived. My specimen was 13 years old when I gave it to a friend with a much larger tank than mine, and it lived with him for several years thereafter. While needing to be fed only about three times a week, this fish has a hearty appetite. A large one will consume six to ten feeder goldfish at a sitting and then beg for more. As with the other lionfishes, providing a suitable food supply should be your prime consideration. This fish exhibits uncanny intelligence; mine could distinguish me from another person, coming to the top for food when I would walk up, but just sitting there when someone else approached.

Sea Basses

A large number of really good saltwater aquarium fish come from closely related families, collectively known as the *sea basses*. The true sea bass family, Serranidae, has members ranging from large predators to small ones. The other related families are the fairy basslets (Grammidae), anthias (Anthiidae), and the dottybacks (Pseudochromidae).

True Sea Basses (Serranidae)

Only some of the members of the predatory sea bass family are suitable for the community aquarium.

Sea Basses at a Glance

- Only a few species of sea basses are suitable for a small tank, as most grow quite large.
- Sea basses generally lie in wait for suitable prey and cannot be trusted with shrimps or small fishes as tank mates.
- If fed daily with a varied diet, sea basses are generally hardy and easy to keep.

Serranus tigrinus (harlequin bass)

This little bass from the tropical western Atlantic reaches only 4 inches, and so poses no threat to any fish or crustacean it cannot swallow. It will, however, consume shrimps or small fishes, so choose tank mates with care. The dorsal half of the body is pearly white, while the throat and belly are yellow. Stripes and bars are formed from splotches of black pigment, effectively camouflaging the fish as it lies in wait for careless prey. Hardy and adaptable, it is aggressive toward its own kind, unless you have a mated pair. Feed daily with a varied diet of meaty seafood.

Snappers (Lutjanidae)

The snapper family includes some of the most desirable table fishes in the sea, but only a few are suited to the home aquarium.

Lutjanus kasmira (bluelined snapper)

Shaped like a textbook sketch of a "typical" fish, this snapper is bright yellow with four or five brilliant blue stripes decorating its flanks. The face is also blue. It reaches over a foot in length, and, typical of its family, feeds aggressively on both crustaceans and fishes. Tank mates small enough to swallow will become lunch for the snapper. Despite the fact that it often lives in large shoals in the wild, keep only one per tank. It may be aggressive toward more docile species and therefore should be considered only for a tank exhibiting species with bolder personalities.

Surgeonfishes (Tangs) (Acanthuridae)

Surgeonfishes are often called *tangs* in the aquarium trade. Both *tang* and *surgeonfish* refer to a sharp, bladelike spine on the caudal peduncle. In many species, this structure folds away into the body like the blade of a penknife. Employed in territorial scuffles, the blade is capable of inflicting a serious wound, and these fish should always be handled with caution. While keeping tangs can sometimes pose problems, they are hardy if their needs are understood, and they make good choices for a larger aquarium. Tangs should either be kept as solitary specimens, or in groups of at least three individuals. Note that alone a tang is more likely to be aggressive to its non-tang tank mates than if in a group of its own kind. They must also be given a large tank, at least 4 feet in length. Among the best of choices is the

Snappers at a Glance

- Snappers are aggressive predators of both crustaceans and fishes.
- Keep only one snapper per tank, or they may fight.
- Snappers grow to a large size and need a correspondingly large aquarium.
- Good tank mates for snappers should be equally robust, aggressive species, such as groupers.

yellow tang (*Zebrasoma flavescens*), collected almost exclusively in Hawaii. The most popular species, perhaps, is the regal surgeonfish (*Paracanthurus hepatus*). The former species is largely vegetarian, while the latter feeds more commonly on plankton. The major drawbacks to keeping tangs in captivity are their large size (up to 6 inches for the species mentioned, and much larger for several others), a requirement for abundant algae on which the vegetarian species can constantly graze, and a tendency to develop common parasitic infestations when conditions are stressful.

Acanthurus coeruleus (Atlantic blue tang)

Among the hardiest of the family, this tang reaches about 9 inches in diameter and therefore needs a large aquarium. It feeds almost exclusively on algae, and should receive a varied diet rich in seaweeds. Juvenile *A. coeruleus* are yellow, with a blue tail and a blue ring around the eye. An intermediate color phase, blue with a yellow tail, gives way to the adult coloration of overall deep blue. The intensity of the blue coloration varies from one individual to another, and may be a reflection of the fish's relative level of calmness. The bluer they are, the less stressed-out they are.

Naso lituratus (naso tang, orange-spined unicornfish)

Reaching nearly half a meter (about 18 inches) in length, this spectacular fish is mostly slate-gray in color. The face bears yellow and black markings, the lips are bright orange, and the belly and anal fin are yellow-orange. This tang bears two blades on its caudal peduncle. They are marked in bright orange and separated by a white patch. The outer margin of the tail is yellow. Because of its size, it is best suited to a large tank that provides plenty of swimming room. Feed several times daily with a diet consisting mostly of vegetable matter, supplemented with small, meaty seafood pieces. It seems to require more animal food than the other members of its family.

Paracanthurus hepatus (regal surgeonfish, palette surgeonfish)

I confess great fondness for this fish, with its royal blue body marked in black, and bright yellow belly and tail. Unlike most surgeons, this one feeds largely on plankton, and should have a varied diet of meaty seafoods chopped into appropriately small pieces. Supplement the diet with live or frozen brine shrimp, frozen foods designed for herbivores, and frozen mysis shrimp. Poor diet will lead to a condition known as *head and lateral line erosion* (see page 185). Reaching a foot in length in nature, it seldom grows beyond 6 inches in the aquarium, but needs a roomy tank nonetheless. Juveniles can be kept in groups, but adults usually don't get along. This fish is equally at home in a minireef or fish-only aquarium, and does not bother sessile invertebrates. Habitually hiding in branching coral heads, regal tangs are adept at finding the smallest, most remote crevice in the tank in which to hide should they become alarmed. Chasing one with a cup is a pointless exercise in frustration. To extract the tang from the tank, you'll need to remove the entire coral head in which the fish is hiding. Holding the coral over a bucket of water usually encourages the tang to let go, and it falls into the bucket.

Surgeonfishes at a Glance

- Surgeonfishes often live in large shoals in the ocean but are usually maintained singly in an average-size aquarium.
- Surgeonfishes all possess a sharp, blade-like spine at the base of the tail that is used in territorial scuffles with other surgeonfishes. This structure can inflict a serious wound, so these fish must be handled with caution.
- While the majority of surgeonfishes crop algae from the reef all day, many include a substantial portion of animal matter in their diets. These species-specific dietary patterns must be taken into account in providing an aquarium diet.
- Surgeonfishes patrol the reef far and wide in search of algae "meadows" in which to graze. They may suffer stress from claustrophobia if maintained in an aquarium that is too small. Provide a tank at least 4 feet in length.
- Keeping a shoal of surgeonfishes, provided the tank is sufficiently large, is better than placing only a pair of individuals together. One fish will constantly harass the other if only a pair is present, but aggressiveness is spread among many individuals when a group is maintained together.
- Surgeonfishes have a reputation for being delicate in captivity, although this may have more to do with the stresses of confinement than with any inherent weakness in the fish.

Zebrasoma flavescens (yellow tang)

As a rule, members of the genus *Zebrasoma* are among the most adaptable surgeonfishes. This one is by far the most popular tang, and nearly every aquarium shop has a few specimens on hand. It needs only proper attention to its diet, which must consist mostly of vegetable matter. Feed several times daily, as with other grazing species. Improper diet will lead to loss of weight, head and lateral line erosion, and other ills. In nature, it usually lives in huge shoals, but keep only one per aquarium. An established specimen can become quite aggressive, particularly if the tank provides inadequate space. Creating a shoal under aquarium conditions requires a large tank, preferably over 200 gallons, and the introduction of all the yellow tangs simultaneously. After a few days spent working out a suitable "pecking order" among themselves, the fish will then settle down and cohabit peacefully. Done well, this type of aquarium is an awesome sight.

Triggerfishes (Balistidae)

The hardiness and aggression of these fishes spawns many a fish tale at aquarium club meetings. Both the dorsal and anal fins bear a thick spine that can be locked in an erect position, allowing the fish to wedge itself inextricably into a crevice or coral head, defying all attempts at removal. When the "trigger" holding the spine in place is released, though, the erect spine collapses and the fish swims away, presumably after a frustrated predator has given up. All triggerfishes are bold, greedy eaters, requiring a mixed diet and plenty of it. Most reach over 10 inches in size, and so require a suitably large tank. Armed with strong jaws for crushing the shells of invertebrates, a large triggerfish can inflict a severe bite. They are unsuitable, therefore, in a household with small children. Quite intelligent, they learn to recognize their owners, though they may literally bite the hand that feeds them.

Balistoides conspicillum (clown triggerfish)

Always popular because of its jaw-dropping coloration, this triggerfish should always be obtained at a size greater than 3 inches, because juveniles adapt far less readily than adults do. The upper half of the body is jet black, while the throat and belly are black, overlain with enamel-white polka dots. A bright yellow bar camouflages the eye. The caudal peduncle is white, with a yellow patch on top and numerous black dots arranged in rows to form stripes. The central portion of the tail fin is yellow, and the posterior portions of the dorsal and anal fins bear neon blue and chrome yellow pigments. Once settled in, it feeds voraciously on anything and everything, and it grows rapidly.

Balistapus undulatus (undulate triggerfish, orange-lined triggerfish)

I seldom think of this fish without wondering what makes them so popular with aquarists, because its boisterous behavior sometimes obscures its undeniable beauty. Deep orange, with a pattern of wavy blue stripes from snout to tail fin, it's a gorgeous fish that adapts quickly, eats anything, and grows to about a foot in length. It may, however, attack anything else in the tank that moves, and will rearrange the decorations, moving chunks of coral twice its size. It demands an aquarium of its own. Found in the Indo-Pacific, like its cousins it is quite capable of delivering a serious bite. Though few, its charms do include the ability to learn to recognize its owner.

Rhinecanthus aculeatus (Picasso triggerfish, humahuma triggerfish)

The common name of this triggerfish refers to the modern art pattern of coloration. "Brush strokes" in yellow, blue, pure white, and black adorn the cream-colored to brown body. Triggerfishes are basically diamond-shaped, especially this one. Intelligent, it quickly learns

Triggerfishes at a Glance

- Triggerfishes are too large and aggressive to be placed in a community of more docile species but will often get along with similarly robust tank mates.
- A large triggerfish is capable of delivering a serious bite with its powerful jaws, hence these fish are not recommended around small children.
- Triggerfishes will feed aggressively on virtually any reasonable aquarium food.
- Some triggerfish species are too aggressive for any tank mate and must be kept in solitary confinement.
- Triggerfishes are long-lived and intelligent, and so make excellent pets in a single-species tank.

to recognize its owner, coming to the surface to beg for food each time you approach the tank. Easily maintained on a diet of meaty seafood offered several times a day, it grows to about 10 inches. The other common name derives from a Hawaiian word meaning "fish that carries a needle."

Wrasses (Labridae)

Ichthyologists (biologists who specialize in the study of fishes) are not terribly fond of wrasses, at least when it comes to trying to classify them. These fish have multiple sexual phases, and the different phases are different in color, often markedly so. This can make identification confusing and the job of identifying each species a chore. For a given species, though, most of the wrasses collected for the aquarium are of only one color phase. The family name, Labridae, derives from *labrum*, or "lip" in Latin. This is a reference to the thickened lips all wrasses possess. All are more or less elongated fish, with terminal mouths, and one or more pairs of sharp canine teeth. The canines protrude and are obvious on many species. All wrasses begin life as females, bearing an initial color phase. This color phase may be shared by non-sex-reversing males, but the brightly colored terminal phase male has a strikingly different pattern. It was once believed that the initial color phase males did not breed, but this has been shown to be a misinterpretation of wrasse ecology. All wrasses spawn pelagically, meaning eggs and sperm are released into the surrounding water where fertilization occurs. Typically, the display and courtship behavior of the supermale attracts a small shoal of females, and both they and the supermale discharge gametes into the water simultaneously. We have learned, however, that some sexually mature males bearing the female color pattern, thus disguised, are able to participate in the spawning. This, of course, maintains the "sneaky male" trait in the next generation of wrasses. Wrasse larvae have been reared to adulthood in the laboratory by using eggs and sperm harvested from parents caught in the wild. Great potential exists, therefore, for producing these hardy and adaptable fishes through captive propagation.

The wrasses described in the following section are but a glimpse of this varied family. Other commonly imported ones you might consider include: *Novaculithes taeniorum*, the dragon wrasse. Although it grows rather large, the unusual color pattern of this species makes it well worth keeping in a fish-only tank. *Halichoeres* is a large genus, with many aquarium choices, such as *H. chrysus*, the canary wrasse; *H. iridis*, the radiant wrasse; and *H ornatissimus*, the ornate wrasse. Two species of *Thalassoma* are described, but there are many others. A good one is *T. lunare*, the lunar wrasse. It reaches about 10 inches but is a hardy and adaptable species if you have the room. Another beautiful species is *T. lutescens*, the sunset wrasse. Two commonly imported Caribbean wrasses are called "hogfish." *Bodianus pulchellus*, the Cuban hogfish, and *B. rufus*, the Spanish hogfish, are durable, easily maintained choices for a large tank. The former reaches about 6 inches, while the latter can grow over a foot.

Reef-Compatible Wrasses

Some of the more interesting and lesser known wrasse species are good for reef tanks. *Pseudocheilinus tetrataenia* and *P. hexataenia*, the four-lined and six-lined neon wrasses, respectively, are small, colorful, and useful choices in the reef aquarium. They feed on parasitic snails that attack tridacnid clams, and generally leave corals and other invertebrates alone. When the snail supply runs low, they greedily accept a variety of seafood. Fairy wrasses, genus *Cirrhilabrus*, are frequently offered. There are many species, some as yet undescribed by scientists. Many will adapt to the aquarium if a male is kept along with a harem of two females. *C. jordani*, the bright red species known as the flame fairy wrasse, is collected in Hawaii. It is a good choice for starting out with this somewhat delicate genus. Flasher wrasses, genus *Paracheilinus*, also offer numerous possibilities for reef tanks, and remain small in size. They adapt readily when larger fishes that might harass them are excluded. These wrasses don't do too well in fish-only aquariums, and so are covered in the section on reef-compatible fishes, below.

Choerodon fasciatus (harlequin tuskfish)

This beautiful but aggressive fish is a superb choice for a large tank of similarly aggressive species. All wrasses have canine teeth, but the harlequin tusk goes out of its way to advertise their presence: its teeth are bright blue! White with eight to ten red bars edged in blue, it feeds greedily on just about anything within reason. Although commanding a somewhat higher price, specimens collected in Australia tend to be more colorful than those from other areas of the Indo-Pacific.

Coris gaimard (yellowtail wrasse, red coris)

Among the many colorful wrasses imported from the Indo-Pacific, the gloriously beautiful terminal males of this species take the prize for showiness. The lemon yellow tail is carried at the end of a brilliant blue body marked in neon blue polka dots. Light blue lines on the fins and a pattern of green and peach on the head complete the picture. Females are bright red, with several white saddles outlined in black. Although larger specimens can be aggressive, this is an easy and adaptable species for an aquarium containing similar-size tank mates.

Labroides phthirophagus (Hawaiian cleaner wrasse)

Although brightly colored males continue to be offered for sale in aquarium shops, this wrasse is an obligate cleaner, meaning it will only feed by removing parasites from the skin surface of other fishes. It seldom adapts to the aquarium and should be avoided.

Gomphosus varius (Hawaiian bird wrasse)

A good candidate for a large, fish-only tank, males are sea-green, while females sport a charming brown and white pattern. With an elongate snout, this wrasse grabs even small minnows and scrapes them against rocks until they are in pieces small enough to swallow. It does not bury itself at night, as do many members of the family. Provide a large tank with plenty of swimming room.

Thalassoma bivitattum (bluehead wrasse)

From Florida and the Caribbean, the initial color phase of this wrasse is bright yellow; collectors call it the "banana" wrasse. Terminal males, on the other hand, are iridescent green with bright blue heads. This species seldom exceeds 5 inches under aquarium conditions. It

Wrasses at a Glance

- Wrasses are all carnivorous. Only smaller species are safe with crustaceans. Large wrasses can eat bait fish.
- Many smaller wrasses bury themselves in the substrate at night. The tank must have a sufficiently deep substrate layer.
- Certain wrasse genera have highly specific feeding requirements that usually cannot be met in the aquarium. These genera should be avoided by aquarists. Examples are *Anampses*, *Stethojulis*, *Labroides*, and *Macropharyngodon* species.
- Wrasses sometimes get lazy, and will spend long periods of time during the daylight hours simply resting motionless in a favored spot. To keep them swimming around more, try reducing the amount of food you provide.
- Captive diets for wrasses should include an array of ingredients derived from marine invertebrates and fishes. Brine shrimp are an excellent dietary supplement but should not be fed exclusively. Wrasses are opportunistic, and get a wide variety of foods in their natural habitats.
- All wrasses have sharp canine teeth and can administer a bite, the severity of which will be in proportion to the size of the wrasse.
- Most of the wrasses sold for marine aquariums are terminal color phase males. Try requesting that your supplier also provide fishes with the juvenile/female coloration, so you can combine multiple individuals in the same tank.
- Some wrasses, such as the two species of *Pseudocheilinus*, are useful in preventing invertebrate parasites from attacking giant clams. Cleaner wrasses, genus *Labroides*, which remove parasites from fishes, on the other hand, often do not adapt well to the aquarium, even though they might be considered valuable in controlling parasites. The small fish population cannot host enough parasites to keep the cleaner wrasses well-fed.
- It may be difficult or impossible for two terminal male wrasses of the same species to be accommodated in the same aquarium. The best approach is to limit each tank to a single species.

is hardy and adapts readily to a diet of frozen foods. Like most wrasses, it swims almost constantly, pausing only now and then to rest.

Thalassoma lucasanum (paddlefin wrasse)

From the eastern Pacific, collectors in Costa Rica offer this active species that reaches about 6 inches. The common name derives from its mode of swimming, in that it uses its pectoral fins to row through the water. Males are pinkish-purple, with teal on the head and tail. A bright lemon yellow bar lies behind the head. The strikingly different females are marketed as "Mexican rock wrasse." They are dark brown with two bright yellow stripes, and a flaming red stripe extending from the middle of the body to the lower lobe of the tail fin. A group of females and one male makes a striking display in a large tank. Like most species, this wrasse is easy to keep. Feed several times a day with meaty seafood, varying the diet as much as possible.

Reef-Compatible Fish Species

For me, these are the loveliest and most desirable of fishes available to saltwater hobbyists. Reef-compatible fishes are generally small, nonaggressive species. In particular, they will not make a meal of corals and other invertebrates displayed in the same aquarium. Any of the ones mentioned could also be kept in a fish-only community tank. If you only have room for a small aquarium, consider these your best choices.

Anthias (Anthiidae)

Beautiful fishes that frequently congregate in vast schools over Indo-Pacific reefs, most anthias are a challenge to keep. They require frequent feedings with foods that mimic the zooplankton (free-swimming invertebrates only a few millimeters in length) on which they naturally feed. Many anthias are shoaling fishes. A solitary form from deep water, the sunburst anthias (*Serranocirrhitus latus*) is an excellent choice for the community aquarium, however, although beginning hobbyists may find it too expensive.

Pseudanthias bicolor (bicolor anthias)

Considered easier to keep than many of its relatives, this anthias is divided lengthwise into intense yellow (dorsal) and pale pink (ventral) halves. Long, flowing fins in pink and blue enhance its exotic appearance. Reaching about 5 inches, it is a deep-water species that needs slow acclimation to the bright illumination of a reef tank, or it can be kept in a dimly lit fish-only tank with other nonaggressive species. Feed several times daily with food intended for zooplankton feeders.

Pseudanthias ventralis hawaiiensis (Hawaiian longfin anthias)

This exquisite anthias is a good choice from among the shoaling species. Males are adorned with lovely streamers extending from the pelvic and anal fins. The males' coloration is hot pink, with a yellow head and purple caudal fin, while females are yellow, with lavender sides. This fish lives at depths of over 100 feet and must be carefully decompressed as it is brought to the surface or it will not fare well subsequently. Only purchase this species from a trusted source. Once properly acclimated it is easily maintained. As with many deep-water fish, *P. ventralis* will take a variety of foods. It grows only to about 3 inches, and should be kept in a harem consisting of one male and several females.

Serranocirrhitus latus (fathead anthias, sunburst anthias, hawkfish anthias)

This is another deep-water anthias that does very well in a dimly lit tank, or it can be slowly acclimated to more light and maintained in a minireef. Feed the same as for other anthias. Hot pink belly coloration gives way to deep red on the cheeks and gill covers. Bright gold pigment begins to intrude on the pink about a third of the way up the flanks, and the dorsal coloration is uniformly gold. Truly a breathtaking species, it needs plenty of places to hide and should not be placed in the same community with aggressive species.

Anthias at a Glance

- Anthias are all schooling or harem-forming species that need to be with others of their kind to feel secure. In the aquarium, the best arrangement is one male and two or three females.
- Because they feed on planktonic invertebrates, anthias need several daily feedings of small, meaty seafood, such as brine shrimp and mysis shrimp.
- Being an exception to the schooling rule, the deep-water sunburst anthias can be maintained singly. Its high price often dissuades beginners from trying it.
- Many good aquarium anthias come from deeper waters and must be acclimated to the bright illumination of a minireef aquarium.

Blennies (Blenniidae)

The often droll-looking blennies are either vegetarians or midwater plankton feeders.

Acanthemblemaria sp. (sailfin blennies)

Any of these blennies will occupy holes in the rocks and "explode" out of hiding like popcorn popping when food is added to the aquarium. The individual species are sometimes difficult to identify, but for aquarium purposes are all the same. Care is as for the canary blenny, described below.

Ecsenius bicolor (bicolor blenny)

Reaching a maximum length of only 4 inches, this one is a good example of the vegetarian blennies. The anterior two-thirds of the elongated body is dark brown to blue-black, and the posterior third and tail fin are bright orange. Ignored by tank mates as it spends its days cropping algae growth from any accessible surface, this fish is extremely aggressive toward members of its own species and may harass closely related varieties or those similar to it in size and habit. Probably this behavior is an attempt to protect its feeding territory, which must be large in comparison to the size of the fish, in order to provide ample algae growth. Bicolor blennies seldom thrive in brand-new aquariums lacking a good growth of filamentous algae. Also offer frozen and dried aquarium preparations meant for vegetarian fishes.

Meiacanthus atrodorsalis ovaluensis (canary blenny)

This blenny is a good choice among the plankton feeders. It is bright yellow and is found only around the Fiji Islands. It ignores other fishes as well as invertebrates. It needs frequent feedings with small pieces of food that mimic its natural diet.

Blennies at a Glance

- Blennies fall into two groups, with important implications for aquarium care. "Comb-toothed" blennies feed on filamentous algae and are territorial, while "fanged" blennies feed on small invertebrates and are gregarious.
- Fanged blennies cannot take large prey and need frequent feedings with small pieces of ocean-derived foods.
- Because most remain under 4 inches in size, blennies are good choices for aquariums as small as 30 gallons.
- Many blenny species will take up residence in a hole in the coral or an abandoned worm tube. Always provide suitable cover for them when you arrange the aquarium decorations.

Cardinalfishes (Apogonidae)

Among the many families of marine fishes in the aquarium trade, perhaps none is more underappreciated than the cardinalfishes, family Apogonidae. Cardinalfishes are mainly small, hardy species that are easily fed, so the reasons for their lack of popularity are difficult to fathom. All cardinalfishes have two dorsal fins, large eyes, a large mouth, and double-edged preopercles, the stiffened flaps that form part of the covering of the gills. They occur in both the Atlantic and Pacific, with many more species, approximately 60, found in the latter. The name is derived from the red coloration seen in many species, although some are quite drably colored. The drab ones are seldom imported for the aquarium. Several species, including the more popular ones, are striped. Cardinalfishes are generally nocturnal, as is evident from the large eyes and red coloration. (Red is the color least likely to be seen at night by a predator.) Most species spend the daylight hours in hiding, resting in caves or under ledges, and dispersing over the reef at night to feed on small organisms such as mysid shrimps, or benthic crustaceans such as copepods. Their catholic tastes in food make them easy to accommodate on an aquarium diet. Some species are gregarious, gathering in large shoals, hovering just above the protection of a large coral head. In the aquarium, cardinalfishes are seldom more than a few inches away from a preferred hiding place. Consequently, they should be provided with a suitable refuge by arranging live rock or coral skeletons to provide caves and ledges.

Apogon cyanosoma (orange-striped cardinalfish)

This species occurs from the Red Sea to the Great Barrier Reef and north to southern Japan. Seldom exceeding 3 inches, it is yellow with horizontal stripes of iridescent blue. Less retiring than other species, it spends much of its time in open water, a behavior that no doubt accounts for its popularity with hobbyists. It feeds both day and night in the wild, and is one of the species that forms shoals. A group of five to seven individuals is suitable for a larger reef tank, or a single individual could be maintained in a small aquarium.

Apogon maculatus (flame cardinalfish)

From Florida and the Caribbean comes this single aquarium species. Its elongated body is cherry-red, with a black spot on the gill cover, one just beneath the second dorsal fin, and a black blotch disguising the large eye. This species has a tendency to be aggressive toward its own kind and toward other cardinalfishes. It is nocturnal, spending most of its time at the entrance to its chosen cave. A proper diet seems to be important to maintain the bright coloration of this species. Consequently, it should be given seafood that has been enriched with preparations containing vitamin A. Look for commercially available fish foods with labels touting "color enhancers."

Pterapogon kauderni (Banggai cardinalfish)

Here's the most famous cardinalfish, introduced to the aquarium trade in the 1990s by Dr. Gerald Allen, who discovered a population off the island of Banggai in Sulawesi, Indonesia. It is apparently restricted to Indonesian waters. It is found in shallow areas dominated by sea grasses, often forming aggregations when young. For this reason, it is easy to catch, and the species is potentially threatened by overcollection. Its saving grace, however, lies in its breeding behavior. Males of most cardinalfishes brood the fertilized eggs in their mouths, but the Banggai cardinalfish takes this a step further, retaining the young until they are free-swimming, nearly a quarter of an inch in length. The young are able to eat live brine shrimp nauplii as soon as they are released by their father, making them ideal candidates for captive propagation. Although young specimens tend to aggregate, they disperse as they mature, often becoming aggressive. Several individuals should be maintained together only if the tank is large. The requirement for lots of room for maturing specimens unfortunately results in a higher cost for captive-reared specimens.

For all its quirks, the Banggai cardinalfish rewards the beholder with some of the most elegant decoration to be found among aquarium fishes. The pale body is boldly marked with three vertical black stripes, one running through the eye, one from the first dorsal to the pelvic fins, and the third from the second dorsal to the anal fin. Each stripe is outlined in silver. The fins are elongate and pointed, with the black stripes extending to the tips of the first and second dorsal fins. The pelvic, anal, and caudal fins are black, decorated with silver dots. Similar dots are scattered in the spaces between the black stripes. The caudal fin, in particular is striking, because the silver dots are arranged in a neat row outlining the border, converging anteriorly to form silver stripes. This fish is an ideal choice for a 30-gallon species tank devoted to it. The tank can be decorated with plastic plants or genuine seaweeds, to mimic the habitat the Banggai cardinalfish prefers.

Sphaeramia nematoptera (pajama cardinalfish)

The head is greenish-yellow with a bright red eye. The middle portion of the body is covered in white scales from the first dorsal fin to the pelvic fins, with each scale outlined in black to produce a cross-hatched pattern. The rear third of the body is pearly white with reddish polka dots. The second dorsal, anal, and caudal fins are bluish-white. It reaches about 3 inches in diameter, although it appears larger because of the fins. Its aquarium care is identical to that of the other species in the family.

Cardinalfishes at a Glance

- Cardinalfishes accept a wide variety of commonly available aquarium foods. Feed dry foods intended for marine fish, along with brine shrimp, worms, and frozen chopped seafood products.
- Since cardinalfishes are nocturnal, feeding, at least initially, should be undertaken after the tank lights are turned off.
- Cardinalfishes generally leave tank mates alone. With the exception of small shrimps, or other mobile creatures too large to swallow, invertebrates are ignored.
- Being mouth brooders, cardinalfishes are good choices for hobbyists who want to attempt breeding. Because many varieties of cardinalfishes are naturally gregarious, several individuals of a single species may be maintained together.
- Because of their nocturnal habits, cardinalfishes must be provided with an area in which to retire during the daylight hours. Create rock ledges or caves for this purpose.
- Many specimens will quickly learn to feed during the day, once they have adapted to captive conditions.
- Cardinalfishes are seldom aggressive, and are thus subject to harassment by more robust species. They are thus more appropriate choices for a minireef than a typical fish-only aquarium.
- Many cardinalfishes are small and can be successfully kept in a 30-gallon aquarium. Four or five specimens can be maintained in a 50-gallon tank.
- The Banggai cardinalfish is in danger from overcollecting. Only specimens produced through captive breeding should be purchased.

Damselfishes

Often the first fish that a saltwater aquarist keeps is a damselfish. Hardy and beautiful, damselfishes accept a variety of foods. Damselfishes occur in many reef habitats, from shallow lagoons to the blue waters of the outer reef. In terms of aquarium care, they can be divided into two groups, species that form shoals and feed on plankton in open water, and solitary species that feed on benthic invertebrates and algae.

Juveniles are reasonably gregarious, but adult benthic-feeding damselfishes often exhibit strong territoriality. To minimize disputes, keep only one kind of these damselfish per tank. For some common ones, such as the humbug damsels in the genus *Dascyllus*, if several individuals of the same species are housed together, each fish must be provided with its own cave or coral head. This spot will be vigorously defended by the resident damselfish, even unto death. Problems often arise when the novice aquarist adds three or four juvenile damselfishes as the first residents of his or her new aquarium. If enough nooks and crannies exist to accommodate each fish with a hidey-hole, they will initially get along just fine. However, as the fish grow in size and mature sexually, their innate territoriality will emerge, and the likelihood of fighting increases enormously. Unfortunately, the usual outcome in this situation positions one surviving damselfish as the "king of the aquarium." This individual will have systematically harassed its tank mates to death, and now will defend the entire aquarium against the intrusion of any other fish, even one considerably larger than itself.

The numerous species of *Chromis* represent the other end of the spectrum. *Chromis* are damselfishes that form shoals in open water over reefs, where they feed on plankton. Have I successfully given the impression that with few exceptions the single most important concern in the aquarium care of the varied family of damselfishes lies in consideration of their species-specific aggressive tendencies? Most eat nearly anything of suitable size offered to them. Most survive water quality that would quickly kill many other species. Most endure temperature fluctuations that would certainly precipitate disaster among a tank of less-hardy species. Most regularly and repeatedly spawn in home aquariums, producing relatively large offspring that can be successfully reared. Most remain relatively small in size, allowing them accommodation in tanks as small as 30 gallons, even as adults. And too many of them may systematically kill every other fish in the tank, if mismatched with retiring, docile species. Among the damselfishes, an understanding of the peculiarities of each one becomes essential to captive care.

C. vanderbilti (Vanderbilt's chromis)

This fish features horizontal lines of bright blue dots overlain on an orange body. It is collected in Hawaii and widely available. An excellent aquarium fish, it is identical to the following species in terms of care. Most aquarium specimens remain under 3 inches in length.

Chromis viridis (green chromis)

An excellent choice from the Indo-Pacific, six or seven individuals housed in a large aquarium will form an impressive display, as they tend to stay near the surface. In the sea, this behavior may be due to the increased visibility in the upper reaches of the water column, which would aid these fishes in pursuit of their prey, various members of the plankton community. If provided with a rich and varied diet that includes both plant and animal matter, all derived from marine sources, this and other *Chromis* can be expected to thrive and grow to an adult size of about 4 inches. The green *Chromis* sports an iridescent shade that can only be called "sea-green."

Chrysiptera cyanea (orange-tailed blue damselfish)

This species is perhaps the best choice among the entire family. Only the mature male fish has the orange tail, which nicely complements his electric-blue body. Females and juveniles are completely blue, with a black dot at the base of the dorsal fin. These fish are found in shallow lagoons, where the male guards a territory shared by his harem. Creating an aquarium for this species alone, together with an assortment of the invertebrates that also live in the lagoon, results in an almost foolproof miniature ecosystem. Feeding should consist of a variety of aquarium foods, offered two or three times a day.

Damselfishes at a Glance

- Feed damsels dry foods intended for marine fish, along with brine shrimp, worms, and frozen chopped seafood products. They thrive on feedings in small amounts offered rather frequently. *Chromis*, for example, need three or more light feedings daily.
- Mature damselfishes of certain species, particularly *Dascyllus*, seldom leave tank mates alone. With the exception of small shrimps they ignore invertebrates.
- The most popular damselfishes produce a nest of large eggs and provide parental care until they hatch, making them good choices for hobbyists who want to attempt breeding.
- Damselfish are capable of surviving conditions intolerable to most other aquarium species.
- Because of their territorial habits, damselfishes other than *Chromis* must be provided with an area in which to retire during the daylight hours. Expect each damselfish to select a spot and defend it against all comers.
- Damselfish pairs can be successfully maintained in an aquarium with a capacity of 30 gallons.

Dascyllus species (humbug damselfishes)

Common in the trade, the "humbug" damsels of the genus *Dascyllus* are often too aggressive for anything but a single-species aquarium. Unfortunately, they may constitute the majority of fishes sold as a first fish for beginning hobbyists, being so commonly imported and inexpensive. Admittedly, the little ones exude charm, oaring about with their pectoral fins. The amusing bobbing swimming pattern belies their close relationship to the anemonefishes. Indeed, juvenile *Dascyllus* may associate with large anemones, so focused are they on laying claim to a territorial hideout. Alas, they may be so successful in their endeavors as to become the size of a man's hand, driving off and killing anything that comes close to their private estate. Pairs will readily spawn in captivity, however, and the young are easily raised. They make superb candidates for a species tank, and their hardiness in such a situation approaches legendary proportions. The commonly imported *Dascyllus* share a black-and-white color scheme, differing only in pattern. *D. aruanus*, *the three stripe humbug,* has three vertical black bars alternating with three white ones. *D. melanurus*, known as the black-tailed humbug, is similar, but while *D. aruanus* has a white tail fin, that of *D. melanurus* is black on the outer edge, giving this species a total of four black bars. *D. trimaculatus*, the three spot humbug, on the other hand, opts for solid black coloration relieved of its monotony only by a white spot on the forehead and another larger white spot on its mid-dorsal flanks.

Pomacentrus alleni (electric-blue damselfish)

Widely regarded as the most beautiful example of the family, this species was named in honor of the world's most renowned student of the damselfish family, Dr. Gerry Allen. It is downright docile and can be recommended to anyone. Like other species in the genus, it consumes a fair proportion of algae as part of an omnivorous diet. The electric-blue body, bright yellow belly, and colorless caudal fin with a prominent black spot on the peduncle render this fish unmistakable. Several other species of *Pomacentrus* appear from time to time in shipments. Most are some variation on the yellow/electric-blue color scheme and have the same care requirements.

Anemonefishes

Perhaps the most popular marine fishes, anemonefishes are also among the best choices for the aquarium, with the possible exception of their close relatives, the damselfishes. Anemonefishes are often the first saltwater fish that a hobbyist chooses to keep, and with good reason. Anemonefishes are hardy, remain relatively small, accept a variety of aquarium foods, and exhibit bright colors and interesting behavior.

Anemonefishes constitute a subfamily, Amphiprioninae, of the damselfish family, Pomacentridae. Unlike other pomacentrids, they have evolved the habit of associating with large sea anemones. An inkling as to how this relationship may have developed can be seen in the behavior of some damselfishes. Juveniles associate with anemones, but later as adults they do not. Among the anemonefishes, adults are rarely found more than a meter's distance from the host anemone.

This unique dependence on giant sea anemones has resulted in an equally unique way of coping with the problems of reproducing the species while avoiding inbreeding. All anemonefishes start life as males. Soon after hatching, larval fishes spend a period of time drifting with the plankton. At metamorphosis, the juvenile anemonefish must now locate and successfully join an established family of its own species, already in residence in a suitable host anemone. As if this were not a sufficient challenge for a fish less than 1 inch in length, the resident male fish will drive off new arrivals that do not meet his criteria for adoption. Assuming the newcomer is accepted, he may yet never have the opportunity to fulfill his biological destiny, for reasons that become clear when one understands how female anemonefishes develop.

The resident pair will consist of a large female and a much smaller male. (The dominant male will nevertheless be larger than the juvenile males that constitute the remainder of the clan.) When the breeding female anemonefish dies, her former husband rapidly develops into a functional female, and one of the juvenile males now takes the role of breeding male. This arrangement guarantees that an anemone, once occupied, will never lack a source of eggs for continued propagation of the species. The pair may live to be over 10 years old, and during that time will produce thousands of offspring, only a tiny fraction of which will survive to maturity. Thus, a newly metamorphosed fish may succeed in locating a suitable anemone and be accepted by the resident pair only to remain for life an undeveloped male. The anemonefish lifestyle has not only achieved the goal of species survival, but has led to the evolution of some twenty-eight species of anemonefishes that are distributed throughout the Indo-Pacific region.

Because they normally spend their lives in the restricted area near the host anemone, anemonefishes are "pre-adapted" to captivity. They are undemanding in their requirements, needing only appropriate water conditions and a good diet to thrive and even spawn in aquariums as small as 30 gallons. The anemone need not be present.

Amphiprion clarkii *(Clark's anemonefish)*

Reaching about 4–5 inches, this fish is often misidentified as *sebae* anemonefish although the true *A. sebae* is rare in the aquarium trade. Hardy, long-lived, and disease resistant, it comes in several geographic color variations. In the most common one, the body is dark brown with a vertical white bar behind the eye and another below the middle of the dorsal fin. The snout and tail are pale, and the paired fins are yellow. In captivity, it will accept any of the host anemone species.

Amphiprion frenatus (tomato anemonefish)

This fish is so fearless, colorful, and hardy it is often described as "bulletproof." One individual of my acquaintance lived to be over 15 years old. Blood-red with an enamel-white bar behind the eye as an adult, it often has a white bar midbody as a juvenile. Like other anemonefishes, it feeds readily on a wide variety of aquarium foods. Never try to keep this one with another species of anemonefish. The tomato won't put up with the competition, and they are surprisingly vicious fighters. Natural host anemones are *Heteractis crispa* and *Entacmaea quadricolor*.

Amphiprion melanopus (cinnamon anemonefish, red and black anemonefish)

This one may also become somewhat aggressive as it matures, especially toward other anemonefishes, which it no doubt looks upon as a threat to its possession of the host anemone. It associates with *Entacmaea quadricolor*, and *Heteractis crispa*. It ranges from Indonesia eastward to the Marshall Islands, inhabiting the waters of numerous archipelagos. Juveniles are red-orange with a white bar behind the eye and a black spot on the upper body behind the dorsal fin. With maturity, the black spot enlarges to cover most of the rear two-thirds of the body, leaving the tail red-orange.

Amphiprion ocellaris (common clown anemonefish)

This one was a legendary favorite long before the Disney movie *Finding Nemo*. Bright orange, the common clown anemonefish has an enamel-white bar behind the eye and a bar behind the dorsal fin that is roughly triangular in shape. The fins are edged in black, and there may be a black line edging the white bars. Combined with the bobbing swimming pattern, the bright coloration makes the fish irresistible. It associates with *Heteractis magnifica*, *Stichodactyla gigantea*, and *S. mertensii* anemones. Wild-caught specimens are so disease prone that they have largely been replaced by tank-raised ones.

Amphiprion percula (percula clown anemonefish)

Percula clowns look so much like the preceding species that most *A. ocellaris* are identified as *percula* in the aquarium trade. Usually, though, the black edging on the white bars is much wider in *A. percula* than it is in *A. ocellaris*. Ichthyologists distinguish the two by minute

Anemonefishes at a Glance

- Anemonefishes are widely available from hatcheries and are among the best marine fish for beginners.
- It is not necessary to keep anemonefishes with an anemone. Beginners may find the anemone's needs too challenging, anyway.
- About all an anemonefish needs to survive for 10 or more years in the aquarium is proper water conditions and a varied diet that includes both plant- and animal-derived foods.
- Because juvenile anemonefishes change sex as they mature, any group will eventually produce a mated pair, thus facilitating the efforts of would-be breeders.
- Anemonefish have been spawned and reared to adulthood by home aquarists, so they are the best choice for a first attempt at breeding.
- After they become adults, anemonefish seldom tolerate another species of anemonefish in the same aquarium.

details of the finnage and teeth. For all practical purposes, they are the same fish. But don't try to keep the two species together, as *they* can tell the difference readily, and will fight. *Heteractis magnifica*, *H. crispa*, and *Stichodactyla mertensii* are the natural hosts.

Premnas biaculeatus (maroon anemonefish)

Maroon anemonefish are in a separate genus because they have two cheek spines instead of only one, which is the case in *Amphiprion*. Ichthyologists are always drawing distinctions over little details like this. *Premnas* grows larger, often over 6 inches, and is aggressive in proportion to its size. Never try to keep this one with other anemonefishes, nor indeed with any small, nonaggressive fish. I've had my hand bitten numerous times by a maroon. It lives with *Entacmea quadricolor* on the reef, usually as a pair consisting of the spunky little male and a female about three times his size. With or without the anemone, it adapts readily to captivity and feeds on nearly anything offered. The body is a deep wine-red, with a white bar behind the eye, another below the dorsal fin, and a third at the base of the tail. The fins are also deeply pigmented in red. A color variation with lemon-yellow bars is highly valued by aquarists.

Dartfishes (Microdesmidae), *see* Gobies (Gobiidae).

Dottybacks (Pseudochromidae)

While some dottybacks reach a considerable size and can potentially feed on their smaller tank mates, the seven or eight most widely available species reach a maximum length of about 4 inches. Aside from a propensity toward intolerance of their own kind, any of these fishes pose few problems for the home aquarist. Dottybacks respond well to simple care. They accept a broad selection of foods, including frozen foods, brine shrimp, blackworms, and flake foods. They pose a threat only to small crustaceans, such as shrimps, that could fit into the fish's mouth. They will not harm corals, anemones, or other invertebrates such as algae snails. Many offer potential for hobbyist breeding projects.

Hatchery managers have learned that for all species of dottybacks, two males will not get along, but a mated pair, or a male and several females, can share the same aquarium. *P. fridmani* is an especially good choice for breeding purposes, because the sexes can be distinguished. The male has a more elaborate tail fin than the female. This species has been studied extensively, and more is known about spawning and rearing them than possibly any other marine fish.

Only one dottyback tolerates its own kind in captivity. This is the orchid dottyback (*Pseudochromis fridmani*), native to the Red Sea. For the remainder, such as the brilliant blue and orange neon dottyback (*P. aldebarensis*), the rule is one to a customer unless a mated pair can be obtained. All these fish remain under 4 inches in length. Not only colorful and easy to keep, this family is widely propagated in captivity, so tank-raised specimens are commonly available. Dottybacks are all hardy if maintained with similarly small species and fed once or twice a day with meaty seafood.

Pseudochromis aldebarensis (Arabian dottyback, neon dottyback)

Although inclined to be considerably more aggressive than most members of the family, this fish is so lavishly colored it is hard to pass up. The base coloration is bright yellow-orange, but the face and back are black. Overlain on the black are stripes of the most vivid, neon blue you are likely to see in an aquarium fish. A blue stripe runs the length of the spine, and there are similar markings on the face, the dorsal and anal fins, and the tail. Beware, as it may attack smaller tank mates for no apparent reason.

Pseudochromis diadema (diadem dottyback)

This dottyback is yellow all over, except for the purple crown that gives rise to its name. Keep only one to a tank, although this species is not as aggressive as most.

Dottybacks at a Glance

- Unless you have a mated pair, dottybacks are best maintained singly.
- Dottybacks are easily fed on a varied diet of seafood.
- Dottybacks spawn readily in captivity, and the fry have been successfully raised. They are good choices if you are interested in breeding saltwater fish. Try the orchid dottyback for a first attempt.
- Although they make good community fish, dottybacks can sometimes become aggressive toward more docile tank mates. Other than moving the fish that's being picked on, there is little you can do about this.
- With the exception of shrimps small enough to be eaten, dottybacks generally ignore invertebrates.

Pseudochromis fridmani (orchid dottyback, Fridman's dottyback)

Extremely hardy, easy to feed, and a stunning orchid-purple in color, this dottyback was once among the most expensive fish in the store, even though it seldom reaches 3 inches in length. Now widely available at reasonable prices owing to the success of captive breeding efforts, it is the most sociable member of its family and can be kept singly, in pairs, or in groups. Just be sure to provide sufficient space and plenty of hiding places. It fares equally well in a minireef or a community of smaller, nonaggressive fishes.

Pseudochromis paccagnellae (bicolor dottyback, Pacific royal gramma)

The color pattern is similar to the popular Caribbean species, *Gramma loreto*. On closer inspection, these species appear distinctly different, and no experienced person should confuse them. *P. paccagnellae* is purple from the head to about midway along the body, when the color abruptly changes to lemon-yellow, as if it had been dipped, tail first, in yellow paint. The line of demarcation between the two colors is not so abrupt in the royal gramma.

Pseudochromis porphyreus (purple dottyback, strawberry dottyback)

This species is quite territorial and should be provided with a crevice or cave in which to retire. Most of the time, the fish will forage for food a short distance from the entrance to this retreat. Other fish that approach the den will be vigorously driven away. It's coloration is a uniform reddish-purple with transparent fins.

Pseudochromis springeri (Springer's dottyback)

Like the orchid dottyback, this one is found in the Red Sea and was quite expensive prior to the introduction of captive-bred specimens. The body is jet-black with electric-blue markings on the face. Reaching a mere 2 inches in length, it is nevertheless somewhat aggressive and should be kept only with equally robust fishes. It won't bother most minireef invertebrates, but may find a small shrimp too tempting to resist.

Dragonets (Callionymidae)

Only two species of dragonets are typically offered to aquarists, and both are quite spectacular in coloration. Dragonets should only be kept in an established aquarium with plenty of live rock, as they feed only on tiny bottom-dwelling invertebrates. Such food organisms will grow naturally in a thriving minireef. When their requirement for appropriate food is met, the mandarin, *Pterosynchiropus splendidus*, and the psychedelic fish, *Synchiropus picturatus*, are ideal specimens for a minireef. In all dragonets, the male can be distinguished from the female by the greatly elongated first spine of his dorsal fin and by his larger size. You can keep dragonets of the same species together as trios consisting of one male and two females. You can also keep the two species together. Never put two male dragonets of the same species together, however; they will fight until one is killed. Dragonets are seldom bothered by other fishes, perhaps because they are poisonous if eaten. They ignore other tank occupants, apart from their tiny food sources. *Synchiropus picturatus* prefers to seek its food among growths of filamentous algae, while *P. splendidus* cruises over rocks and coral skeletons. Only in exceptional cases will these fish accept substitute foods. It is therefore prudent to introduce them only into an aquarium that has been established for a while, and therefore will have a thriving population of copepods and similar organisms on which the mandarins can dine. For the same reason, it is unwise to place these fish in a tank of less than 50 gallons capacity (for each one you intend to maintain). Otherwise, the natural production of suitable food items may not keep up with the fish's appetite. Never purchase either of these species if the animal appears hollow-bellied. This is indicative of a specimen that has not been properly fed during its sojourn in the holding tanks of the collector, wholesaler, and/or dealer. In my experience, starved specimens do not recover, even when placed in optimal circumstances.

Pterosynchiropus splendidus (mandarin)

The basic body coloration of the mandarin is deep blue-green overlain with swirls and squiggles in coppery-red. The throat is often yellowish or light orange, and just behind the gill covers is a patch of yellow dots. Pectoral and tail fins are marked like the body, while the dorsal and pelvic fins are blue. It reaches nearly 5 inches in length and is more common than the following species.

Synchiropus picturatus (psychedelic fish)

Smaller than the mandarin, this fish reaches only about 3 inches in length, and so can be accommodated in a 50-gallon tank with one or two other fish. It is not as commonly imported as the mandarin and can be very difficult to acclimate to nonliving foods. No doubt many have starved in the hands of novice hobbyists. It should not be housed in the same tank with sea anemones or it will eventually wind up as dinner for one. The body is lime green with large polka dots. Each polka dot has a turquoise center, surrounded with concentric rings of orange, black, and teal. There are dark markings on the dorsal fin and at the base of the tail fin.

Dragonets at a Glance

- Dragonets are not for beginning aquarists.
- Dragonets feed only on tiny, living invertebrates that they pick from rocks all day long. They may starve rather than accept artificial foods.
- Male dragonets of the same species will fight until one is killed, but the different species tolerate each other.
- One male and two females of a single dragonet species can be maintained in a well-established minireef holding about 50 gallons.
- Dragonets will not harm most desirable invertebrates, but should not be kept with anemones. Eventually, the dragonet will be captured and eaten by the anemone.
- Dragonets avoid predation in the sea by being poisonous, advertised by their bright, gaudy, warning coloration. Placing one in a tank with a predatory fish may result in the loss of both.

Fairy Basslets or Grammas (Grammidae)

I confess a certain prejudice toward the royal gramma (*Gramma loreto*), the most common member of this family in the aquarium trade. It has long been a favorite of mine for a variety of reasons. In the first place, it comes from the Caribbean region and is therefore usually available from east coast wholesalers. This is a decided advantage for both dealers and hobbyists who live east of the Rockies, because it means quality, healthy specimens are relatively inexpensive and readily obtained. Second, it is among the least demanding of saltwater fish, provided its tank is maintained properly. Third, apart from a tendency to feed on smaller shrimps, it never bothers invertebrates and can be included in a minireef. Fourth, although males may exhibit aggressive behavior, a group of these fishes may be maintained in the same tank and will usually remain relatively close to each other, often taking shelter upside down under an overhanging rock. Even male to male aggression rarely leads to a damaging fight, as one fish always backs down and moves out of the winner's territory. Because adult grammas are small, usually only about 3 inches or less, this means that more than one territory can be defended within the confines of a suitably large aquarium, say 4 feet or more in length. With good reason, this is arguably the most popular Atlantic-Caribbean species in most dealers' inventories.

Gramma loreto is closely related to the dottybacks (Pseudochromidae). Indeed, the bicolor dottyback (*P. paccagnellae*), which is strikingly similar in coloration to the royal gramma, is often called Pacific royal gramma by aquarium dealers. Grammas and dottybacks are separated geographically. Dottybacks are confined to the Indo-Pacific. Grammas are found only in the Atlantic-Caribbean region, though only rarely in the Florida Keys. Most specimens are collected in the waters off Caribbean islands. Other members of the genus are confined to depths of 30 to 60 meters. *Gramma melacara*, the black capped basslet, is the only one seen with any regularity in aquarium shops. It is deep royal purple all over, except for the black cap. Slightly smaller than the royal gramma, it is identical in terms of care. Rare deep-water fairy basslets also occur in the tropical Atlantic. These, such as *G. lincki*, are seldom seen in the United States, but Japanese aquarists reportedly are willing to pay up to several thousand dollars for specimens.

The royal gramma was one of the first marine fishes to be introduced into the aquarium trade in the 1960s, and it retains enormous popularity today. Its striking coloration no doubt accounts for much of the interest among hobbyists. The bright yellow body appears as if the fish were held by the tail and dunked in purple paint, the colors blending about two-thirds of the way toward the tail fin. A few yellow scales form lines that merge with the purple anterior. There is a black dot on the purple dorsal fin, and the paired fins are also purple. Yellow streaking surrounding the eyes decorates the head. (Separating the royal gramma from its Pacific counterpart, the bicolor dottyback, is easy, because the line demarcating the color change is well-defined in the dottyback, but more uneven in the gramma. Further, the dottyback has no yellow on its head, and the dorsal fin and paired fins are colorless.) A fairy basslet closely related to the royal gramma occurs off Brazil. *Gramma brasiliensis* is slightly larger than *G. loreto* and lacks the yellow lines on the head. Although not often seen in the trade, the Brazilian gramma is a good aquarium fish, despite a tendency to aggressiveness toward smaller tank mates. Its care is identical to that for the royal gramma, except that only one specimen or a mated pair should be maintained together, to avoid fighting.

Because of its diminutive size, the royal gramma can be easily accommodated in tanks as small as 30 gallons, although a larger tank will be necessary for a group. Water conditions typical for any tropical marine aquarium should be maintained, despite the notable resistance of this fish to the more common parasitic infestations that plague marine hobbyists from time to time, usually when water quality declines. Virtually any aquarium food of suitable size is greedily accepted, including chopped fish or shellfish meat, mysid shrimps, brine shrimp adults, and various commercially available frozen food recipes. Daily or twice daily feedings are recommended.

Although adult aggressiveness is limited, the royal gramma will vigorously defend its chosen territory, usually a rock crevice or hole in the coral, against any intruder. This can lead to damage, and the offending party should be removed to a separate tank if aggression is frequent. Male grammas, which are usually larger than females, display aggressive behavior by opening their disproportionately wide jaws and pushing against each other, lips touching. This behavior is similar to that exhibited by the familiar freshwater fish, the kissing gourami, *Helostoma temmencki*. Observing such behavior in the aquarium is a sure way to recognize a male fish, if breeding them is your goal.

Royal grammas have been bred repeatedly in captivity. Mated pairs can be obtained by keeping one larger fish (or one previously identified as male) in a tank with several smaller individuals. The fish will pair off naturally. When ready to breed, the male builds a tube-shaped nest slightly larger than his body, using pebbles, seaweed, and bits of debris. Sometimes, the pair chooses a hole or cave, placing stones in front of the opening to restrict access, presumably for the protection of the developing eggs. A strand of seaweed placed in the nest serves as a substrate upon which the female deposits her eggs, which are immediately fertilized by the male.

Fairy Basslets (Grammas) at a Glance

- If the tank is sufficiently large, grammas can be kept in a group. They will often aggregate under a rock ledge.
- Feed grammas two or three times a day with a varied diet, mostly containing seafood.
- Despite their tolerance of poor water conditions, grammas do best in a minireef with optimal water quality.
- Spawning of the royal gramma often occurs in hobby aquariums, but the fry are difficult to raise to maturity.
- The royal gramma was one of the first saltwater fish sold in aquarium shops.

Other species of fairy basslets sometimes appear in aquarium shops. All are similar to the royal gramma in terms of size, feeding, and aquarium care.

Gobies and Their Relatives

Gobies, the entire suborder Gobioidei, are among my favorite fish. The six families that comprise this suborder are well represented in the aquarium trade, always lumped under the common name *goby* regardless of the actual taxonomy. Freshwater and brackish water gobies are found throughout the world, but it is around coral reefs that the group achieves its finest development. The majority of the 2,000 species in the suborder are in the family Gobiidae. The other important aquarium family, Microdesmidae, is known as dartfishes. I include both families in the discussion below, as aquarium care is similar for all of them.

Gobies (in the general, not scientific, sense) are mostly small fishes with two dorsal fins. Many have the pectoral fins fused into an attachment organ that allows them stability in water currents. Family Microdesmidae offers two, rarely three or four species to the aquarium trade. The most common of these is known as the firefish, *Nemateleotris magnifica*. Many specimens are imported from Hawaii, and the species occurs throughout the Indo-Pacific region. Sometimes seen is the purple firefish, or decorated dartfish, *N. decora*. Rarely, *N. helfrichi*, Helfrich's dartfish, is available to aquarists.

Occasionally, the excitable and inclined-to-jump *Ptereleotris zebra*, usually called zebra hover goby, makes an appearance. These are all elongate, agile species, seldom exceeding 4 inches in length, that are adapted to life in midwater, feeding on zooplankton, able to "dart" into a nearby hole or crevice should danger threaten. All are good jumpers and will leap out of the tank if startled. *P. zebra* is particularly prone to this behavior and is seldom imported as a result. Excellent reef species, any of the dartfishes needs a suitable "bolt-hole" or refuge among the rocks and a steady supply of small, meaty seafood that mimics their natural diet.

Family Gobiidae, the "true" gobies, includes at least 500 species in the Indo-Pacific region, with numerous other representatives throughout the world, including the coastal rivers and estuaries of California and the mountain streams of Tennessee and North Carolina. The true goby clan is the most numerous in the sea, in terms of the number of species, and new ones are still being discovered. All are bottom dwellers that feed on small invertebrates, but beyond that their lifestyles are extremely varied. Before you purchase an unfamiliar one, it is best to research its specific needs.

It is only possible to speak about the true gobies in generalities; a thorough discussion would occupy an entire book. The identifying characteristics of the clan are easy to remember: They remain under 4 inches, are elongate, possess a large mouth, and lack a swim bladder in all but a few species. Many kinds are regularly imported for the aquarium, and members of the genus *Gobiosoma*, the shark-nosed gobies of Florida and the Caribbean, are produced in hatcheries. Goby eggs are placed on a solid surface and guarded by the male until they hatch. The group thus offers some nearly perfect subjects for marine aquaculture.

Among the most interesting of all gobies are those that associate symbiotically with alpheid shrimps (snapping shrimps). At least eight shrimp species partner with ten or more genera of gobies. The shrimp constructs a burrow that both occupy, while the goby acts as a sentinel, alerting the blind shrimp to potential threats. The arrangement affords protection to the shrimp while permitting the gobies, unable to dig a burrow themselves, to occupy a

habitat that would otherwise be unavailable to them. By far the most common of these gobies in the aquarium trade is *Cryptocentrus cinctus*. Less often seen are species of *Amblyeleotris*, such as *A. randalli*, Randall's shrimp goby, which is cream-colored, with a distinctive false eye pattern on the large first dorsal fin.

Several species of gobies that habitually sift the substrate for food have been imported and are popular with aquarists whose reef tanks feature a live sand substrate. *Amblygobius phalaena*, the rather drab brown-barred goby, is a hardy species that gets larger than the average goby, about 5 inches. *Valenciennea puellaris* and *V. strigatus* are also somewhat larger than average. The former is cream-colored with orange spots and stripes marking its body, while the latter is pearly with a bright yellow head and a distinctive blue streak below the eye. These sand-sifting gobies may be hard to feed in captivity. *Amblygobius hectori*, Hector's goby, and *A. rainfordi*, Rainford's goby, are two colorful species that appear to need regular access to living algae if they are to do well in the aquarium.

Chances are, any goby you might encounter will remain small, can be safely accommodated in a reef tank, and will eat many different kinds of seafood, including frozen prepared mixes, as well as mysid shrimp, brine shrimp, chopped seafood from the grocery store, and possibly some green algae.

Amblygobius rainfordi (Rainford's goby)

This goby is olive-green with four bright red stripes running the length of the body. It is a grazer and needs a well-established aquarium with a good growth of filamentous algae. Supplement its diet with small, meaty seafood, as recommended for planktivores. It needs hiding places and is likely to be picked on by more aggressive species. Keep only one per tank, as it will not get along with another of its kind.

Cryptocentrus cinctus (yellow watchman goby, yellow shrimp goby)

Here we have an example of one of the most remarkable relationships to be found in the sea. It lives in areas of coral rubble and pebbles, where there is little in the way of cover. This and several related species have solved the problem by moving in with a burrowing shrimp. The shrimp excavates the burrow with its specially modified claws, and both goby and shrimp occupy it. What's in it for the shrimp? A pair of eyes. The burrowing shrimps are all blind. The goby earns its keep by issuing a warning when danger threatens. When they venture forth, the shrimp keeps one antenna in contact with the goby at all times, ready to sense the flick of the tail that says "Danger!" When this occurs, both disappear into the safety of the burrow. Unfortunately, the goby and shrimp are offered as a pair only infrequently, because collectors seldom keep both together during the long trek from reef to tank. However, the relationship can be established easily in the aquarium simply by placing an appropriate pair in the same tank. They'll immediately recognize each other and set up housekeeping. Better dealers should be sought out if you want to locate a goby-shrimp pair. The yellow watchman goby, true to name, is uniformly dusky-yellow, with tiny neon blue dots all over. Don't try to keep more than one per tank, and avoid mixing with other species of shrimp goby, as they do not tolerate each other.

Gobiodon okinawae **(yellow clown goby) and *G. rivulatus* (banded coral goby)**

Clown gobies love to perch in coral heads or atop a prominent rock. From this lofty position they survey the entire tank like a sentinel. Bright lemon all over, they rarely reach a length greater than 1½ inches. The closely similar-banded coral goby, *G. rivulatus*, is turquoise-green with brick-red bars, and also remains under 2 inches in size. If you have a large aquarium with many coral heads, you can try keeping several of these fish together. If conditions suit them, they will sort themselves out into male-female pairs and spawn regularly. Each couple establishes a territory in a single coral head, to which the egg cluster is also attached. Reportedly, the *Gobiodon* genus secretes mucus with noxious properties that cause predators to keep their distance. These fish are nonaggressive and should be kept in a minireef with similarly well-behaved species, or they may be harassed.

Gobiosoma

Gobisoma oceanops was among the first saltwater fishes to be spawned in captivity, and today thousands of them are reared for the aquarium trade. Just over 1 inch in length, black in color with brilliant blue and white horizontal stripes, it is at home even in a small tank. Related species, the green-banded goby (*G. multifasciatum*) and the red-headed goby (*G. puncticulatus*), are also sometimes available as captive-propagated specimens. Feed any of the *Gobiosoma* species with a variety of foods daily.

Gobies at a Glance

- Because different gobies may have very different lifestyles, any goby you choose for your aquarium must be correctly identified. That way, you can find out what it needs to thrive.
- Sand-sifting gobies are often difficult to maintain, because they have trouble getting enough to eat in an aquarium.
- Virtually all gobies remain under 6 inches, and most rarely exceed 4.
- Exact food preferences may vary, but gobies generally accept any kind of aquarium food that is small enough to swallow.
- Shrimp gobies can be exhibited with their partner shrimps if you can obtain both. This makes a fascinating display for a small saltwater tank.
- The most popular gobies are dartfishes, but remember that they can jump out of the tank, which therefore should be kept covered.
- Some gobies, such as Rainford's, need a good growth of filamentous algae to graze and don't fare well without it.
- Signal gobies can be a challenge because of their sand-sifting feeding behavior but will usually adapt to aquarium foods if kept as a mated pair.

Nemateleotris magnifica (common fire goby, common dartfish)

The common fire goby, collected from several locations in the Hawaii/Indo-Pacific region, has a cream-colored body with a brilliant flame-red tail. It hovers in midwater with its elongated dorsal fin held erect. Feed a plankton substitute several times a day. It is an excellent choice for a minireef.

Pterelotris heteroptera (blue gudgeon)

This is an elongated species, baby blue with a single black splotch in the fork of the tail. It will spend more time out in the open if kept in a group. Singles often hide. They do not squabble among themselves, as is sometimes the case with fire gobies. The diet suggested for other planktivores is also suitable for the blue gudgeon. These fish may jump from the tank if startled.

Signigobius biocellatus (signal goby, twinspot goby)

Here's another example of the remarkable adaptations of the goby clan: This species mimics a crab. The dorsal fin is large and bears a pair of dark eyespots, each encircled in yellow. The remainder of the body is cream-colored with orange-brown patches that obscure its outline against the background. As the fish moves along the bottom seeking tiny organisms that constitute its diet, it looks exactly like a large, aggressive crab. This apparently fools predators, who swim off to seek prey less likely to put up a fight. It is usually found in male-female pairs on the reef and does not do well if kept singly in the aquarium. Unfortunately, this is among the more challenging gobies to feed, and many slowly starve in captivity. It takes in a mouthful of sand, along with any food lying on or living in the substrate. After a bit of "chewing" during which time anything edible is separated and swallowed, the sand is spit out. This process is repeated all day long, and probably explains the difficulty of getting adequate nourishment in the aquarium. If you are tempted to try this fascinating fish, I suggest the pair be the only fish in a very well-established minireef of about 50 gallons.

Jawfishes (Opistognathidae)

The most readily available species from the jawfish family is the yellowheaded jawfish (*Opistognathus aurifrons*) from Florida and the Caribbean. Jawfish can be kept singly or in groups (a group is more fun to watch) in any size aquarium that will accommodate the number of fishes desired. They will excavate vertical burrows in the substrate, about twice as deep as the fish is long, so the aquarium must contain a deep layer of sand, shells, and pebbles. Often the burrow is excavated beneath a large shell or rock that provides a secure roof. Don't be concerned that the deep substrate will become dirty and pose problems, as the excavations of the jawfish will keep things stirred up nicely. Jawfish feed on planktonic organisms snatched from the water column, and accept a variety of fresh and/or frozen foods. They are notorious for jumping from the tank, especially during the first few days and nights of captivity or when startled. Keep the tank covered and try not to disturb them unnecessarily, and you should not have any problems.

Jawfishes at a Glance

- Only one species of jawfish is commonly seen in aquarium shops.
- Each jawfish constructs a burrow about twice its length. Provide a deep substrate to permit them to do this in the aquarium.
- Jawfishes are easily fed on small pieces of seafood and frozen aquarium preparations.
- Jawfishes are extremely nervous, and may jump out of the tank when alarmed. Keep the tank well covered and do not disturb them needlessly.
- It is not unusual for the high-strung jawfish to remain in hiding for a week after it is introduced into a new aquarium. During this time, do nothing to coax it out of its retreat.

Some Fish to Avoid

I have some definite recommendations on fish to avoid. For the most part, these are species that are so specialized in their feeding requirements that providing a suitable aquarium diet is virtually impossible. Others make the list because they are dangerous, grow extremely large, or both. With all the adaptable species available, it makes little sense to purchase a fish that poses a nearly hopeless challenge to a home hobbyist.

- Some butterflyfishes feed only on coral polyps. Many will accept only a specific type of coral. These fish usually starve in captivity. The species include exquisite butterflyfish, *Chaetodon austraicus*; triangle butterflyfish, *C. baronessa*; Bennett's butterflyfish, *C. bennetti*; foureye butterflyfish, *C. capistratus*; orangeface butterflyfish, *C. larvatus*, red-finned butterflyfish, *C. lunulatu*; Meyer's butterflyfish, *C. meyeri*; eight-banded butterflyfish, *C. octofasciatus*; ornate butterflyfish, *C. ornatissimus*; bluespot butterflyfish, *C. plebius*; Rainford's butterflyfish, *C. rainford*; oval spotted butterflyfish, *C. speculum*; and the Indian Ocean red-finned butterflyfish, *C. trifasciatus*. All these turn up from time to time in dealer tanks.
- Another coral-eater is the orange-spotted filefish, *Oxymonacanthus longirostris*. A beautiful fish with a charming way of swimming in and out of the coral, it will only rarely accept food other than its natural food.
- The rock beauty angelfish, *Holocanthus tricolor*, is regularly imported from the tropical Atlantic. It feeds mostly on living sponges and seldom adapts to aquarium fare.
- *Pygoplites diacanthus*, the regal angelfish, is also a challenge to feed.
- Several types of regularly imported wrasses have food requirements that are difficult or impossible to satisfy. These include various *Anampses* species that feed on benthic invertebrates, cleaner wrasses, *Labroides* species that feed on parasites infesting other fishes, and *Macropharyngodon* species that feed on tiny invertebrates.
- *Platax pinnatus*, known as the "pinnatus batfish" in the aquarium trade, is regularly offered by dealers. It feeds mostly on sessile invertebrates and only rarely will an individual learn to eat in captivity.

- The various species of sweetlips, *Plectorhynchus*, seldom adapt. What a shame, also, that the stunningly beautiful Moorish idol, *Zanclus canescens*, rarely lives out a year on a captive diet.
- Other families in which most members are difficult include boxfishes and cowfishes (Ostraciidae), seahorses (Hippocampidae), pipefishes (Syngnathidae), and shrimpfishes (Centriscidae).
- Seahorses, a fish sometimes suggested as an appropriate subject for a small, fish-only aquarium, are nearly impossible to maintain for a complete life cycle, even in a research laboratory.
- Ribbon eels (family Rhinomuraenidae) are undeniably beautiful, but they almost always refuse to eat in captivity. Even once enticed to feed, the fish may not fare well. Moray eels, on the other hand, seldom refuse to eat. In fact, they may attack anything placed in the tank, such as your hand. The main problem with a moray, though, is its wanderlust. I have scarcely heard of one of these eels in a home aquarium that did not eventually escape, later to be discovered desiccated on the carpet. Examples include Hawaiian dragon moray, *Enchelycore pardalis*; snowflake moray, *Echidna nebulosa*; zebra moray, *Gymnomuraena zebra*; comet moray, *G. meleagris*; and Atlantic green moray, *G. funebris*. These are all commonly imported species.
- Sharks and rays typically grow much too large for the home aquarium. Even if you have a giant tank, I'd urge against attempting these fish, as they are easily subject to injury and are difficult to treat if disease should strike. Shark populations are declining. Why take one more from the ocean when it's not likely to thrive at home? Another nontrivial consideration is that a 3-foot baby shark can easily bite off your finger.
- Stonefish, *Synanceia* species, are sometimes imported along with lionfishes. The sting, however, is far more severe, and has caused human deaths.
- A few fish simply have disagreeable personalities that warrant passing over them for others. In this group is the Atlantic red-lipped blenny, *Ophioblennius atlanticus*. Its drab coloration and aggressive behavior offer little in the way of recommendation. Blennies in the genus *Plagiotremus* are called "mimic" blennies because they share the coloration of several kinds of cleaner fish. Thus disguised, they are able to approach other fish with impunity, because the targeted fish thinks it is going to have its skin freed of parasites. When *Plagiotremus* gets close enough, though, it bites a chunk of flesh from its hapless victim and dashes to the security of a coral head. Similarly disappointing, though quite commonly seen in dealers' tanks, the neon damselfish, *Neoglyphidodon oxyodon*, starts life as a perky, retiring juvenile, black-bodied and marked attractively in brilliant blue and white stripes. It matures into a large, dirty brown adult with a truly obnoxious disposition.

Questions to Ask When Considering a Fish Purchase

How big does it get? (Choose specimens you can accommodate in the size tank you have.)

____

____

What does it eat? (This is probably the single most important factor in long-term care.)

____

____

Will it get along with the fish I already have in the tank?

____

____

Will it get along with the other fish I plan to purchase later?

____

____

Does this species pose any special challenges? (For example, jawfishes, while easy to feed and hardy, are extremely nervous and high-strung. They might not do well if your aquarium is situated where they are likely to be disturbed frequently.)

____

____

I have small children. Is there anything I should know about this fish that might be an issue for an inquisitive child? (Lionfishes, for example, can sting. Triggers and several others can bite.)

____

____

continued

How long have you had this fish? (Try to buy fish that have had a chance to recover from the trauma of capture and shipment.)

____

____

Where did this fish come from? (Fish that originate in the United States are likely to be in better shape than those from far away, all other things being equal. Some locations are notorious for using chemicals to collect fish. See the discussion of this in chapter 1.)

____

____

Is this specimen captive-propagated? (Hatchery fish always adapt better to captivity than their wild counterparts.)

____

____

What You Now Know . . .

- Some species of saltwater fish are best maintained in a fish-only tank, while others do best in a minireef, and a few are at home in either.
- The fish recommended for minireefs are mostly small species that feed on a variety of easily available foods and are therefore the best choices for beginners.
- Many fish are aggressive and can only be kept with equally robust tank mates.
- Very large, aggressive species are often intelligent and hardy, and make good choices for a single-species aquarium.
- Some saltwater fish are so finicky or dangerous or grow so large that they should be avoided by home aquarists altogether.

Chapter 5

Stocking Your Tank II: Invertebrates

What's Inside . . .

- Learn to recognize the various groups of aquarium invertebrates.
- Learn how to use live rock and live sand to create a natural aquarium.
- Learn to distinguish invertebrates according to their roles in the aquarium community.
- Learn which invertebrates should be avoided by aquarium hobbyists.

Some saltwater organisms are more amenable to domestication than others are. This is particularly true in the case of invertebrates. Representatives of every major group of invertebrates, except insects, can be found on the coral reef. Recognizing the major groups and being familiar with their typical lifestyles are important skills for anyone who plans to maintain invertebrates in an aquarium.

Invertebrate Groups

The coral reef is home to more species of marine invertebrates and fishes than any other habitat in the sea.

Invertebrates comprise roughly 95 percent of the animal kingdom, and they exhibit enormous diversity. With the exception of the representatives of some minor groups that one might find growing on a piece of live rock, only five invertebrate phyla command most of the attention of saltwater aquarists. These are: corals and their relatives (phylum Cnidaria), segmented worms (phylum Annelida), mollusks (phylum Mollusca), crustaceans (phylum Arthropoda), and echinoderms (phylum Echinodermata). Representatives of each of these groups that are good choices for a beginner's minireef are listed in the table on page 100. For each species, its food, habitat preferences and geographic range are given.

Recommended Invertebrates

	Food	Habitat	Found In
Coelenterates			
Disc Anemones			
Discosoma sp., mushroom polyp	Photosynthetic	Widespread in dim light and calm water	Indo-Pacific
Rhodactis sp., blue hairy mushroom polyp	Photosynthetic	Partially shaded areas in quiet water	Tonga
Sea Anemones			
Bartholomea annulata, curlicue anemone	Photosynthetic, but strongly carnivorous; feed as for other anemones	Grass beds and hardbottom flats, with seaweeds. Often hosts symbiotic shrimp	Florida and Caribbean
Condylactis gigantea, Haitian pink-tipped anemone	Photosynthetic, supplemented with occasional feedings	Turtle grass, with column slightly buried in soft bottom	Florida and Caribbean
Entacmaea quadricolor, bubble-tip anemone (clownfish host)	Photosynthetic, but feed once or twice a week with a small piece of seafood	On rocks in shallow water, sometimes with column in soft sand	Indonesia
Sea Mats			
Parazoanthus sp., yellow colonial polyp	Photosynthetic	Loose rubble on sand in bright, shallow water	Indo-Pacific
Soft Corals			
Brierium viridis, green star polyp soft coral	Photosynthetic	Lagoons, bays, outer reef slope	Indonesia
Sarcophyton sp., leather soft corals	Photosynthetic	Shallow lagoons in cloudy water	Indo-Pacific
Stony Corals			
Trachyphyllia geoffreyi, open brain coral	Photosynthetic	Shallow areas on soft bottom of mud or sand	Indo-Pacific
Annelids			
Fanworms			
Sabellastarte, giant feather duster worm	Suspended particles including bacteria and plankton	In quiet, shallow water	Florida and Hawaii have similar species
Spirobranchus, Christmas tree worm	Suspended particles	Moderately deep, turbid water	Tampa Bay area

	Food	Habitat	Found In
Mollusks			
Bivalves			
Tridacna derasa, ponderous giant clam	Photosynthetic	Outer reefs in deep water depending upon water clarity	Indo-Pacific
Tridacna gigas, giant clam	Photosynthetic	Grass beds or open areas on sand or among rubble	Indo-Pacific
Tridacna maxima, blue giant clam	Photosynthetic	Usually embedded in rocks in shallow water	Indo-Pacific
Snails			
Astraea, Turbo, and others	Algal films and filamentous algae	Anywhere with enough light to permit algae growth	Worldwide
Arthropods			
Hermit Crabs			
Clibanarius tricolor, blue-legged hermit crab	Algae and dead animal matter	In tide pools and among rocks in shallow, inshore areas	Florida and Caribbean
Paguristes cadenanti, scarlet hermit crab	Algae primarily, but whatever it finds	Many areas near the reef and on it	Florida and Caribbean
Shrimps			
Hippolysmata wurdemanni, peppermint shrimp	An omnivore, it will eat small anemones and is capable of reproducing in the aquarium	Shallow, quiet water among sessile invertebrates	Florida, similar species worldwide
Lysmata amboiensis, scarlet cleaner shrimp	Almost any small, organic item, including bits of dead skin from your fingernails.	Cleaning "stations" anywhere that provides shelter and many fish	Several similar species worldwide
Periclimenes sp., anemone shrimp	Depending on species, the same as above or on fish parasites primarily	In association with sea anemones	Similar species worldwide
Stenopus hispidus, banded coral shrimp	Same as previous shrimp; aggressive, it can catch unwary small fish	On back reefs at shallow to moderate depth	Florida, with similar species worldwide
Snapping Shrimps			
Alpheus armatus, curlicue snapping shrimp	Anything and everything, but not a predator	Burrows into coral gravel at the base of curlicue anemone in shallow water	Florida and Caribbean
Alpheus sp., goby shrimp	Small bits of organic matter stirred up by its excavations and the goby	Burrows into gravel on reef flats	Various species throughout the Indo-Pacific

continued

Recommended Invertebrates (continued)

	Food	Habitat	Found In
Echinoderms			
Brittlestars			
Various species, often difficult to identify	Scavenges after dark	Among rubble and boulders in shallow water	Worldwide
Sea Cucumbers			
Various species	Organic debris	Burrow into soft sand or mud in shallow water	Worldwide, most aquarium specimens come from Florida
Sea Stars			
Fromia elegans, little red sea star	Algal films and detritus	Shallow, inshore areas	Indo-Pacific
Sea Urchins			
Various species	Algae	Among rocks with algae growth	Worldwide

The table is arranged taxonomically, in order to show how the different groups of invertebrates are related to each other. Each of the phyla is subdivided, based on specific traits. Recognizing the group to which a particular invertebrate belongs will automatically tell you something about its needs in the aquarium. Sea urchins, for example, are active in the daytime and feed on algae, while brittlestars, which like urchins are placed in the echinoderm phylum, without exception hide from the light. Each of the important subdivisions of the prominent aquarium phyla are discussed briefly so you can recognize the specimens you encounter in aquarium shops.

Coelenterates (Phylum Cnidaria)

All coelenterates are animals with only two layers of cells composing the body. A single body opening serves as both mouth and anus. Organs are lacking or rudimentary. Unique to the phylum, specialized stinging cells, or *cnidoblasts*, are present. Two body plans, the *medusa*, or jellyfish form, and the *polyp*, or flower-animal form, exist among coelenterates.

Separation of the three classes is based on which of the two body forms is predominant during the life cycle. Class Hydrozoa, is comprised of coelenterates with alternation between the polyp and the medusa stages at different times in the life cycle. This class includes only one species of potential aquarium interest, fire coral (*Millepora*), an atypical hydrozoan that builds a calcified skeleton. It sometimes appears on live rock. Usually tan in color, it fares well in the aquarium under bright illumination. Beware, though: it can deliver a sting worthy of its name.

Class Schyphozoa includes jellyfish, in which the medusa is the dominant form and the polyp stage is brief. Jellyfish are very challenging as aquarium subjects, since they are creatures of the open sea.

Class Anthozoa, or *flower animals* are coelenterates in which only the polyp form occurs. Subclass Hexacorallia includes six-tentacle corals, solitary or colonial anthozoans with tentacles in multiples of six. Several important aquarium invertebrates are in this group.

Anemones

Sea anemones are solitary anthozoans that lack any sort of calcified skeletal elements. Two anemone genera, *Calliactis* and *Adamsia*, are found attached to the mollusk shell housing a hermit crab. In the case of *Adamsia*, the relationship is obligate and quite specific, with only one species of hermit a suitable host, and the anemone is never observed except attached to its host's shell. *Calliactis parasitica*, on the other hand, associates with at least three species of hermits and can survive even attached to an uninhabited shell. Since these species are found along the temperate Atlantic coast, they do well in a cooler aquarium but are poor choices for a tropical minireef.

Other Six-Tentacled Anthozoans

Among the six-tentacled anthozoans that are not anemones are disc anemones (also called mushroom corals and false corals), sea mats, and stony corals. Disc anemones, usually colonial and lacking a skeleton, are flattened discs with reduced tentacles. Sea mats are always colonial and also lack a skeleton. In most species individual polyps are connected by a sheet of tissue that spreads over the substrate. In the stony corals the distinctive feature is the calcified skeleton. Structural details of the skeleton serve to distinguish corals from other anthozoans.

Eight-Tentacled Anthozoans

A second major group of anthozoans possess tentacles in multiples of eight, and so are called *octocorals*. All of them are colonial. Sea pens are octocorals with a fleshy body and a skeleton of loose elements. Usually the lower portion of the animal is buried in sand and the upper portion gathers planktonic food. To the delight of aquarists, some sea pens are brilliantly luminescent at night. Unfortunately, they can be challenging to maintain in captivity, owing to their demand for abundant planktonic food. One large subgroup of the polyps arises from a creeping mat of tissue, and the skeleton, if present, is made of loose elements. Alcyonarians are soft corals in which the skeleton is made up of loose elements, resulting in a "flabby" individual. Gorgonians are soft corals in which the skeleton consists of a stiffened, axial rod of protein and calcareous spicules growing upright like a shrubbery.

Annelids (Phylum Annelida)

Annelids are familiar to most of us in the form of earthworms and leeches. In the sea, however, this phylum is represented by thousands of species of *polychaetes*, annelids with numerous rudimentary appendages, usually a pair on each segment. The vast majority of polychaetes are of little interest to aquarists, but the sedentary fanworms are quite popular. Fanworms live in a protective tube that they secrete, and only their feeding appendages, the "fan" that gives them their name, are visible. These are often brightly colored. The fan is instantly withdrawn into the worm's tube when danger threatens.

Mollusks (Phylum Mollusca)

Around 100,000 species of mollusks exist. No one knows for sure, as new species are constantly being discovered. Despite the incredible diversity of this group, relatively few species are of interest to aquarists. Basic mollusk anatomy reveals a bilaterally symmetrical body, meaning it has distinguishable left and right sides. The body is often enclosed in a calcareous shell secreted by a structure called the mantle.

In the *chitons*, the shell consists of eight calcified plates. Chitons are adapted for clinging to wave-scoured rocks, from which they scrape algae. They are seldom deliberately collected for the aquarium, but often hitchhike on live rock. They are hardy and useful herbivores and are considered to be very primitive mollusks.

By contrast, the most recently evolved mollusks—octopus, squid, and nautilus—are collectively called *cephalopods*. These are suitable subjects only for specialized aquaria designed for their needs and will not be discussed further.

Gastropods, or snails, constitute the largest class of mollusks. They exhibit a range of diversity scarcely found elsewhere in the animal kingdom. Most gastropods have a tubular, spiral shell. Some, however, have no shell at all.

Prosobranchs are gastropods with the mantle cavity and organs located in the front part of the body. The shell is usually closed by a door, or operculum, and the sexes are usually separate. Primitive prosobranchs with two gills include the important aquarium herbivores *Turbo* and *Astraea*, and various limpets.

Forms with only one gill (always the left one, by the way) are known as mesogastropods. Periwinkles, conchs, and coweries are sometimes seen in aquarium shops.

Opisthobranchs have only one gill and often exhibit loss or reduction of the shell. Only three of the twelve orders of opisthobranchs are collected as aquarium specimens. A fourth is of interest because its members are pests. Pyramid snails parasitize other mollusks. When the host is a tridacnid clam (discussed later in this section) aquarists take notice of them. The other opisthobranchs are sea hares, saccoglossans and nudibranchs. In sea hares the shell is reduced and internal. Saccoglossans are sluglike, and generally feed on algae. Sometimes they show up unannounced, having been brought along on a piece of live rock. Another group of shell-less mollusks usually called sea slugs is the nudibranchs ("naked gill"). Many are strikingly beautiful, but these specialized creatures seldom survive for long in the aquarium. They are carnivorous, and usually have highly specialized dietary requirements. Providing the appropriate food can be a problem. Most nudibranchs complete their life cycle in one year or less.

Bivalve mollusks have a hinged pair of shells enclosing the body. The majority are filter feeders and are among the most familiar of marine invertebrates. Clams, oysters, scallops, and mussels are all gastronomic delights, and tropical species are frequently collected on live rock. The genus *Lima*, or file shells, includes the Caribbean flame scallop as well as Indo-Pacific species that are sometimes available to aquarists. One group in particular, characterized by a few large, interlocking teeth along the hinge line, includes the giant tridacnid clams, which garners the vast majority of minireef hobbyist interest.

Arthropods (Phylum Arthropoda)

This huge assemblage includes all organisms with jointed appendages, an exoskeleton composed of chitin (a tough, but flexible protein similar to fingernails), and a segmented body. The most commonly recognized arthropods are the terrestrial insects and spiders. In the ocean, however, it is the crustaceans that are the dominant group. The crustacean group includes brine shrimp, amphipods, copepods, mantis shrimps, true shrimps, hermit crabs, true crabs, and lobsters, along with several other types of marine arthropods of little interest to the aquarist. Because of the many species of crustaceans, the class is split into numerous subdivisions.

Brine shrimp (subclass Branchiopoda) are familiar as a food source for many types of aquarium organisms. Amphipods (order Amphipoda) and copepods (subclass Copepoda) are seldom added to the aquarium deliberately as specimens, but these tiny shrimplike creatures often turn up in tanks that have been established for several months, and frequently cause concern because they may undergo a population explosion. This concern is unwarranted, as these organisms are harmless. Their presence in the aquarium may indicate that detritus is accumulating, because it is a source of food for them. Otherwise the appearance of amphipods and copepods is no cause for alarm. Many fishes feed on amphipods and copepods.

Mantis shrimps (order Stomatopoda) are another type of crustacean that may turn up unexpectedly in the aquarium. They usually come hidden in a crevice in a piece of live rock. Many are harmless but all are predatory and should be removed if possible. Krill shrimps (order Euphausiacea) are important in ocean food webs, and are widely sold in frozen and freeze-dried form for fish food, as are mysid shrimps (order Mysidacea).

The crustaceans of most interest to aquarists are the hermit crabs, true crabs, true shrimp, and lobsters. These are all in the misnamed group Malacostraca. The name means "soft shelled," although most members have hard, calcified shells. All the aquarium types look more or less like the familiar edible members of their respective groups, that is, aquarium lobsters resemble the Maine lobster, aquarium crabs resemble the blue crab, etc.

Echinoderms (Phylum Echinodermata)

The echinoderm phylum is the only one found exclusively in the sea, with no members in freshwater or terrestrial habitats. As such, all of them are sensitive to poor water conditions and are especially intolerant of low salinities. They are characterized by radial symmetry, with the familiar starfish a classic example. Rather than being divided into left and right sides, the body parts radiate from a central point. Several orders of echinoderms are recognized, including the crinoids (also known as *sea lilies*), sea stars, brittlestars, sea urchins, and sea cucumbers. Crinoids are delicate and difficult to feed and are not suitable aquarium subjects, except perhaps in large, public aquarium displays. The other echinoderms include many great choices, even for beginning aquarists.

Invertebrate Roles in the Aquarium Community

Taxonomic classification helps demonstrate the relationships among invertebrates. For aquarium purposes, another way of "classifying" invertebrates may prove more useful, especially for someone with no background in biology. We can group them according to the role they will play in the aquarium community. Looked at this way, the groups are:

- Live rock
- Live sand
- Utilitarian invertebrates
- Photosynthetic invertebrates
- Clownfish host anemones
- Nonphotosynthetic invertebrates other than the utilitarian ones
- Seaweeds

The remainder of this chapter will provide details on each of these groups, highlighting their members that make especially good aquarium subjects.

Live Rock

An essential component of the minireef aquarium, live rock consists of dead coral skeletons or fossil coral limestone that is removed from the ocean with encrusting plants and animals attached. The nature of live rock can vary due to the kind of rock, the collecting locality, the depth from which the rock is taken, the numbers and kinds of organisms present at the time of collection, and the method of storage and transport between the collector and the hobbyist.

Live rock is harvested from shallow, inshore areas. Collection of natural live rock is prohibited in Hawaii, Florida, and Puerto Rico, but cultivation of live rock takes place in Florida under special permits. Live rock is cultivated in the central Gulf of Mexico, as well as in the Florida Keys. Cultivation involves dumping quarry rock at sea and retrieving it a year or two later, when encrusting organisms have colonized it.

Curing Live Rock

As soon as rock is received, it should be briefly rinsed in a bucket of seawater to dislodge any loose material and then immediately placed in the quarantine tank. There should be about 2 gallons of water per pound of live rock.

The rock remains in the quarantine tank for 2 weeks, or longer if necessary, to allow beneficial bacteria to restore the rock to health by breaking down dead organisms and replacing the original biomass of the rock with their own microscopic cells. A community of organisms tends to become reestablished on the rock. This results from a process of artificial selection: small invertebrates and microorganisms able to survive and reproduce under conditions in the rock curing process are permitted to flourish.

These beneficial organisms are subsequently transferred to the display aquarium after curing, and form the foundation of the captive ecosystem. When the curing process is complete, the rock has a fresh, ocean smell and is free of dead, decaying organisms.

Besides a thriving population of beneficial bacteria that have fed on the abundant nutrients released in the process of decay, the rock will have numerous colonies of pink, mauve, and purple encrusting coralline algae present. Live rock may develop an assortment of green or red seaweed growth that looks especially good if kept well-pruned by herbivorous fish.

Regardless of the source, of utmost importance is the treatment that the rock receives between collection and retail sale. You will generally be unable to obtain this information with certainty and must rely on your dealer to stock good quality live rock and to care for it properly. Collectors do not ship live rock in water. Live rock is packed in wet newspaper and shipped in insulated cartons. Despite these precautions, there will always be a significant amount of die-off of the encrusting organisms. The degree to which the organisms that were originally present on the rock arrive intact in your aquarium depends on how long the rock has been out of water on its journey.

When the rock is placed under water once again, organisms that have died begin to decay. This creates a lot of ammonia pollution and generates large amounts of organic debris. This process, which usually takes about three weeks, is called *curing*. Curing must take place in a container separate from the display aquarium. Otherwise, the pollution and debris will seriously harm the fish and invertebrates.

Some dealers hold live rock long enough to allow the curing process to proceed to completion. Others do not, and leave it up to you to do the curing at home. You do this in your quarantine tank (see page 137). Since live rock is the first addition you will make to the minireef, using the quarantine tank at this stage won't interfere with the need for it when fish arrive.

Few large organisms will be apparent immediately after curing, although the rock harbors spores, holdfasts, and other portions of organisms, from which new invertebrates sometimes grow once the rock becomes part of a maturing minireef. Sponges, tubeworms, and other small, encrusting organisms often begin to appear after the completed minireef has had the opportunity to develop by itself for several months.

Live Sand

Live sand is analogous to live rock in that it is harvested from the sea bottom and contains a natural population of beneficial small organisms. Simply placing a layer of coarse sand on the bottom of the aquarium and allowing it to develop a population of bacteria, worms, and microcrustaceans appears to be all that is necessary for enhancing the microbial community of the minireef. The use of natural live sand as a source of seed organisms that will colonize a new sand bed is clearly beneficial. Incorporating a layer of sand into the minireef aquarium may speed up the establishment of a system that is in nitrogen equilibrium (see page 42). Whether it is essential to provide a plenum under the sand layer, as in the Monaco-style minireef, is debatable.

Utilitarian Invertebrates

Some invertebrates may be added to either the minireef or the fish-only aquarium simply for the chores they do. Hermit crabs are the classic saltwater aquarium housekeepers. Small ones can be included in any minireef. They keep filamentous algae under control and spend much of their time seeking out and devouring bits of food missed by the fish. Larger hermit crabs are best suited to a fish-only tank. They can be boisterous and may rearrange the decorations. Occasionally, a large hermit will luck out and catch a small fish.

Among mollusks, snails that eat filamentous algae are welcome in any aquarium. Beware of placing them in a tank with fish that might eat them, such as wrasses and triggerfish. In the minireef, however, it is not excessive to have two snails per gallon. Two genera, *Astraea* and *Turbo*, are most often collected for algae control, but numerous herbivorous mollusks live near coral reefs, and any of them can turn up in your local shop. The warty sea hare, *Dolabrifera dolabrifera*, is a small species that can be useful, as it will eat films of diatoms and cyanobacteria. It is found in the Caribbean. Saccoglossans are another group of shell-less mollusks that are useful for algae control. They generally remain much smaller than sea hares, which can be as big as a real, mammalian hare and consume prodigious quantities of seaweed. Some species of saccoglossans will reproduce themselves in the aquarium. Sea hares do not. Most frequently, saccoglossans are not added deliberately, but hitchhike on live rock and turn up in the aquarium later, as if by magic.

Cleaning shrimps are often added to fish-only tanks to do what they do naturally, remove parasites from the skin of fishes. In the confines of the aquarium, cleaners are not completely safe from being eaten, although in the wild they have been photographed working inside the mouths of large predators with impunity. One of the best choices is *Stenopus hispidus*, the banded coral shrimp. It is robust and aggressive enough not to be bothered too much by fishes.

A less aggressive but more entertaining cleaner is *Lysmata amboiensis*, the scarlet cleaning shrimp, also known as the "scarlet lady." Bright red, with a white stripe down the middle of its back, this 2- to 3-inch shrimp seems bent on cleaning anything and everything that moves about in its territory. It will hop on your hand and give it a good going over, once accustomed to aquarium life. Either of these shrimps gets along just fine by scavenging, so skin parasites are not essential in their diet. Both make fine minireef subjects.

Among echinoderms, small sea urchins are useful for controlling algae growth and various kinds of brittlestars make great scavengers. Active mostly at night, brittlestars stay hidden under rocks during the daylight hours. They are efficient at removing all sorts of debris, such as uneaten fish food. Along with the brittlestars, certain species of sea cucumbers are valuable for keeping the aquarium substrate stirred up. These burrowers not only feed on detritus encountered as they tunnel along, their excavations allow vital oxygen to reach all parts of the substrate, facilitating healthy bacterial activity. In aquariums where an undisturbed layer of anaerobic sand is desired, a sheet of plastic netting can be placed above the anaerobic layer before adding the remainder of the substrate, to prevent later access by burrowers.

Photosynthetic Invertebrates

Photosynthetic invertebrates may be classified, for aquarium purposes, into a few key groups that are conveniently correlated with habitat preferences. Among the most widely available coelenterates are the anemones, soft corals, sea mats, disc anemones, and large-polyped scleractinian (LPS) corals that inhabit shallow, inshore waters. Important characteristics for this habitat are intense lighting (shallow water allows maximum penetration of solar radiation), moderate currents (inshore regions are protected by the reef from the pounding of the open sea), and tolerance of organisms for elevated nutrient levels (lagoon waters tend to accumulate nutrients). Another broad group, small-polyped scleractinian (SPS) corals, is generally found on the outer reef. In this habitat, water movement can be extreme, and nutrient levels are nearly immeasurable. Lighting needs can vary from high to low, depending on depth, although many SPS corals need very bright light.

Although clownfish host anemones are also photosynthetic, we will consider them separately in the next section. Many beginners want to exhibit the clownfish-anemone relationship in their aquariums but fail to understand how challenging it may be to keep the host anemone. Hence, I've covered them in considerable detail.

Disc Anemones

Tentacles are absent from many of the Pacific disc anemones or mushroom corals, of which there are several species from the genera *Rhodactis*, *Actinodiscus*, and *Discosoma*. All are flat, rounded polyps with very short columns. Mushroom corals typically do well in moderate light and can be placed near the bottom of the aquarium or in tanks where lighting is below 10,000 lux. Also called "false corals," they come in many colors, with blue-green, brown, and green being the most common. Some have striking blue or red pigments. Their pigmentation may change if the lighting conditions in the tank are significantly different from those under which the specimen was growing in the ocean. Moderate currents are preferred, and elevated levels of nutrients are tolerated. As a general rule, the false corals are easy to keep, and will grow and multiply in the aquarium. One deserves special mention—the elephant ear, *Amplexidiscus*. Nearly a foot across, its only negative trait is a propensity to eat small fishes that may be unwary of its stubby tentacles. Most other false corals rely either on photosynthesis or eat small planktonic organisms. Any species is a good choice for a tank depicting quiet waters with subdued light. Companions might include *Trachyphyllia*, a stony coral (see below).

Anemones That Do Not Host Clownfish

For our purposes, there are two groups of anemones, those that host clownfish, and those that do not. The clownfish host anemones are discussed separately below. In this section I cover other widely available anemones.

The curlicue anemone, *Bartholomea annulata*, commonly collected in Florida, is a highly suitable aquarium subject. There are interesting symbiotic associations in which this anemone is a participant, and I would regard this species as ideal for a small habitat tank. It requires bright light, but is tolerant of warm, nutrient-rich aquarium water. It hosts the symbiotic shrimps *Periclimenes pedersoni* and *P. yucatanensis*. A snapping shrimp, *Alpheus armatus*, makes its home exclusively at the base of this anemone. These relationships can form the focus of an interesting small aquarium devoted to the anemone and its partners.

Another interesting anemone, *Telmatactis*, is found in Hawaii. It lives symbiotically with the teddy bear crab, *Polydectus*. Only juvenile anemones are carried by the crab, probably as an aid in food gathering and for defense. *Triactis producta* is seen by aquarium hobbyists only when clenched in the chelae of the pom pom crab, *Lybia*. Two species of this unusual crab, *L. edmonsoni*, which is confined to Hawaii, and *L. dubia*, which is found elsewhere in the Indo-Pacific region, carry *Triactis,* and use it both as a food-gathering tool and a defensive weapon. *Lybia* is a more popular aquarium crab than *Polydectus*, perhaps because it is more colorful and less secretive. These specimens are easy to keep and adapt well to a small minireef.

Lebrunia danae, the stinging anemone, is collected in the Florida Keys. It has specialized tentacles that give rise to its other common name "antler anemone." Despite its ability to deliver a nasty sting, this species is at home in an aquarium devoted to the shallow waters from which it is collected, alongside the curlicue anemone, above, and it can be exhibited.

Phymanthus crucifer, usually called *flower anemone*, is found only in shallow water (less than 20 feet) in Florida and the West Indies. It may be brightly colored, owing to the presence of zooxanthellae and accessory pigments, and makes a fine aquarium specimen. It is very hardy and tolerant of suboptimal water conditions, although it must be given bright illumination. *Phymanthus* is usually buried in sand and retracts completely when disturbed. Here's a tip: Providing soft sand, rather than coarse crushed coral or shell fragments, may be important for anemones that bury themselves. The coarser materials may be irritating and prevent the anemone from locating itself properly. If the anemone cannot attach itself and expand its tentacles, it cannot receive sufficient light, oxygen, or planktonic food.

There are two common and attractive anemone species in the Atlantic-Caribbean region, *Condylactis passiflora* and *C. gigantea*, that are regularly seen in aquarium shops. *C. passiflora* is the smaller of the two. It occurs in turtle grass beds where its column is buried in sediment, and it does not host symbiotic shrimps. It is identified in the trade as Florida pink-tipped anemone. *C. gigantea* occurs among rocks on the fore-reef and in lagoons. It is larger, almost always has a colorful column, and hosts the symbiotic shrimps *P. pedersoni*, *P. yucatanensis*, and *Thor amboiensis*. It is known in the trade as Haitian pink-tipped anemone. *C. gigantea* is common, but it does not occur in concentrated groups. Conversely, *C. passiflora* can be as numerous as one per square foot in turtle grass. Color is variable, but the tentacles of both species are often tipped in magenta or pink, and the column of *C. gigantea* is often salmon pink. Both these anemones are good aquarium subjects and are quite hardy.

Sea Mats

Sea mats look like a colony of small anemones connected at the base by a sheet of tissue spreading over the substrate. One that is not interconnected is a *Parazoanthus* species sold as yellow polyp sea mat or yellow polyp colony. This species is an excellent choice for the minireef, and its bright lemon-yellow color is both unusual and attractive. It is collected in the Indo-Pacific. There are many other sea mats. Their coloration is usually restricted to the center of the oral disc, with the column and tentacles being dull gray, brown, or greenish. Disc colors range from greens to blue and even pink. Some specimens are green with orange centers, and there is also a lovely pinkish-purple form. The species are difficult to identify, but most of the ones you'll see probably belong to the genera *Isaurus*, *Palythoa*, and *Zoanthus*.

Soft Corals

Photosynthetic soft corals are very popular as aquarium subjects. They are amenable to propagation by simple division. Some can literally be raised from cuttings, like houseplants. They fall into three groups, the leather corals, the pulse corals, and the stoloniferans.

Leather Corals

The many species of *Sarcophyton*, usually called leather corals, are among the most suitable of alcyonarians for aquarium care. In all of them, the body is brownish or yellowish in color, with pale yellow to bright green polyps embedded in it. Leather corals generally prefer high light intensities. They often grow in abundance in shallow lagoons. They also need a stable, high pH. These conditions are also favored by many seaweeds, and leather corals look good in tanks with lots of green growth, being a nicely contrasting color. It is not unusual for the polyps of leather corals to remain contracted for several days after a change in water conditions, such as moving them from one aquarium to the other. Several other genera of soft corals are available. *Lobophytum*, or "devil's hand," has only a few short polyps protruding from its flattened body. *Sinularia*, known as "lettuce" or "cauliflower" coral, has large, prominent skeletal elements that give it a spiky feel. *Cladiella* is a large, bushy species that produces a lot of mucus when handled. Other genera that are regularly available include *Lemnalia* and *Litophyton*.

Pulse Corals

Several species of soft corals exhibit continuous pulsing movements. These are collectively referred to as *pulse corals*, and may be species of *Xenia*, *Heteroxenia*, *Cespitularia*, or *Anthelia*. In *Xenia*, the columns of the individual polyps are long and thin, and the crown of tentacles reminds one of a daisy. They are brownish in color. In *Anthelia* the feathery, white polyps are attached at the base to form a cluster anchored to a rock or other hard surface. *Heteroxenia* specimens may stop pumping when currents, which transport nutrients to the animal and carry away wastes, are too strong. It does not possess nematocysts and so cannot catch plankton. Thus, it probably relies on photosynthesis exclusively for growth. Pulse polyps are hardy and reproduce themselves readily in the aquarium.

Stoloniferans

Starburst soft coral, *Briereum viridis*, is also called *green star polyp*. In these alcyonarians, the skeleton is a rubbery, flattened sheet that encrusts a solid substrate. Each polyp resides in a short tube that projects upward from the sheet about ¼ inch. The polyps themselves are pale green with bright green centers, or are an overall lime-green color. When expanded, this is a very beautiful species. It is also, happily, one of the hardiest and most durable, and can be recommended to the rankest beginner. Its only special requirements seem to be current and very bright light, under which it will grow and spread.

Stony Corals

The stony corals seen in the aquarium trade fall neatly into two groups that may be easily differentiated. Small-polyped scleractinian (SPS) corals, famous among advanced hobbyists because of the ease with which they may be propagated, are generally thought of as species of the outer reef. Lagoon species have mostly large polyps. There are, of course, species of stony corals that occur over a range of habitats, and many of these may alter their growth form to take advantage of a particular microenvironment. This can make identification of species extremely difficult, and all identifications to the species level should be considered suspect. This is why only genera are mentioned here, with few exceptions. Stony corals require excellent water quality, good water movement (*chaotic* is a term often used to describe the type of water movement favored by many corals), and suitable illumination.

Shallow-water stony corals are often large, single polyps contained within a cone-shaped skeleton that sits partially buried, pointed-end down, in the soft bottom sediments. Lagoon corals are more tolerant of high nutrient levels, higher temperatures, and sluggish water movement than are their cousins on the fore reef.

Heliofungia actiniformis, or plate coral, needs a soft, sandy substrate and plenty of room. It is spectacular in a tank designed with its special needs in mind. It is the only commonly available coral capable of moving from place to place. Symbiotic shrimps, *Periclimenes holthusii* and *Thor amboiensis*, are found on this coral in nature. It lives in shallow water subject to intense illumination.

Herpolitha, or slipper coral, is a close relative of *Heliofungia* and needs similar conditions. Provide average light intensity and moderate but not forceful current. It should be placed on the floor of the aquarium on sand.

Goniopora, or flowerpot coral, is considered to be a difficult species to maintain. A related genus, *Alveopora*, is sometimes imported. Despite the fact that these species are challenging, they will sometimes produce offspring in the form of small buds. Nevertheless, I cannot recommend them to beginners.

Trachyphyllia geoffreyi, or open-brain coral, is a hardy and attractive species that is regularly imported. This coral is a single large polyp, a design that seems to be associated with ease of aquarium care. The skeleton is in the form of an inverted cone, often attached at the apex to a hard substrate when the coral is young, but later breaking off, allowing the coral to sit upright in soft sand or silt. As a result of this growth form, it is easily collected without damage, which may explain why aquarium specimens do so well. *Trachyphyllia* prefers the same conditions favored by false corals, mentioned earlier, and is a good companion for them.

Cynarina, or button coral, is also a single large polyp, and should receive the same care as *Trachyphyllia*. Another similar genus, *Lobophyllia*, is recognizable by the "teeth" at the margin of the colony, which are lacking in *Trachyphyllia* or *Cynarina*.

Catalaphyllia jardinieri, or elegant coral, is one of the most popular, hardy, and spectacular stony corals. Like *Trachyphyllia*, this species is a single polyp that lives in mud and is easy to collect in undamaged condition. In addition, the polyps can withdraw completely into the skeleton where they are adequately protected during transport, and the coral rarely arrives at its destination in damaged condition. It is somewhat rare, however, and commands a premium price. However, if I were going to have only one coral, this would be my choice. Specimens can double in size in 6 months.

Several species of *Euphyllia* are available to aquarists, and all make good additions to the reef tank. All have relatively long tentacles and must not be placed close to other invertebrates, which they may sting. They need bright light. *Euphyllia ancora*, known variously as anchor coral, hammerhead coral, hammer coral, or ridge coral, has a curved extension at the end of each tentacle, giving the appearance of little hammers or anchors. *Euphyllia divisa*, or frogspawn coral, gets its colorful common name from the appearance of the tentacles. They sport numerous tubercles and white spots, suggesting a mass of frog's egg. It is another good aquarium species, although specimens are often lost due to shipping damage. Torch coral, *Euphyllia glabrescens*, looks like several cone-shaped torches, attached at the apex. The elongated tentacles with pale, rounded tips extend from the torch like flames.

Turbinaria, or chalice coral, cup coral, or wineglass coral, is so named because the skeleton is shaped like a goblet with a fat stem by which the coral is attached to a hard substrate. Thin, brownish tissue covers the entire surface. The large, flowerlike polyps are borne only on the inside of the goblet. *Turbinaria* is interesting in appearance and easy to keep. Sometimes an attractive mustard-colored variety is available.

Plerogyra sinuosa, or bubble coral, may be pale blue, brownish, or green in color. This is a commonly available and popular species. A related genus, *Physogyra*, which looks very similar, is called pearl bubble coral. These corals do well in moderate light.

SPS Corals

Small-polyped scleractinian corals reach their greatest abundance and vigor on the fore-reef, where bright light, nutrient-poor conditions, and strong turbulence are the rule. In contrast with their lagoon counterparts, SPS corals exhibit branching form and can be readily propagated by removing fragments and securing them to an appropriate substrate. Under proper care, the fragments develop into new colonies. SPS corals are usually hermaphroditic, and sexual reproduction is often simultaneous among the majority of the species in a given area, a phenomenon though to be under the control of environmental factors such as temperature, photoperiod, and lunar cycles.

SPS corals include the genera *Acropora*, *Pocillopora*, *Seriatopora*, *Stylophora*, *Hydnophora*, *Pavona*, *Anacropora*, *Porites*, *Favites*, *Favia*, and *Goniastrea*. The first three of these have received the majority of attention, but there are many species in cultivation. Collection of stony corals is prohibited in many countries, and the question of whether stony coral species should be collected for the aquarium is debated. Captive spawning of stony corals may be a very rare event, but propagation from cuttings of all the branching stony coral species is successful. Coral "farms" have sprung up all over the United States and in some other countries. The supply of corals will one day probably come exclusively from such sources.

Billions of larval corals are released into the sea only to die for every one that finds a suitable spot and grows into a visible colony. Coral spawnings of many species occur seasonally and predictably, with the waters surrounding the reef clouded with millions of eggs and sperm. An idea that takes advantage of this phenomenon is the placement of artificial substrates, such as ceramic tiles, in hopes of collecting coral larvae that will grow into aquarium-size colonies.

Tips on Coral Placement

Corals (and anemones) in which the ends of the tentacles are pink or purple in color, and corals with a lot of pink in the tissue, such as the red form of *Trachyphyllia geoffreyi*, were likely collected in shallow water where they received very bright light. It is believed that the pink and purple pigments help to protect the coral from UV light. Branching corals grow nearest the surface of the ocean, high up on the reef, where light and oxygen are abundant. Massive, rounded corals grow at moderate depths. Platelike growth forms are characteristic of areas where light is lowest, resulting in the coral spreading out to expose maximum surface area to the sunshine. You will note an analogy here to plants: plants with very fine leaves usually live in full sun, while those with big, flat leaves grow in shadier spots. Variation in form in a single species can lead to confusion about which species are found where. It is therefore probably more useful to consider the growth form of a particular specimen, rather than its putative species designation, when deciding whether the specimen would be suitable for shallow water habitat or an exposed, turbulent one. Using these criteria, here are tips on placing the corals described in this section:

- Brightly pigmented specimens of all types should be placed near the top of the aquarium where they receive maximum light exposure.
- Leather corals, pulse corals, and stoloniferans all need bright light and moderate to high levels of water movement. Place them no deeper than a foot below the water surface, or exhibit them in a shallow tank.
- Sea mats, especially brightly pigmented ones, should also receive bright light.
- Disc anemones do well in moderate to low light levels near the bottom.
- *Heliofungia* and *Herpolitha* need bright light but must be placed on the bottom, lest they topple off the reef and suffer damage.
- All of the anemones mentioned in this section live in shallow water and need very bright light.
- Large-polyped scleractinian corals, including *Trachyphyllia, Euphyllia, Turbinaria*, and *Plerogyra*, adapt well to moderate light levels. If they bear intense, colorful pigments when you purchase them, place them near the surface where they will receive bright light. If they are paler, they can be placed lower in the tank.
- Small-polyped scleractinian corals without exception need intense illumination and plenty of water movement, which is best managed by placing them near the top of the reef.
- If your light levels are sufficient, all photosynthetic invertebrates should grow noticeably over a period of, say, 6 months. If they don't, they need more light. Similarly, if new growth appears to be gravitating toward the light, the specimen probably needs more light. Conversely, if growth is headed toward the bottom, the light level may be too high for the specimen in question.

Giant Clams

Giant clams, or tridacnids, are the only photosynthetic aquarium invertebrates that are not coelenterates. Rather, they are unusual mollusks that derive all of their food from their photosynthetic zooxanthellae. Of the eight species of giant clams found in the Indo-Pacific region, seven are available from hatcheries for the aquarium trade. These are *Tridacna derasa*, *T. crocea*, *T. squamosa*, *T. gigas*, *T. maxima*, *Hippopus hippopus*, and *H. porcellanus*. The mantle of these mollusks is filled with zooxanthellae, which form interesting patterns that no doubt account for their appeal to aquarists. Coloration of the mantle ranges from bright green to blue and purple. Each individual clam looks a little different from every other one, and all are quite beautiful. The aquarium husbandry of all species of giant clams is the same. The clam relies exclusively on its zooxanthellae, and so needs no additional food. It absorbs both inorganic and organic nutrients from the water, probably for the primary benefit of the zooxanthellae. Such nutrients include both ammonia and nitrate. Nitrate removal can be dramatic if large numbers of clams are introduced into the aquarium. Phosphates are also absorbed. Thus, tridacnids actually enjoy levels of nitrate and phosphate that would be considered unsuitable for a coral reef aquarium, in general. Nevertheless, attention should be paid to water quality for these clams, which require sufficient oxygen, a high stable pH, and alkalinity of 3.5 meq/L or more. Appropriate high-intensity lighting is also necessary. Clams need protection from irritants and parasites, also. Small parasitic snails that sometimes infest tridacnids can be controlled by keeping a neon wrasse, *Pseudocheilinus hexataenia* or *P. tetrataenia*, in the tank, although this fish is not often seen in shallow water. All of the shallow-water clams are frequently encrusted with coralline algae, sponges, and other small invertebrates. Live-rock organisms may establish themselves on the shells of clams in the aquarium, and this creates a natural look. As a general rule, place giant clams where they will receive bright light and gentle currents. Strong directional water flow can tear the delicate mantle tissues. Clams not already attached to a rock when you buy them will attach themselves by means of a mass of threads known as the *byssus*. Damage to the organ that secretes this structure, as when the clam is removed from its rock, can result in death. If it is absolutely necessary to move an established clam, carefully free it by clipping the individual byssus threads near the rock with a pair of nail scissors. If possible, move rock and all instead.

Clownfish Host Anemones

The anemones that host clownfish are such popular aquarium subjects, and yet so widely misunderstood; one should consider their special needs in detail before committing to creating an aquarium for them. When designing an aquarium for one of them, the anemone is always the pivotal species.

Heteractis aurora, or beaded sea anemone, is perhaps the easiest of this group to identify, as the tentacles are ribbed with swellings that are often a contrasting color. It hosts seven clownfish species.

Heteractis crispa, or leathery sea anemone, hosts eleven clownfish. *H. crispa* has a decidedly firm column. It is sometimes confused with *H. malu*, which in the aquarium trade is usually known as the sebae or Singapore sebae anemone. *H. malu* is most easily recognized by the white tentacles, seldom over an inch in length, that are tipped in bright magenta.

Heteractis magnifica, or magnificent sea anemone, still goes by its old name of *Radianthus ritteri* in the aquarium industry, and is often called simply Ritteri anemone. It is host to ten clownfish species, including *Amphiprion ocellaris* and *A. percula*, for which it is the most frequently suggested aquarium host.

Stichodactyla gigantea, the giant carpet anemone, is host to seven clownfish species and can be separated from the other two *Stichodactyla* species by its noticeably longer tentacles, often strikingly colored.

Stichodactyla haddoni, or Haddon's carpet anemone, is called the saddle carpet in the aquarium trade, because of the affinity of the saddleback clownfish, *Amphiprion polymnus*, for this host. The very short tentacles that are frequently of two colors, giving the oral disc a mottled appearance, serve to distinguish this species from the other two carpet anemones. Besides *A. polymnus*, five other clownfish species associate with Haddon's carpet.

Merten's carpet anemone, *Stichodactyla mertensi*, is called a Sri Lanka carpet by aquarium dealers and is sometimes bright green in color. Its stubby tentacles, often more like little knobs, are uniform in color, and often a contrasting ring of purple pigment encircles the mouth. This species holds the oral disc size record for clownfish hosts, and can be over 3 feet in diameter.

Clownfish host anemones in this family have a mixed record of success in the aquarium, and the majority of specimens probably die before reaching anything approaching their natural life span. On the other hand, I know personally of a specimen of *H. malu* that survived 12 years in a hobbyist's aquarium, under conditions that today would be considered less than ideal, and more than doubled in size in a 55-gallon tank. It succumbed to loss of water quality during a prolonged power outage, unfortunately. Barring this disaster it might well be alive today. Other aquarists of my acquaintance have not had such good luck with *H. malu*.

Heteractis magnifica is known for its habit of wandering all over the aquarium, often being killed or damaged when sucked into a filter intake. It appears that the availability of light, planktonic food, and water movement are important to this species. The fact that it is often beautifully colored and that the most popular clownfish species prefers it may explain why many aquarists are tempted to buy it despite its reputation for being a challenge.

The carpet anemones also pose husbandry problems. Only *Stichodactyla mertensii* is found on the reef proper, while *S. haddoni* and *S. gigantea* occur in sandy, shallow-water habitats. All three species require intense lighting, as can be noted from the presence of brightly colored pigments in many specimens. Attention should also be paid to the nature of the substrate preferred by the anemone. *Stichodactyla haddoni* and *S. gigantea* prefer clean sand, deep enough to allow the anemone to retract completely. By contrast, *S. mertensi* lives on hard surfaces on the reef slope. Also preferring to live buried in soft sediment are *Heteractis aurora*, *H. malu*, and *H. crispa*, although the latter may also be found with the pedal disk attached to branching coral. The other two are found in shallow, quiet waters. *Heteractis magnifica* is always found attached to a solid object in a fully exposed position, such as atop a coral head. Its requirements for light, oxygen, and turbulence are thus similar to those of the branching corals of the outer reef. It may wander about in search of appropriate conditions, as previously mentioned.

In contrast to the previous list, hardiness is a characteristic of the two remaining anemones that host clownfishes. These are *Macrodactyla doreensis* and *Entacmaea quadricolor*. *Macrodactyla* is known as long-tentacle anemone, often abbreviated LTA. The red column topped with bluish-gray verrucae is distinctive, although in a proper habitat tank the column will be buried in the substrate. The long tentacles, gray, bluish, or pinkish in color, often twist into a spiral shape. It hosts only three clownfish species in nature, but in the aquarium is accepted by additional ones. The majority of specimens are collected in Indonesia, and as a result it is widely available. It is reasonably hardy but does need a suitable substrate in which to bury the column. Lacking this it will wander around, fail to attach, and eventually die. It is most frequently found in mud, in water less than 15 feet deep. Mud implies moderate current, and shallow water suggests the need for bright illumination. Fine sand is a suitable aquarium substrate.

Entacmaea quadricolor, called the bulb, bubble tip, or maroon anemone in the aquarium trade, holds the record for clownfish species hosted, at thirteen. The inflated tips of the tentacles, looking something like the nipple on an old-fashioned glass baby bottle, are characteristic. No other anemone has this feature. Interestingly, the bulbs occur more commonly on anemones that have clownfish in residence than on those that do not. The majority of specimens I have seen have the bulbs. There are two subtypes of *Entacmaea*, which may have important implications for aquarium care. In shallow water a "clonal" form occurs. Generally less than 2 inches in diameter across the oral disc, this form lives in large aggregations, with individuals often so close together as to give the appearance of a single anemone. The "solitary" form is found in deep water. These individuals can be over a foot across. The shallow-water form is called the clonal form because the aggregations are thought to arise as a result of simple division of individuals, leading to a collection of genetically identical offspring—clones of the original anemone. The solitary form apparently does not divide in this fashion. Possibly the solitary individuals are responsible for sexual reproduction. This makes sense. A larger individual has more resources on which to draw in order to carry out the demanding job of producing eggs and sperm. It is known that sexes are separate in *Entacmaea*, and the female anemones brood eggs, which are fertilized by sperm carried on the water currents. It appears that the clonal form reproduces readily by asexual reproduction, whereas the solitary form does not. These lifestyle differences have been exploited to produce captive-propagated specimens for the aquarium trade by cultivating the readily dividing clonal form.

Clownfish Host Anemones at a Glance

- *Entacmaea quadricolor*: Tentacles inflated at tips, with white band and pink tip (usually). Attaches to hard surface. In nature hosts maroon and bluestripe anemonefishes. In aquarium will also host tomato and Clark's anemonefishes.
- *Macrodactyla doreensis*: Column always red or salmon-pink, with verrucae underneath oral disk. Buries column in substrate. Seldom confused. Natural symbionts are Clark's and pink skunk anemonefishes; in aquarium often accepted by maroon, bluestripe, and tomato clowns, as well.
- *Heteractis crispa*: Column tough, leathery, and buried in substrate. Tentacles long and pointed, often purple. Not common in trade. Hosts Clark's, bluestripe, percula, pink skunk, and saddleback anemonefishes.
- *H. aurora*: Not common in aquarium trade. Buries column in substrate. Tentacles with raised white ridges unmistakable. Only common anemonefish hosted is Clark's.
- *H. malu*: Column and oral disk uniform pale color, with stubby tentacles usually tipped in magenta. Seldom confused. Hosts only Clark's clownfish in nature, but may host tomato and bluestripe clowns in the aquarium.
- *H. magnifica*: Seldom mistaken. Attaches to hard surfaces in good current and bright light; may wander if not happy. Column smooth, often colorful; tentacles always slightly inflated, with yellow or white pigment at tips. Hosts Clark's, bluestripe, ocellaris percula, and pink skunk anemonefishes.
- *Stichodactyla gigantea*: Tentacles longer than those of other carpet anemones, and slightly pointed at tips. May be green, yellow-brown, blue, turquoise, or purple in color. Hosts Clark's, ocellaris, and percula anemonefishes.
- *S. haddoni*: Tentacles almost always two colors, imparting a mottled appearance. Hosts saddleback and Clark's anemonefishes.
- *S. mertensi*: Tentacles stubby and knoblike, and uniform brown or occasionally bright green in color. Hosts Clark's and ocellaris anemonefishes.

Anemone Conservation Issues

Whether the clownfish host anemones should be collected in large numbers should be given consideration. In the first place, authorities seem certain that survival of larvae to become adult anemones is rare. Very few small individuals of any anemone species are observed in the field. Further, low recruitment rates are characteristic of species that are long-lived, and there are documented instances of captive anemones living to be quite old. Many of the larger anemones are over a century in age. That such long-lived creatures often survive only a few months in captivity is strong evidence that aquarium hobbyists should become more adept at keeping them, or should avoid these specimens altogether in favor of species more likely to live out a natural life span in captivity. Anemones for the aquarium should be smaller specimens. Larger individuals adapt less readily to captivity, and these individuals may represent the brood stock. I recommend that aquarium hobbyists select only *Entacmaea* and *Macrodactyla* as the clownfish hosts of primary interest, and avoid the other species. *Entacmaea* seems to me to be the most appropriate clownfish host. It is the most abundant host anemone in nature; it is widely distributed, occurring from the Red Sea to Samoa; it is host to many species of clownfish, and it can be propagated in the aquarium. *Entacmaea* settles into the aquarium quickly and does not, like *Macrodactyla*, require substrate into which to bury the column, preferring instead to attach to a rock or other solid object. This species clearly deserves attention from aquarists capable of providing for its needs—good illumination and cooler water (70 to 75 degrees F).

Nonphotosynthetic Invertebrates

Fanworms

The Christmas tree worm derives its common name (and its generic name, too, in fact) from the appearance of specialized structures, the *radioles*, that are used in both feeding and respiration. (The generic name comes from two words meaning "spiral gill.") The worm spends its life housed in a calcareous tube attached to a rock or coral head, extending the radioles into the surrounding water column. The radioles consist of a pair of tentacles with feathery appendages wound around them in a tapering spiral. When extended from the mouth of the tube, the radioles look like a pair of Christmas trees sharing the same stand. The brilliant colors and symmetrical appearance of these structures are responsible for the popularity of this annelid with aquarists. The worms are often gregarious, with individuals bearing radioles of strikingly different colors growing side by side. When a chunk or rock or coral inhabited by a number of these worms is collected for the aquarium, it is usually sold as *worm rock*. Undeniably attractive, these specimens need special attention to their requirements. It is helpful to explore the natural history of this species.

Spirobranchus giganteus occurs in both the Indo-Pacific and the Atlantic-Caribbean regions. Recognizing the source of a particular specimen is simple, as there are apparently two subspecies of this worm. Specimens from the Indo-Pacific usually have smaller radioles and always come embedded in living coral. Specimens from the Atlantic-Caribbean region are not necessarily associated with corals and are about twice as large as the Indo-Pacific form. The radioles reach just over an inch in length.

A different range of color variation exists between the two geographic forms of *Spirobranchus*. Bicolor forms appear to occur more commonly in Atlantic-Caribbean specimens, while bright blue specimens appear to be more abundant in the Indo-Pacific type. The fact that the worms come in different colors may be an adaptation to avoid predation. Predators do not learn to locate the worms by color. The worm's most useful defense, however, is its ability to quickly withdraw the radioles into the protective tube at the first hint of danger. The opening of the tube is capped with an operculum bearing fierce-looking horns. Close examination will show that the horns are nearly identical in the two geographic types, providing evidence of their affinity. The coral that harbors *Spirobranchus* in the Indo-Pacific is *Porites*. The worms appear to require the presence of the coral for survival, and, unfortunately, the coral itself is not often successfully maintained by aquarists. The Atlantic-Caribbean type does not always occur embedded in colonies of *Porites* coral in shallow, wave-tossed waters.

In all the world, only in the central Gulf of Mexico is this worm found on a substrate other than living coral. Most specimens collected for the aquarium trade come from the middle Gulf of Mexico, miles from the nearest coral reef. Worm rock from the Gulf harbors a wide variety of coralline algae and invertebrates, often in bright, attractive colors, in addition to the worms themselves. Such specimens are very beautiful, but too often the appearance of the worm rock declines after perhaps 6 months in the aquarium. Specimens should be provided with dim lighting, cool water temperatures, and frequent feeding with a plankton substitute. Given proper attention, few invertebrates can rival Christmas tree worm rock for color and diversity of the encrusting organisms.

Another type of fanworm produces a leathery tube rather than a calcified one. Collectively called *feather dusters* these fanworms are aptly described by that name. The "handle" is hidden in the tube. It comprises the body of the worm, which greatly resembles a large earthworm. The "feathers" are the radioles. As with the Christmas tree worm, these are the colorful and attractive part of the creature, and are withdrawn into the tube in a flash if the worm is disturbed. Depending on the species, the feathers may be anywhere from a quarter of an inch to several inches across. Individual species are difficult to identify, but many aquarium specimens are in the genera *Sabella* and *Sabellastarte*. A chocolate-brown variety from Florida, commonly seen in shops, is *Sabellastarte magnifica*. Its crown of feathers can be 4 inches in diameter. These fanworms are hardier than the Christmas tree worm, probably because they feed mostly on bacteria and fine debris suspended in the water. The radioles function as food traps as well as gills.

Crustaceans

The hermit crabs *Aniculus strigatus*, *Calcinus latens*, and *C. elegans* are imported from Hawaii. There are many other suitable species from the Indo-Pacific region. The tiny, inshore tricolor hermit crab, *Clibanarius tricolor*, is a valuable Caribbean species. Other hermit crabs that are commonly available from Florida and the Caribbean include *Calcinus tibicen*, *Paguristes cadenati*, and *Pylopagurus operculatus*. These hermit crabs all remain small in size and do not become destructive. If a hermit crab should grow too large and rambunctious for your minireef, you can transfer it to a fish-only system. Hermit crabs make good scavengers. One species, *Clibanarius vittatus*, the striped hermit, found along the Atlantic from Florida to Cape Cod, is an excellent choice for a tank with larger fish.

The anemone crabs are close relatives of the hermit crabs, but with important differences. First, while hermit crabs are often scavengers, anemone crabs are filter feeders. They have specially modified legs that are used to sweep the water for floating debris and plankton. Second, as the name implies, anemone crabs are found with

anemones. The two species usually imported for the aquarium associate with giant anemones, such as the clownfish host species. Sometimes clownfish will live peaceably with an anemone crab sharing the anemone, and sometimes not. Often the crab is evicted by the clownfish, and usually does poorly thereafter if another suitable anemone host cannot be found. The most commonly available anemone crab is *Petrolisthes maculatus*, with an attractive pattern of wine-red polka dots on its otherwise white carapace. Less frequently seen is *P. oshimani*, with many fine red dots scattered uniformly over its back and claws. Mated pairs of both species are sometimes available and will share an anemone.

Only a few of the true crabs are suitable for the aquarium, since most are too large, too boisterous, too destructive, or too secretive to be of interest. Nevertheless, perhaps the most interesting of all invertebrates is the pom pom crab, *Lybia edmonsoni*, from Hawaii. As already described, *Lybia* presents a very rare example of tool-use among invertebrates. The crab has specially modified claws in which it grasps two tiny sea anemones, *Triactis producta*. The crab uses the anemones as mops to gather detritus and other edibles that cling to the anemone's tentacles. When threatened, the crab puts its anemones to another use, brandishing them as weapons. The stinging tentacles of the anemone are apparently sufficient to ward off most of the crab's enemies.

Few lobsters are suitable for the minireef, as they grow to an unwieldy size and cannot be trusted to leave their tank mates unharmed. In addition, they are generally secretive and spend most of their time out of sight. Spiny lobsters, in the genus *Panulirus*, are reasonably well-behaved but do spend most of their time in hiding, emerging mainly at night to feed. They can be interesting additions to a fish-only display.

Among the crustaceans, the widest variety of species suitable for the aquarium is found among the shrimps. For our purposes, we can divide the many members of this group into two categories: those that are free-living and those that associate with anemones or other organisms. The association of shrimps and the curlicue anemone was described in the section on photosynthetic invertebrates. *Periclimenes brevicarpalis*, from the Pacific, is associated with anemones as well as the large plate and slipper stony corals. It is remarkably similar in appearance to its cousin *P. yucatanensis*, which lives in the Atlantic with the curlicue anemone.

P. brevicarpalis has distinctive white saddles along the back as well as orange circles surrounded by black on the top of each tail segment. In *P. yucatanensis*, the saddles are purple. In both species, males are much smaller than females, and are pale in color. In the females the white saddles are quite obvious; in males they are present, but not large and distinctive.

Both species are thought to be "false cleaners," meaning they mimic the color patterns and behavior of true cleaning shrimps and thereby gain a measure of protection from predatory fishes. Because of their beneficial behavior, cleaners are seldom eaten. The cleaning behavior of the scarlet lady shrimp was described in the section on utilitarian invertebrates. *Periclimenes pedersoni*, found in association with the curlicue anemone, is a true cleaner like the scarlet lady. Its nearly transparent body would be invisible except for distinct white and purple stripes and its long white antennae. White antennae seem to signal to fish that the shrimp is a cleaner as opposed to food. Cleaner shrimps of all species have white antennae and usually perform a characteristic "dance." This set of movements is thought to reinforce in the fish's dim awareness the shrimp's status as a cleaner, allowing it to approach otherwise fearsome predators with impunity.

Another species, *P. holthusii*, is uncommon, but should be sought out. It is transparent, though attractively marked in small red and white dots. It has white antennae, and may be a cleaner. It is found in association with large anemones as well as plate coral (*Heliofungia actiniformis*). This shrimp has the amusing habit of holding its chelae (pincers) in position and moving them back and forth as if it were cradling a baby. This has earned it the common name of rockabye baby shrimp.

The most spectacular of the Indo-Pacific shrimps is the fire shrimp or blood shrimp, *Lysmata debelius*. Bright red in color, it bears four pairs of white polka dots, one pair between the eyes, another pair just behind and below the eyes, a third pair centered on the thorax, and a fourth pair on the first abdominal segment. The tips of the legs and the antennae are white. It is probably a cleaner.

Snapping shrimps, family Alpheidae, include the curlicue anemone shrimp, *Alpheus armatus*, which as already mentioned lives in association with the curlicue anemone. Instead of standing on the anemone's oral disk and advertising cleaning services to passers-by, it burrows under the anemone to make a home for itself and a mate. Apparently the stinging tentacles of the anemone offer the shrimp protection from predators. In return, anything approaching the anemone too closely may be repelled by a loud pop emitted by the shrimp. Snapping shrimps possess specially modified chelae that produce the sound much like you do when you snap your fingers. Underwater, the noise is audible for a long distance, and divers can hear the cacophony produced by the thousands of snapping shrimps living on the reef, especially at night. Several other snapping shrimps are of interest, especially those that associate with certain species of Indo-Pacific gobies. These are mentioned in chapter 4.

There are literally thousands of species of crustaceans. Those I discuss here are generally available, attractive, interesting, and suitable for the aquarium. Some, like the pom pom crab, are fascinating enough to merit a tank of their own.

Mollusks and Echinoderms

Aside from the particular ones already discussed, numerous varieties of snails, clams, sea urchins, starfish, sea cucumbers, and brittlestars turn up in aquarium shops. Most are collected simply because they are small and colorful, without regard to their suitability for the aquarium. It is always wise to identify any critter like this that you might be considering, and find out what you can about its lifestyle. This can make all the difference in your ability to successfully maintain it. For example, there is a little yellow sea cucumber that adapts so well to the aquarium it often produces offspring. It's worth purchasing one or two of them any time they are available. On the other hand, certain Indo-Pacific cone snails can deliver a painful, potentially harmful sting. These mollusks are a poor choice for most home aquariums. Not only might you get stung, so might your favorite bottom-dwelling fish. Cone snails are predators that hunt at night. I cannot emphasize enough the importance of prior research when considering any unfamiliar saltwater invertebrate.

Seaweeds

Seaweeds are algae, of course, not invertebrate animals. Because of their important role in the minireef, they are covered here. An aquarium for shallow-water photosynthetic invertebrates coincidentally provides the right conditions for several interesting and attractive species of calcareous seaweeds. The aquarium should have a layer of substrate to better support these algae, which are rooted by a holdfast. *Penicillus*, *Rhipocephalus*, *Udotea*, and *Halimeda incrassata* are typical and often occur together in the lagoon. *Halimeda opuntia* and *Cymopolia barbata* are not usually rooted in the substrate, but rather are attached to rocks or simply lie on the bottom. Seaweeds reach their greatest diversity and abundance in shallow habitats over a sandy or muddy bottom. Besides the species just mentioned are various forms of *Caulerpa*. This seaweed is not calcified and leaks organic matter into the water, so the aquarium housing it needs adequate foam fractionation. Soft corals of the more tolerant varieties, such as *Sarcophyton*, and stony corals such as *Trachyphyllia*, are at home in a habitat with abundant *Caulerpa*. A dense growth dominated by *Caulerpa* also comes close to duplicating a patch denuded of turtle grass and subsequently recolonized by the more rapidly growing seaweeds. Such areas are often home to photosynthetic gorgonians towering above the carpet of *Caulerpa*. A pair of dottybacks (*Pseudochromis*) of any species would also be appropriate here. Male dottybacks may use pieces of the algae to construct a nest. Seaweeds come in a beautiful diversity of forms. They supply the lush, green color of chlorophyll, so pleasing to the eye. Wisely chosen and properly grown, they are appropriate additions to any natural reef aquarium.

The single most important requirement for the cultivation of seaweeds is sufficient light. Refer to chapter 2 for information regarding selection of artificial lighting systems for the aquarium. The optimum light intensity for shallow-water tropical seaweeds is about 16,000 lux. The major and minor nutrients required by seaweeds are nitrogen compounds, phosphate, potassium, sulfate, iron, manganese, thiamine, biotin, and vitamin B_{12}. Nitrogen compounds and phosphate are generally always available in the aquarium, often to the extent that one must take measures to remove them. Other major elements (potassium, sulfate, and manganese) are present in seawater mixes. Iron and iodine, important trace elements, can be added in chemical form. If iron supplementation is used, test the water daily with an iron test kit, and add enough supplement to maintain a concentration of 0.05 to 0.1 mg/L. Iodine supplements should also be used. Seaweeds with calcareous skeletons are especially sensitive to pH, alkalinity, and calcium concentration (see page 168).

Some fishes and invertebrates are not compatible with seaweeds. Tangs, angelfishes, sea urchins, and many mollusks will readily consume a carefully tended underwater garden.

One problem that may develop in an aquarium with abundant seaweeds is an elevated pH. This occurs as the growing algae remove carbon dioxide from the water for photosynthesis. Vigorous aeration for increased gas exchange, or control of pH with an automated carbon dioxide injection system, may be necessary.

Some Invertebrates to Avoid

Harbor Anemones

Quite content in warmer water with a heavy load of nitrate, phosphate, and organics—in fact thriving under such conditions—are the various species of *Aiptasia* anemones. These smallish brown polyps can multiply in the aquarium to plague proportions. Since they are able to sting giant clams and other aquarium habitants with deleterious results, hobbyists sometimes go to great lengths to eliminate them. Various remedies have been suggested, including (1) introduction of anemone-eating fishes, such as the raccoon butterflyfish, *Chaetodon lunula* or the copperband butterflyfish, *Chelmon rostratus*; (2) injection of individual anemones with poisons; or (3) introduction of anemone-eating shrimps, such as *Rhyncocinetes uritai*, the dancing shrimp, or *Lysmata wurdemanni*, the peppermint shrimp. None of these methods is entirely satisfactory. Predatory shrimps often do not limit themselves to *Aiptasia*, so other invertebrates may be in jeopardy. If a fish placed in the aquarium for anemone control develops a taste for something more exotic, the aquarist is faced with the problem of removing the offender to a new home. Injection of individual anemones with poison, or removing them one by one is incredibly tedious. Scraping them off the aquarium glass and decorations with a razor blade or fingernail is not always effective, either. The anemones can regenerate easily from even a tiny piece left behind, and the problem soon returns. What then, is one to do?

Taking care not to introduce *Aiptasia* in the first place is the best solution. However, this is more of a challenge than it sounds. Any individuals that go unnoticed will be producing offspring in a few months. *Aiptasia* is common in many localities from which live rock, and various other specimens that are sold on a rock base, such as sea mat and mushroom polyp colonies, are collected.

Aiptasia multiply rapidly when the aquarium is too warm or too rich in nutrients. This explains why it is commonly found in harbors, where such conditions prevail, and is not so abundant on the reef itself, where temperatures are more moderate and the nutrient concentration of the water is low. Maintaining the correct temperature and keeping nutrient levels low in your minireef works against the interests of the *Aiptasia*, and may help to limit their multiplication.

If you can find it, the nudibranch *Dondice occidentalis* eats *Aiptasia*, and nothing else.

Mystery Mollusks

Accurate identification of any gastropod mollusk is essential to discovering its lifestyle, and consequently, to designing an appropriate aquarium environment. If in doubt about identification, it is best not to put the specimen in the aquarium. Eggshell coweries (*Ovula ovum*) and flamingo tongue snails (*Cyphoma gibbosum*) are two examples of undesirable mollusks regularly offered to aquarium hobbyists. The former feeds only on alcyonarians such as *Xenia* and *Sarcophyton*, while the latter preys on gorgonians exclusively.

Mantis Shrimps

Mantis shrimps can be troublesome. They can be tricky to catch, but if the mantis shrimp's lair can be located, it can sometimes be extracted with a wire hook. Failing this, it may be necessary to remove the entire rock to a bucket of seawater, which will give you a better opportunity to extract the shrimp. The presence of a single small mantis shrimp in the tank is hardly cause for panic. Drastic measures should be taken only if you determine for certain that the mantis shrimp has actually done some damage to one of your specimens. Mantis shrimp are active mostly at night, and this is a good time to observe the tank for their presence. The particular species is not important, as all look basically similar in body form, shrimplike, with large, stalked eyes that can be rotated in all directions to search for food or recognize danger, and characteristic forelegs like the raptorial appendages of a praying mantis (hence the name mantis shrimp). A large, destructive mantis shrimp may lash out with these and cause a nasty cut, so do not attempt to handle it with your bare hands. One large species found in temperate seas is called "thumb splitter" by fishermen, who use them for bait.

Giant Hermit Crabs

Every now and then a dealer may display a really large hermit crab. *Petrochirus diogenes* is found in the south Atlantic region, and grows to 8 inches or more. It is aggressive, messy, gluttonous, and a potential threat to any fish that nears its formidable pincers.

Filter-Feeding Echinoderms

Known in the aquarium trade as "feather stars" and "basket stars" these are echinoderms with the arms divided into feathery branches used for trapping plankton. Graceful, colorful, and lacelike in appearance, these animals need daily feeding with abundant, living zooplankton. They are challenging even for public aquariums and should be avoided in favor of the more easily accommodated brittlestars.

Big Starfish

Starfish are predators. A large one, when hungry, can stalk, capture, and kill a fish half its size. It usually does so at night, when the fish is sleeping. The normal diet of most common starfish is bivalve mollusks, but they will dine on almost anything that cannot escape, given the chance. Only in a fish-only tank with large inhabitants can a big, predatory starfish be trusted to behave.

Sea Hares

A type of gastropod with an internal shell, sea hares can grow almost as large as their furry terrestrial namesake. They graze continuously on seaweeds, and require prodigious quantities of food, making them too demanding for the home hobbyist. Add to this a propensity to eject a thick, purple ink when alarmed, often overwhelming the filter system. Pass, no matter how cute you think they are.

Nonphotosynthetic Coelenterates

Some corals, soft corals, and gorgonians have no zooxanthellae, and rely exclusively on capturing plankton. Lacking an appropriate plankton substitute in ample quantity, they soon weaken and die in captivity. Unfortunately, these are some of the most colorful invertebrates found in the aquarium trade, often appearing in shades of bright red, lemon, orange, or pink. Despite their undeniable appeal, these organisms are best left to the professionals, as they seldom succeed without daily attention.

Questions to Ask When Considering an Invertebrate Purchase

Is it photosynthetic? (Without an adequate lighting system, these species simply will not survive long in captivity.)

____

____

What does it eat? (As with fish, this is probably the single most important factor in long-term care.)

____

____

Will it get along with the fish I already have in the tank? (Anemones, for example, may sting and capture certain fishes.)

____

____

Will it get along with the other invertebrates I plan to purchase later? (Larger, more aggressive crustaceans may attack and eat smaller, more docile ones, for example.)

____

____

continued

Does this species pose any special challenges? (For example, soft corals that lack zooxanthellae require daily feeding with zooplankton or they will slowly wither away.)

____

____

I have small children. Is there anything I should know about this species that might be an issue for an inquisitive child? (For example, all anemones can sting. Some are especially painful.)

____

____

How long have you had this specimen? (Try to buy invertebrates that have had a chance to recover from the trauma of capture and shipment.)

____

____

Is this specimen captive-propagated? (Captive-propagated coelenterates and a few other invertebrates are available. Not only do they adapt well, they are also often desirable color forms that are otherwise hard to find.)

____

____

What You Now Know . . .

- The five invertebrate groups of interest to aquarists are coelenterates, annelids, mollusks, arthropods, and echinoderms.
- The best way for hobbyists to sort out the diversity of invertebrates is to group them according to their aquarium roles.
- Grouped by roles, invertebrates may be separated into live rock, live sand, utilitarian, photosynthetic, and nonphotosynthetic species.
- Photosynthetic invertebrates require bright illumination and excellent water quality to thrive and grow. Seaweeds also do well under these conditions.
- Several types of invertebrates should be avoided by hobbyists because they are difficult to feed or behave too aggressively toward tank mates.

Chapter 6

Stocking Your Tank III: Putting It All Together

What's Inside . . .

- Learn how to create a stocking plan for your aquarium.
- Explore example stocking plans.
- Create your own stocking plan.

Just as you planned the physical layout of the aquarium, you'll need to develop a plan for stocking it. You cannot put in everything at once, because this will quickly overload the filtration system and cause problems. Knowing what to add and when structures your stocking plan.

Developing a Stocking Plan

Once the aquarium is filled with seawater and the filtration system is running, live rock and live sand are added first. Live rock is simply placed on top of the substrate, stacked in a realistic-looking arrangement. Add live sand in a layer on top of the substrate. At this point, start operating the lighting system to encourage seaweeds and filamentous algae to grow. After about 2 weeks, you can add utilitarian invertebrates, such as small hermit crabs, algae-eating snails, sea urchins, brittlestars, and burrowing sea cucumbers. A week or so after that, add mobile invertebrates such as shrimps and crabs, unless they need a fish or anemone as a partner. Symbiotic partners, with the exception of anemonefish and their respective anemones, should be added simultaneously, near the end of the stocking period. At this point, you can also place small starfish (*Fromia*, for example) or nonburrowing sea cucumbers in the tank.

When the shrimps and other mobile invertebrates have settled in, seaweeds can be added. Allow them to grow for at least 2 weeks before you add more animals. You may find they grow enough to require a bit of pruning, even in this short time frame.

Now the tank is starting to take on the appearance of a natural reef habitat, and you can begin adding photosynthetic invertebrates. Try to place them where they won't touch one another, and make sure they are located where they will receive plenty of light. Corals that are more upright in structure look good near the top of the tank. Giant clams always look best when they can be viewed from above, showing off their bright colors to best advantage. Corals that typically live on the bottom, such as *Trachyphyllia* or *Heliofungia*, should be placed on the bottom in the aquarium. Be sure to allow room for soft corals, sea mats, and disc anemones to spread, as they frequently do under aquarium conditions.

By now the aquarium should be showing signs of maturity, such as the presence of numerous, nearly microscopic invertebrates in the substrate and on the rocks. These are the copepods and amphipods that will feed some of your most delicate aquarium inhabitants. These tiny crustaceans are, in turn, feeding on microorganisms too small for you to see, but which nevertheless are vital to the aquarium ecosystem.

Once the minireef has reached this stage, there should be enough natural food present to feed nonphotosynthetic, filter-feeding invertebrates such as fanworms. Corals and anemones also benefit from the presence of natural foods. If you plan on cultivating an anemonefish host anemone, now is the time to add it.

Finally the time arrives for the main event. Fish should be added to the aquarium at the end of the stocking period, at about 8 weeks after the live rock is first added. Pay attention to the information on aggressiveness given in the descriptions of fish families. As a rule of thumb, add docile fishes first, giving them an opportunity to stake out a territory, before adding more aggressive species. Bold species, such as surgeonfishes or dwarf angelfishes, should be added last. Anemonefishes can be added as soon as their host is settled in and thriving. If you plan to keep anemonefishes without a host, add them any time.

Don't add new fish more frequently than every 2 weeks. Altogether, it takes about a year for a new aquarium to be stocked completely. Don't try to rush it, and observe the tank carefully for problems shortly after each new addition. Most problems occur within the first 2 weeks that a critter is in the tank.

Some Examples to Get You Started

Creating an aquarium that features invertebrates provides the perfect opportunity to focus on a specific natural habitat and duplicate its characteristics as far as possible. Here are some suggested habitats to get you started.

Depicting Indo-Pacific Habitats

The Indo-Pacific realm is vast, but for aquarium purposes its characteristic environments fall into only a few categories. This is partly because the availability of specimens is limited. Collection of specimens for the aquarium trade tends to focus on specific areas, and collectors tend to harvest only certain organisms for which there is an established market. The tendency to collect what is easily accessible also influences what may be available to aquarists. Thus, lagoon species, which can often be collected by wading at low tide, are more commonplace than species whose range is restricted to the outer reef slope. Marine invertebrates are not strictly limited in their ability to exploit different microhabitats, of course, with many occurring over a wide area. So take my suggestions as just that—suggestions; don't slavishly adhere to my species lists when attempting to re-create an Indo-Pacific microhabitat in the aquarium.

A Minireef for Anemonefish

An aquarium exhibiting the bubble-tip anemone, *Entacmaea quadricolor*, with *Amphiprion frenatus*, would suggest the top of a tiny reef. An aquarium of 75 to 120 gallons would be ideal. Include only one anemone (leaving room for its eventual progeny) with five tank-reared, juvenile anemonefish. Several *Tridacna maxima*, also found near the upper part of the reef, should be included. An assortment of shrimps, including *Lysmata amboiensis* and *L. debelius*, will add interest. SPS corals would also be at home in this aquarium. Choose specimens with pink or purple pigments, indicating that they came from shallow water. Take care to place the corals so that they will not come into contact with the anemone's tentacles, or nettling is possible. Including a neon wrasse, *Pseudocheilinus hexataenia*, will help to protect the giant clams from parasitic snails. A coral goby, such as *Gobiodon okinawae*, will live in the branches of the corals. If the tank is sufficiently large, a small group of the pajama cardinalfish, *Sphaeramia nematoptera*, can be included. They will emerge from hiding among the live rock to feed in the lagoon at night.

A Shallow Inshore Aquarium

For a smaller system than the one just described, a suitable clownfish-host combination might be *Macrodactyla doreensis* with *Amphiprion clarki*. Intense lighting, moderate current, and a layer of fine, soft sand for the anemone to bury in are the prerequisites. A Monaco-style sand bed would be a natural choice. This habitat would also be home to the Mandarin fish, *Pterosynchiropus splendidus*, and its cousin, the spotted Mandarin, *Synchiropus picturatus*. Many other aquarium fishes are collected in shallow lagoons and can be included in this tank. Good choices include the orange-tailed blue damselfish, *Chrysiptera cyanea*; the fuzzy dwarf lionfish, *Dendrochirus brachypterus*; or the yellow watchman goby, *Cryptocentrus cinctus*. Pairing the goby with a suitable burrowing shrimp would be ideal.

Deeper Waters

Outer reefs are the home of the most widely available giant clam, *T. derasa*, which is an adaptable species that I recommended. It is also a good choice to accompany SPS corals. Dartfishes, such as the common firefish, *Nemateleotris magnifica*, and the purple firefish, *N. decora*, occur on the outer reef in pairs. Shoals of anthias hover in the strong currents. The striking purple dottyback, *Pseudochromis porphyreus*, is often very common in this habitat, hovering just above the coral.

The Gulf of Mexico and Other Eastern U.S. Habitats

Compared to the Florida Keys, the Gulf of Mexico is a significantly different habitat, although some tropical species from the Keys area regularly migrate into Gulf waters, and sometimes in the Keys one finds species that are more commonly seen farther north. Since Gulf species are often included in imports of marine livestock from Florida to other parts of the United States, aquarists should be aware of the special habitats that such specimens represent.

A sea mat from the northern Gulf of Mexico, *Palythoa grandis*, is regularly sold in aquarium shops and is commonly kept in tanks along with stony corals and other photosynthetic invertebrates. The large, dark green polyps are attractive and hardy. This is the only species of interest collected in the upper Gulf. Most other northern Gulf species are not well suited to a tropical reef aquarium but are excellent subjects for a specialized aquarium. A good example of such a community is the central Gulf area near Tampa, where the Christmas tree worm, *Spirobranchus giganteus*, is found. While this annelid occurs throughout the West Indies, it is abundant in the central Gulf.

Fish from the Gulf of Mexico include:

- Blue angelfish (*Holocanthus isabelita*)
- Grey angelfish (*Pomacanthus arcuatus*)
- Beau Gregory damselfish (*Stegastes leucostictus*)
- Tiger goby (*Gobiosoma macrodon*)
- Seaweed blenny (*Parablennius marmoreus*)
- Common hawkfish (*Amblycirrhites pinos*)

Among invertebrates are the following:

- Red finger sponge (*Amphimedon compressa*)
- Knobby sea rod (*Eunicea sp.*)
- Purple whip gorgonian (*Leptogorgia sp.*)
- American star shell (*Astraea tectum*)
- Anemone shrimp (*Periclimenes sp.*)
- Peppermint shrimp (*Lysmata wurdemanni*)
- Arrow crab (*Stenorhynchus seticornis*)
- Decorator crab (*Podochela reisi*)

The decorator crab, *Podochela reisi*, is a fascinating and easy-to-keep crustacean. It camouflages itself by attaching bits of living organisms, such as sponges and algae, to its carapace. Each time the crab molts, it will don a new set of clothes, since the camouflage is shed along with the crab's exoskeleton. It may remove some of its favorite attire from the cast-off shell and reattach them. At other times it may select an entirely new wardrobe from whatever is at hand. In this way the crab is always wearing some of the surrounding flora and fauna, maximizing the utility of its camouflage.

Stocking a small aquarium with several pieces of Christmas tree worm rock, one of the gobies, and a selection of the other invertebrates would make an ecologically accurate minireef.

Other Eastern U.S. Habitats

The northern Gulf of Mexico, the Flower Garden Banks in the western Gulf of Mexico, the "Grand Strand" of sandy beaches stretching from Fort Lauderdale to the shores of Delaware, the mid-Atlantic region from the Chesapeake Bay to Cape Cod, and the northern Atlantic coast of New England all offer an array of marine invertebrates, seaweeds, and small fish species that are suited to appropriately designed aquariums. There are many opportunities for creating interesting aquariums featuring the temperate and cold-water species of our Atlantic and Gulf Coasts. Apart from the need to maintain cooler temperatures, these temperate minireefs are set up and maintained just like their tropical counterparts.

Stocking Fish-Only Tanks

Fish-only tanks can stick to species from a specific habitat, or simply exhibit an interesting group of compatible fish. You can use live rock or not, and add a few invertebrates or not, as it suits your taste. Bear in mind that the invertebrates and fish need to be compatible. You cannot, for example, keep a fish with its natural prey. If you choose not to include live rock, you will need to introduce nitrifying bacteria in some other way, and you can begin stocking fish immediately, sticking to smaller, hardier types (see chapter 4). If you do include invertebrates and/or live rock, you begin stocking as described in the previous examples, adding live rock first and the invertebrates next, over a period of about 4 weeks, before you start adding fish.

Either way, I find it helpful to consider fish in terms of their size, aggressiveness, and feeding habits. Rank the fish you have chosen for the aquarium, placing the smallest, least aggressive species at the top of the list, and the largest, most aggressive species at the bottom. For a 30-gallon community tank, the list might look like this:

- Tank-raised neon goby, *Gobiosoma sp.*
- Neon wrasse, *Pseudocheilinus sp.*
- Purple dottyback, *Pseudochromis porphyreus*

For a 75-gallon community tank, the list might look like this:

- Dwarf lionfish, *Dendrochirus sp.*
- Threadfin butterflyfish, *Chaetodon auriga*
- Flame angelfish, *Centropyge loriculus*
- Any wrasse, *Thalassoma sp.*
- Yellow tang, *Zebrasoma flavescens*

Once you've settled on the order, next to each name write down its feeding preferences. Is there anyone in the list that might be eaten by someone else or that won't be able to compete for food with its tank mates? No. Good; now you have a plan. Add a fish about every

2 weeks, beginning with the first one on your list and working down. By putting the more docile or fussy species in first, you give them a head start in establishing a territory and settling in to captive conditions.

I've included an obvious mistake in the 75-gallon plan. Did you catch it? In the species accounts in chapter 4, I mentioned that dwarf lionfish need small, live foods for which they await in ambush. With competition from a swift, active wrasse, even a well-established lionfish may have trouble getting enough to eat. If we replace the lionfish with an equally hardy, but more aggressively feeding red-spotted hawkfish, *Amblycirrhites pinos*, we'll end up with a more harmonious community in the end.

A good rule of thumb for selecting a variety of fish to populate a fish-only aquarium is to have only one herbivore, only one predator with a big mouth, and as many generalized feeders as the remaining tank space will accommodate. In the first example, all the fish are generalized feeders and will eat the same foods. In the second, the tang eats almost nothing but filamentous algae and can take care of itself. It makes sense to wait until there is a substantial amount of algae growth in the tank. The hawkfish is a predator capable of swallowing a fairly large chunk, while the others mostly nibble, so I have followed the rule in developing this list.

Create Your Own Stocking Plan

Using the following worksheet as a guide, create the stocking plan for your minireef. Remember that the whole process will take about a year, so allow plenty of time between additions of fish and/or invertebrates. Base your plan on the one-sentence theme you defined for your aquarium.

Aquarium Stocking Worksheet

Tank number: ____________________ Capacity (gallons): ____________________

Theme

Step 1: Do you plan to use live rock? If no, go to Step 2. If yes, how many pounds do you need?

____

Date I plan to add live rock:

____

Step 2: If you plan to include invertebrates in this tank, list them below in the appropriate group. Add the first four groups 2 weeks after you add the live rock. Add small shrimps and seaweeds 2 weeks after that. Add other invertebrates after the tank has been up for 6 weeks and thereafter. Skip to Step 3 if you leave out any or all of these groups.

Algae-eating snails

____

____

Small hermit crabs

____

____

Brittlestars

____

____

Other utilitarian invertebrates

____

____

Date to add above specimens:

____

Small shrimps

____

____

Seaweeds

____

____

Date to add above specimens:

____

continued

Corals, anemones, and all other invertebrates

____

____

Date to add above specimens:

____

Step 3: List the fish you plan to include in this tank, beginning with the least aggressive species and ending with the most aggressive.

____

____

____

____

Step 4: Next to the name of each species, write down the type of food it eats.

Step 5: Check your list against the information in this book or other references. Cross off any fish not compatible with one another or with the invertebrates you have listed.

Step 6: Starting at the top of your list, add one fish every 2 weeks until your community is complete.

Date to start adding fish:

____

What You Now Know . . .

- Developing a plan is the first step in stocking your aquarium.
- Live rock is added first, if used, followed by utilitarian and other invertebrates, over a period of 8 weeks.
- Fish are stocked beginning about 6 weeks after the tank is set up, or earlier if invertebrates are not included.
- Fish should be added beginning with the least aggressive species and ending with the most aggressive.

Foxfaces are often called Rabbitfishes because they constantly eat algae, like a rabbit nibbling grass all day.

Many types of fish, such as this Mandarinfish, thrive only when introduced to an established aquarium.

Small, hardy, easy to feed, and colorful, the Royal Gramma is a great fish for beginners.

Dragonets, such as this Red-spotted Dragonet, are bottom-feeding fish, and their triangular heads support their function.

While it might not be able to tell you jokes or juggle, you'll get hours of entertainment watching this Clown Anemonefish darting around the aquarium.

This Snooty Wrasse tends to be fairly shy and a little skittish, rarely venturing far from shelter, and is often found in pairs in its natural habitat.

Less challenging to keep than many of its larger cousins, the hardy Flame Angelfish lives in deep water and eats a varied diet of sea life.

Groupers, such as this Coral Grouper, can grow fairly large; most species are very hardy and fairly easy to maintain.

Omnivores, such as this gorgeous Golden Butterflyfish, eat a mixed diet, combining algae and meaty food.

Randall's Shrimp Goby provides a colorful example of the gobies that live in association with certain snapping shrimps, a fascinating relationship you can observe in the aquarium.

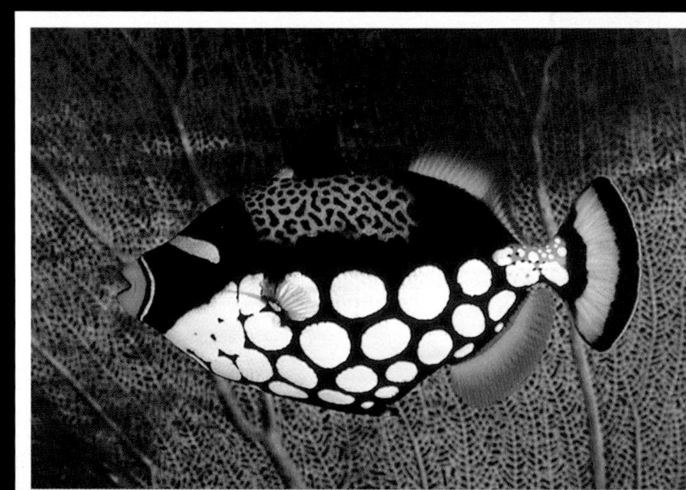

The gaudy Clown Triggerfish can be aggressive and eats almost anything. It is best suited to a large tank of similarly robust fish.

In its natural habitat, this Bangaii Cardinalfish would be found swimming near coral reefs in inshore tropical waters.

Despite its tendency to become aggressive, aquarists love the Blue Devil Damselfish because it is extremely hardy and reaches only about three inches in length. Only males have the

The unusual and beautiful spines of the Volitans Lionfish protect the fish by enabling it to sting and poison predators.

The saltwater aquarium is the perfect place to see fish's natural, fascinating tendancies. This Guineafowl Puffer will puff itself to a larger, balloonlike size when it feels threatened.

Chapter 7

Setting Up Your Tank

What's Inside . . .

- Learn how to set up a quarantine tank.
- Learn basic setup steps for both small and large aquariums.
- Learn how to accommodate an anemone in your aquarium.
- Learn how to create a fish-only tank and a minireef system.

This chapter covers what to do when you get home from the shop with your aquarium and all that equipment. Return to chapter 1 and look at the shopping lists for the under $500 aquarium and my ideal home aquarium. These two systems will provide the examples for installation, discussed separately in this chapter.

Setting Up a Quarantine Tank

In all honesty, the majority of saltwater hobbyists probably omit this step. No one likes the idea of an aquarium that is strictly utilitarian, located out of sight in the basement, garage, or spare room. Nevertheless, if you want a truly hassle-free saltwater aquarium experience, and you have the space, setting up a quarantine tank makes sense. Fish have a long and harrowing journey from the reef to the retailer, usually in poor water conditions. Dealers may hold fish for varying periods of time after receiving them; many will sell fish the day they arrive at the airport. You will have little opportunity to discover all these pertinent facts, so I suggest erring on the side of caution. Buy only one fish at a time, unless you are purchasing a small group of the same species. Place each acquisition in a quarantine tank for a minimum of 2 weeks (a month is better) before relocating it to your display aquarium. Most of the problems that a new fish might develop usually occur within the first 2 weeks after you bring it home.

Your quarantine tank need not be an elaborate affair, but it must be large enough to accommodate the largest individual or group you plan to stock. If your main tank's capacity is less than 150 gallons, a 30-gallon quarantine tank should suffice. This will allow you to stock fish at about 3 inches or less in size.

As a general rule, it is not necessary to quarantine invertebrates. If you for some reason purchase an unfamiliar species or a damaged specimen, it is helpful to isolate it for a while to determine if you can safely add it to the display tank. In that instance, your fish quarantine tank can double as an invertebrate isolation tank. By supplying additional lighting, you can hold photosynthetic species.

The basic equipment needed for a quarantine tank includes:

- **Filter:** You can use a simple recirculating filter that is more commonly used on freshwater aquariums. These filters hang on the back or side of the tank and a pump circulates water from the tank through the filter. Filtration may be as simple as a polyester particle filter pad or elaborate enough to include a protein skimmer. For the quarantine tank, a foam particle filter insert and a protein skimmer are ideal. The foam filter can be seeded with beneficial bacteria to provide biological filtration, and the protein skimmer removes organic matter. Having both forms of filtration provides the best water quality. It is important not to expose your newly arrived fish to suboptimal water conditions, or you defeat the purpose of the quarantine period. Choose a filter that provides water turnover of about five or more times the tank capacity per hour. This ensures adequate gas exchange, provides natural turbulence for the fish, and maximizes filtration capacity.
- **Lighting:** The lighting for your quarantine tank can consist of a single fluorescent lamp in a standard fixture, provided you plan no isolation of photosynthetic invertebrates. In the latter case, double or quadruple the amount of light. This can easily be accomplished by hanging a 4-foot hardware-store shop light above the tank. You may want to use a shop light anyway, because they are so much cheaper than aquarium fixtures. Make sure it is securely suspended 12 to 18 inches above the aquarium.
- **Cover:** As with the display tank, a cover is optional for your quarantine tank. If common sense suggests that a cover would be a good idea, use one. For example, if the tank is in the garage, a cover would prevent foreign objects and dust from falling in the tank.
- **Heater:** Install a thermostatically controlled heater of appropriate wattage to keep the quarantine tank at a constant 74 degrees F. Minimizing temperature fluctuation benefits fish health.
- **Live rock:** Live rock may be added to the quarantine tank if there will be some benefit. For example, fish such as dragonets may need the temptation of the small invertebrates crawling on the rock to begin feeding in captivity. Or you may wish to isolate a piece of live rock before placing it in your main tank. You don't really need to decorate the quarantine tank with live rock, however, because this will make it difficult to clean the tank adequately between tenants. The ideal "decorations" are made from short sections of PVC pipe. Choose a diameter and length that will allow your new fish to hide inside the pipe. Place three or four of these pipe sections in the tank. If you are stocking a group, make sure each member can claim a pipe section.

Substrate material need not be added to the quarantine tank. You want to be able to see debris so it can easily be siphoned out. Quarantine of some goby species and jawfish provides an exception to this rule, because the fish need a substrate to sift through for food or to burrow in, or both.

In the event that you need to medicate a fish, you can use the quarantine tank as a hospital. Depending on the treatment, you may want to shut down the protein skimmer or otherwise modify the setup. (See the discussion of treating fish on page 183.)

Basic Setup for a Small Tank

Setting up any aquarium is mostly common sense. You set the tank in place and install all the equipment before adding seawater. Once the equipment is in place and the tank is filled, it is wise to test all the equipment before you proceed. In this regard, the set-up procedure is the same for either a small tank or a large one.

Installing the Tank and Cabinet

Setup is the same regardless of what type of support the tank is placed upon. I will assume for the remainder of this chapter that the tank will be supported by a base cabinet with access for plumbing and wires, and located against a wall so that the view of the rear of the tank is obscured.

Begin your setup by installing an opaque background. Aquarium shops sell backgrounds in various materials and colors. There are even photographic reproductions of underwater scenes. If these appeal to you, by all means use them. I prefer a simple black or dark blue background. Plastic sheeting, foil, or cloth can be taped to the tank. Ordinary paint provides a more permanent background. Protect areas where paint is unwanted with newspaper and masking tape. Make sure to protect the interior of the tank against stray paint droplets. Thoroughly clean the glass with window cleaner, followed by wiping with a lint-free cloth moistened with rubbing alcohol. Wait for the alcohol to evaporate completely. Apply two coats of exterior-grade enamel from a spray can. Allow to dry according to the manufacturer's directions before proceeding with the aquarium setup. After removing the masking tape and paper, carefully clean the inside of the tank, using warm water to which a small amount of vinegar has been added. Rinse with clean water and dry thoroughly.

With the background in place, the aquarium can be placed on the base. Using a carpenter's level, check to make certain the top of the tank sits perfectly level in both directions. If the top is not level, water will exert more pressure on the low side, increasing the likelihood of a leak. Placing the tank on a sheet of Styrofoam cut to the same size as the tank base offers an easy solution on a sloping floor, carpet, or other nonlevel surface. Lay the Styrofoam on top of the cabinet and place the tank on it. When the tank is filled, its weight will press down on the foam and the tank will level itself.

Fill the tank with tap water from a garden hose and let it sit overnight to make sure there are no leaks and that the weight does not cause any sagging of the cabinet or floor. Fix any problems you discover before proceeding with installation.

Installing the Filtration System and Plumbing

The next step is to install the equipment that will provide water movement and waste removal. If you have found that a heater is needed, it will also be installed at this point. Do not plug in any equipment until later. First, drain some water from the tank so you can easily get your hands and arms in without getting too wet.

Start by installing a submersible heater at the rear of the tank near the bottom, locating it so that the thermostat control is accessible for adjustment. Heaters are usually supplied with suction cups to facilitate installation.

Next, install the protein skimmer according to the manufacturer's directions. A skimmer/filter combination designed to hang on the back of the tank is the best choice for the 30-gallon system in this example. I prefer to have as little equipment as possible visible inside the tank, so I suggest this option over a more inexpensive skimmer designed to be placed inside the tank. If you don't mind looking at it, use the internal skimmer. Either way, you will find it convenient to locate the skimmer at a rear corner of the tank, to facilitate inspection and cleaning. If the unit includes a recirculating filter, make sure you can gain access to it for cleaning, changing filter pads, or whatever. Follow the manufacturer's directions regarding installation.

You will probably want water movement greater than that provided by the skimmer/filter. Place at least one small powerhead (see page 20) along the back wall of the tank with the outflow forward. The powerhead provides extra water circulation. Select one that moves about 150 gallons per hour. Using two powerheads, controlled by a timer known as a *wavemaker*, is an even better idea, though certainly not essential. Wavemakers allow the pumps to be switched on and off on a regular schedule, creating pulsed water movement simulating reef turbulence. Turbulence washes corals with oxygenated water and provides fish exercise swimming against the current.

Installing the Lighting System

The single lamp fluorescent strip light fixture that is sold to accompany most brands of aquarium tanks will work just fine for this setup. Don't forget to buy the fluorescent tube. The usual fixture for a 30-gallon system accepts a lamp about 3 feet long that draws 30 watts of electricity. Dealers sometimes make much ado about the benefits of different types of fluorescent lamps. For this simple system, choose one that gives a pleasing visual effect (use your own judgment) and ignore the hype. From a hardware store, purchase a timer to control the light fixture. Set the timer to provide 12 hours of lighting per day. One important point about fluorescent light fixtures: choose one that will work with the timer. Some fixtures have a "preheat" require-

ment that will not permit this convenience. If in doubt, buy the timer first, and ask for a demonstration, before buying the fixture. Aquarium "control centers" that can regulate both lighting and powerheads are available. Some units provide auxiliary outlets for other aquarium equipment, and plug into an ordinary wall outlet. These handy devices resemble the power centers sold for home computers.

When all of the equipment is in place, refill the tank to the bottom of the plastic trim with fresh water.

Performing the First System Test

When the tank is full again, plug everything in and allow the equipment to run overnight. Adjust the thermostat on the heater to the appropriate temperature. Use an accurate thermometer to check the temperature of the water in the aquarium and make adjustments to reach the target temperature. You may need to readjust the heater several times to achieve the desired result. Several temperature checks over the next few hours will provide an indication of how well the heater is doing its job. The temperature should remain constant within a degree or two.

Adjust the powerhead to direct a diagonal flow from the rear corner of the tank to the opposite front corner. If you are using two powerheads, point them toward each other. The intersecting currents will create turbulence. You may need to reposition the powerheads when live rock is added to the tank later.

Assuming that you have followed the instructions correctly for the skimmer/filter unit, water should be circulating from the tank to the skimmer and back. The skimmer will produce very little, if any, foam at this point. Final adjustments to the skimmer will have to be made after fish and live rock are in the tank. Now is the time to rearrange things, if necessary, to allow easy access to the skimmer controls.

If all goes well, you are ready to proceed with the fun parts, building your miniature "reefscape" and stocking the aquarium with living organisms. First, disconnect the power to all equipment. Drain the tap water from the tank by siphoning it into a bucket with a length of hose. Fill the tank about two-thirds full with synthetic seawater. You can also make the seawater directly in the tank, while you are running the equipment check. After refilling the tank almost full, add dry salt mix and let the pumps run for an hour or so. Check the specific gravity, convert to salinity, and add more salt if the reading is too low. Add more freshwater if the salinity is too high. Recheck the salinity the following day and continue to adjust it to reach a stable level of 35 ppt. This will be the only time that you will add dry salt directly to the tank. Once live organisms are present, this is a no-no.

Adding the Substrate

Covering the bottom of the aquarium with an inch of sand, crushed coral, limestone gravel, aragonite, shell fragments, or (best of all) a mixture of these materials is a good idea. A layer of substrate looks more natural than placing the live rock directly on the bottom of the tank.

Bacteria and small invertebrates living within the substrate aid in maintaining the aquarium's water quality.

In a plastic bucket, rinse 30 pounds of substrate material, a portion at a time, in tap water until the water is only slightly cloudy. This will wash away dirt and the fine powder that accumulates in the sand bag during handling. Skipping this step won't hurt anything, but it may take a while for the tank to clear up. Give it at least a cursory rinse. Sometimes substrate material is contaminated with wood chips or bits of other debris that will float out during the rinse.

Remove some of the seawater from the tank to make room for the substrate. Save the water to top up the tank later. You should end up with a layer of substrate about 1 to 3 inches deep.

Adding Live Rock and Live Sand

Both the look and usefulness of the substrate layer will be enhanced if live sand or live rock pebbles are added on top, at the same time live rock is added.

You will need about 60 pounds of live rock to create a suitable reef structure in the 30-gallon system. You may need to order live rock ahead of time, because of the curing process, so plan appropriately. It is imperative that the aquarium be filled with seawater and that all equipment is operating properly before the live rock is introduced. After adding the substrate, refill the tank to the top if it is going to be a while before live rock is added. Continue to run all equipment and adjust it as needed. Just before adding the rock, you should remove some water and reserve it, to allow for displacement. After all of the rock is in place, the tank can be topped-off with the reserved seawater.

After all the rock has been placed, you can scatter live sand or live rock pebbles on the surface of the substrate near the front of the tank, where they can be seen if they contain interesting or colorful components. Double-check the temperature, specific gravity, and pH. Verify the timer settings on the light fixture. Adjust the wavemaker, if used.

The First Few Weeks

You can stop here and pick up with the rest of the project as time permits, or you can proceed immediately with the next phase. From this point on, however, you are the custodian of a living ecosystem. Even though you cannot see the microorganisms on the live rock, they are already carrying out their vital jobs. Thus, you must maintain the aquarium at optimum over the next several months, in order that these basic biological processes are allowed to develop appropriately. This must be done regardless of the pace at which additional living organisms are added to the aquarium.

For about 6 to 8 weeks from the time you add live rock you can expect a series of algae blooms to occur. Typically, brownish diatoms and reddish-purple "slime algae" (actually photosynthetic cyanobacteria) are the first to show up. Later, filamentous green algae may also

Setup Checklist

Follow these steps in order while setting up your aquarium:

- ☐ Install tank support
- ☐ Install background on tank
- ☐ Place tank on support
- ☐ Check to make certain tank is perfectly level
- ☐ Install the filtration system
- ☐ Install the lighting system
- ☐ Fill tank and test all equipment for 24 hours
- ☐ Add substrate material
- ☐ Add live rock and live sand
- ☐ Double-check water conditions and equipment operation

appear. This is normal, and no special effort needs to be undertaken to eliminate the algae growth. Trying to do so is futile, anyway. With the passage of time the algae blooms will abate and the first few patches of purple coralline algae will begin to grow on solid surfaces. Coralline algae tend to grow best in moderate to dim light. Thus, new colonies often appear on the sides or back glass first. Eventually, several types of coralline algae will coat large areas of the glass and rocks. Use a razor blade to remove the algae from any area of the glass that you want to remain unobstructed, but leave the other colonies undisturbed. The coralline algae is an important component of the minireef's ecosystem. Good coralline algae growth indicates that conditions in the aquarium are suitable for sessile invertebrates.

Because of the inevitable algae blooms early in the life of any aquarium, it is a good idea to choose for the first inhabitants of the aquarium an assortment of species that consume algae. Algae-eating snails are widely available and a good choice. Other good choices include blue-legged hermit crabs, or scarlet hermit crabs. You should have one individual crab or snail for each gallon of water in the aquarium, for effective long-term algae control. Other utilitarian invertebrates can be added early in the aquarium's development. These include scavengers such as brittlestars, small shrimps such as the peppermint shrimp, and detritus-feeding species such as burrowing sea cucumbers.

Add thirty algae-eaters about a week after you have added the live rock, or when the initial algae growth becomes noticeable. The following week add three peppermint shrimps and a brittlestar. Wait another week, and add another brittlestar, a scarlet cleaner shrimp, and a burrowing sea cucumber. Note that the recommended 1-week interval between introductions of animals is somewhat arbitrary. You can wait a longer time, or even put everything into the aquarium simultaneously. The latter approach, however, will not afford you an

opportunity to correct problems early and avoid unnecessary losses of specimens if something is amiss. If the first introduction goes well and you are keeping up with routine maintenance, there should be few problems with future introductions.

After all of the algae-eating and scavenging invertebrate species have been added, you can add a pair of anemonefish.

By now, the aquarium will be about 2 months old and will have a thriving community of creatures. You can leave it at that, or you could add additional invertebrates such as fanworms. Once you have come this far successfully, you will no doubt develop other ideas on your own. I caution only against the temptation to add more than one additional fish. To do so will test the limits of the system's carrying capacity. Because of the small demand they place on the system, adding invertebrates is permissible.

Accommodating an Anemone

To add an anemone for the anemonefish, the only significant difference from the preceding setup is the need for additional lighting. Host anemones are shallow-water species accustomed to bright light. Four fluorescent lamps will be needed. Use two timers to control each pair of lamps separately. You should adjust the timers so that one pair of lamps comes on about an hour before, and goes off about an hour after, the other pair. This will simulate the increase and decrease in light levels at dawn and dusk.

Choose a moderately large bubble-tip anemone, which will be adopted by most anemonefish within a day or two. Gently and carefully place the anemone in the tank, after acclimating it as described on page 146.

With suitable lighting for the anemone, you can add other photosynthetic invertebrates. Your choices include a variety of species collected from shallow water in the Indo-Pacific region, such as green star polyp, leather mushroom soft coral, and disc anemones. It makes no difference how many (within reason) of these species are included, nor does it matter in what order they are added. What is important is that the minireef ecosystem be sufficiently stable. If you follow the instructions provided here, and in chapter 8, maintaining the aquarium, everything should go smoothly. Once established, a system like this can thrive for many years with little additional attention, apart from weekly testing and regular water changes.

Setting Up a Larger System

Setting up a large aquarium requires more planning than does a small tank. You will be working with 100 pounds or more of live rock, 50 pounds or more of substrate, and enough saltwater to fill a small bathtub. If you are to avoid a chaotic mess, plan ahead.

Work with your dealer to schedule the arrival of your live rock. If the dealer is going to cure the rock for you, working out a schedule should be simple. The dealer calls a couple of days before the curing is done, and you go to the store and pick it up. If you are going to cure the rock yourself and the dealer is merely going to order it for you, you'll want the curing tank set up and running at least 48 hours before the rock arrives at the airport. Then you can pick it up, take it straight home, and place it in the curing tank. If you have followed my advice and set up an auxiliary tank, you can use it for curing the rock. If you plan to cure the rock in the main tank, you'll need to arrange for temporary storage for the rock while you overhaul the tank after the curing process is complete.

When setting up a large tank (anything over 50 gallons) make doubly sure the aquarium sits level in both directions. Uneven water pressure on the glass can create a disaster of major proportions. By the same token, make certain the stand and the floor can support the weight. A 75-gallon tank weighs almost half a ton when filled and stocked.

Because of the money and effort involved in setting up a large system, it is important to test everything at each step. Follow the general plan just given for a small tank, but run the equipment and lighting for several days before proceeding to the addition of live rock. This is especially important if you are planning to cure the live rock directly in the tank. You don't want to have to haul out all that rock in a hurry if there's a plumbing leak.

During the curing process, it will be necessary to periodically remove some pieces of rock for extra cleaning. Sometimes a piece of sponge or other living organism attached to the rock dies and a slimy, white patch of decomposition begins to form. When you see this, take out that piece of rock and scrub off the decayed area with an old toothbrush before returning the rock to the water. Brace yourself; the smell can be quite offensive. Usually, after the first week or so of curing, major die-off such as this no longer occurs, and it is not necessary to do anything further. Scrubbing live rock should be done with care, and only when required, as you will also remove beneficial organisms in the process.

Using a Plastic Trash Can for an Auxiliary Aquarium

For curing and storing live rock, mixing large amounts of seawater, and similar uses, owners of large aquariums find 50-gallon plastic trash cans indispensable. They are sturdy enough to hold water without collapsing, impervious to water damage, and cheap. If you have a warm garage or basement room, you can even use several trash cans to cure live rock or act as holding and quarantine tanks. Outfit the trash can with a submersible aquarium heater and a recirculating pump, and you are in business. Hang a couple of 4-foot fluorescent shop light fixtures above your holding system, and you can even keep photosynthetic invertebrates or raise brine shrimp to adulthood.

How do you know when the curing process is complete? As the rock cures, decaying organisms will produce ammonia, which will be converted to nitrite by beneficial bacteria on the rock. As curing proceeds further, additional bacteria will oxidize the nitrite to nitrate. Therefore, simply test the water for nitrite periodically and keep track of the results. You will see an initial rise, a peak, and then a sharp decline to zero. At that point, the curing process has run its course.

Once the live rock has cured, I recommend discarding all of the water from the aquarium and replacing it with freshly made seawater. The old water will be loaded with organic matter and nitrate that have accumulated during curing. You can store the rock in your plastic trash can while you do this, keeping it covered with some of the old water. When the tank is about half full of new water, start replacing the rock and building your minireef. When all of the rock is in position, finish filling the tank. Let the system run with lighting on the normal 12-hour schedule and all filtration in operation for another month. Then, you should change 20 percent of the water before adding the first fish and/or large invertebrates. From that point on, events in a big tank will proceed pretty much as described earlier for a smaller one. As with the smaller system, a large minireef will mature in about a year. During that time, you can add new specimens about twice a month until your stocking plan is completed.

Acclimating New Arrivals

Whether your new aquarium is large or small, I cannot stress enough how much a separate quarantine tank eases the transition from the retailer's holding tank to your new saltwater aquarium. Regardless of whether you quarantine newly arrived fish and/or invertebrates, your critters require a gradual process of introduction into their new home. This is known as *acclimating* the fish to the new tank. Here's how it's done—the first few steps are performed *before* you even bring your fish home:

1. **Perform a series of water tests on your destination aquarium.** Make certain all the numbers check out. You don't want to jinx your new fish by placing it into unhealthful water conditions. There should be no ammonia or nitrite detectable, the pH should be 8.2 to 8.3, and the salinity should be at 35 to 36 ppt. If you find anything out of line, take steps to correct it before you bring home a new specimen. (See later in this chapter.)
2. **Make sure the filtration system has been recently maintained.**
3. **Ideally, perform your monthly 20 percent water change a couple of days before you expect to bring a fish home, then test the water the day you plan to go to the pet shop.**
4. **Make sure adequate hiding places have been provided.** Anything capable of swimming to shelter is likely to do so as soon as you release it from the transport bag.
5. **Bring your fish home.** The aquarium dealer will place the fish or invertebrate in a plastic bag filled about halfway with seawater. Air is trapped in the space above the water

Warning Signs of Fish Distress

Throughout the acclimation process, if the fish shows signs of obvious distress, it is best to remove it from the bag and place it immediately in the tank. Using a quarantine tank is especially advantageous here, because any subsequent problems can be dealt with without affecting the display aquarium.

- Rapid movement of the gill covers. The fish appears to be panting or gasping for "air."
- Dashing madly back and forth in the bag, or attempting to leap from the bag. Some panic movement is normal, but not to such extremes.
- Gasping at the water surface. This is another sign of oxygen distress.
- Inability to control swimming, or floating off-balance in the bag.

to provide oxygen for the trip home. If the trip home extends to more than half an hour or so, the bag should be inflated with pure oxygen. Most dealers know this and will pack your fish appropriately if you tell them how long you expect to be traveling. Don't make the fish store your first stop on an extended shopping excursion. Instead, wait until you are ready to depart. Then go fish shopping and head straight home with your new pet. By all means, don't stop at the supermarket on the way and leave the bag sitting in a hot or frigid car.

6. **As soon as you arrive home, turn off the lights over the aquarium.** Darkness will help to calm the fish, and it keeps many invertebrates from expanding delicate body parts.
7. **Place the unopened bag in the tank, allowing it to float.** Leave the bag undisturbed for at least 30 minutes.
8. **Gently, so as not to alarm the fish too much, open the bag and roll down the top.** Check the temperature of the water in the bag and compare it to that of the tank. If they're the same, transfer a cup of water from the tank to the bag. If not, wait a little longer until the temperature has equalized.
9. **Continue dipping water from the tank to the bag every 10 minutes until the bag sinks, allowing the fish to swim out.**
10. **Get the fish out of the bag.** If you are acclimating a sessile invertebrate, carefully lift it from the bag and place it where you want it. Mobile invertebrates, such as shrimps and brittlestars, as well as fish, will usually swim out on their own. If not, you can prod at them with a finger until they get the idea.
11. **Lift the plastic bag from the aquarium, water and all, and discard the water.**
12. **Top off the tank with prepared seawater.** This small water change helps to offset the wastes contained in the transport water, some of which is unavoidably added to the tank. Some hobbyists do not allow the bag to sink. They scrupulously avoid introducing any of the water from the bag into their aquarium. Instead, they add water from

the tank, cup by cup as just described, until the amount of water in the bag has doubled. Then, they remove the bag and dump it through a net into a bucket, effectively straining out the now-panicky fish. The netted fish is then plopped into the tank. While this does avoid adding any of the transport water to the display aquarium, the stress imposed on the fish by this treatment probably outweighs any possible benefit. You also run the risk of the fish becoming entangled in the net and suffering damage when you have to extricate it.

Fish or mobile invertebrates will likely seek shelter immediately upon escape from the bag. This is normal, and you should leave them undisturbed. Leave the lights off overnight. The next morning, when the lights come on as usual, the newcomer may emerge from its hiding place and start looking for food. If not, don't worry. It may take a few days of rest before it is ready to venture out. Sessile invertebrates, soft corals in particular, may wait a week or more before expanding their polyps. If all indications are that the tank is normal, their reluctance should be no cause for alarm. Many times anemones and large-polyped stony corals will expand fully within a few hours, but they can be reticent, too. Patience and common sense are your best companions during the first few days.

Creating a Fish-Only Tank

Fish-only aquariums are inherently simpler in design than are minireefs. Instead of live rock, for example, you can use dead coral rock to create a reef structure. Instead of living corals, you can decorate the tank with coral skeletons, or even plastic reproductions. With few or no delicate invertebrates to be accommodated, there are fewer things to worry about. Focus on creating an artistic display, rather than duplicating a natural scene precisely.

Choosing Tank Decorations

Please don't set up a fish-only saltwater tank decorated only with the bleached, white skeletons of stony corals. Creating a minireef using dead and artificial materials actually allows you to be more creative than if you were working with live invertebrates whose biological needs must be taken into account. Here are some ideas of what to use.

- Live rock or even plain, dead coral rock makes a much better background for the bright colors and fluid motion of reef fish. Add a small piece or two of dead coral to suggest a more complex reef structure, but don't pile up pieces of coral in a jumble. The fish won't mind, but the overall effect is seldom either natural or pleasing in appearance.
- Dead coral is by no means the only available material for decorating a fish-only saltwater tank, anyway. For starters, coral rock, which is the fossilized remains of ancient reefs, is a cheap, attractive, and widely available choice. You can see the patterns left in the rock by the fossil corals. Coral rock is supplied in boxes or by the piece. Select enough to build your artificial reef, and give it a good scrubbing with a brush under running water before placing it in the tank. Try to build a wall-like structure that is penetrated by several holes through which the fish can swim. Avoid stacking the rock like bricks. This

looks awkward in what is supposed to be a natural scene, and the tight structure impedes water flow and traps excessive sediment. Before you start plunging pieces in the tank, try various arrangements on a tabletop. Chunks of coral rock can easily be connected together to form a complex, highly attractive reef. You can build this outside the tank and then place the whole thing before adding the water. Rocks can be cemented together with underwater epoxy, tied together with lengths of nylon monofilament fishing line, pegged by drilling a hole in each piece of rock and inserting one end of a plastic rod or pipe into either side, and even mortared together with Portland cement. Creative use of these techniques has resulted in some stunning displays with rock arches suspended across a gap in the reef. Under good conditions, dead rock constructions acquire a coating of algae and take on a very convincing natural appearance.

- Numerous manufacturers produce plastic reproductions of living coral and other sea creatures. Many of these are quite life-like, and if chosen with care really enhance a fish-only display. Unless the tank is quite large, you'll have the best results with several pieces of different sizes but similar in color. If you mix a blue one, a pink one, and a yellow one, the effect is distracting. If you have room for several pieces, group similar ones together and try to balance the groupings within the tank. By this I mean, for example, placing a low, mounding group near the front left side of the tank to balance a tall, branching group above or on the opposite end.
- Sea shells are an obvious choice. They add color and interesting shapes, and many types of small fish will use them as a hiding place. Just make sure there are no remains from the animal that once lived in the shell. Otherwise, this material will rot and foul the aquarium. Place new shells in a bucket of fresh water for a couple of days. If a rotten smell develops, use a jet of water from a garden hose to try to flush out the decaying mollusk. When cleaned sufficiently, shells should have no spoiled seafood odor. Letting them dry in the sun helps. Do not use shells that have been coated with a protective layer of acrylic. The acrylic will usually flake off after the shell has been in the aquarium for a while.

Creating Appropriate Hiding Places

Place a flat rock across two rocks of similar height and you've made the simplest kind of shelter for a saltwater fish. Reef fish are generally territorial, and their need for personal space becomes more pronounced in the confines of an aquarium. Therefore, you should provide a suitably large hiding place for each fish you plan to stock.

Besides incorporating caves and ledges into the backbone structure of your artificial reef, add natural enclosures such as sea shells of an appropriate size. I've also seen interesting found objects from the beach used successfully as aquarium décor. My favorite was an old-fashioned Coke bottle found lying on its side in the sand, the top half of which had been encrusted with fire coral. The bottom half of the bottle, protected by the sand, was scratched

Decorating Tips

- Use rock, rather than dead coral, for the basic reef structure
- Add dead coral here and there for decorative effect. Less is more in the case of dead coral.
- Don't stack rocks like bricks.
- Do stack rocks with openings fish can swim through.
- Secure complex arrangements so they won't collapse.
- Add only materials deemed to be safe for a saltwater tank.
- Try to achieve a natural-looking arrangement.

but otherwise transparent. The aquarist placed it on the bottom in the position it had assumed in the ocean. Only part of the unencrusted area of the bottle was buried, providing a view into the lair of the royal gramma that set up housekeeping inside, using the mouth of the bottle for a doorway.

Public aquariums sometimes put manmade objects in their aquariums to make a statement about littering in the sea. Various kinds of bottom-dwelling fishes sometimes even take up residence in these pieces of junk. If the idea appeals to you, it won't hurt to use such objects in your saltwater tank. Broken flowerpots are a popular choice. Just make certain that anything you try is either ceramic, glass, or plastic. Even though big aquariums sometimes add old tires and beer cans, don't put any form of metal into your aquarium. If you are unsure about the safety of a particular object, reject it rather than taking an unnecessary chance.

Avoiding a "Tank-alanche"

Take care to secure all tank decorations as previously described. If you build caves of rock, make sure the supporting pieces are sitting directly on the bottom of the tank, rather than atop the substrate. Burrowing and digging by fish can undermine the rocks and cause the whole thing to come tumbling into a pile. If the rocks are large enough, there is a danger of breaking the tank. Fish or invertebrates can be crushed by such a "tank-alanche."

Also avoid balancing rocks or other objects one upon the other as you would if building a mortarless wall in the garden. The constant vibration from pumps and nearby foot traffic will eventually permit gravity to have its way with your minireef. Use common sense. Place larger pieces on the bottom. Individual rocks should sit as they would in a natural setting, with the broadest portion of the rock down. Flat rocks serving as the roof of a cave or overhang should rest securely on at least three contact points with their supporting stones. Such an arrangement affords maximum stability.

Creating a Reef Habitat

A reef habitat begins with live rock. After the reef structure is built, live sand and substrate material are added to enhance the appearance and provide valuable bacteria and other organisms. The main decorative features are living corals and other photosynthetic invertebrates, giant clams, and a few carefully chosen fish. A minireef usually strives to exemplify an actual natural habitat. Consequently, you'll need to do more research and to put more thought into your design than is the case with a fish-only aquarium.

Choosing Live Rock

You will be able to build a more interesting reef with a few large pieces of live rock, rather than a bunch of little ones. The reef should appear significantly larger than the largest fish in the tank, or the whole thing will look out of proportion. Using chunks of rock about three times the length of the fish in height and about twice the fish's length in breadth will give the most natural-looking result. Odd numbers of pieces look best. The eye will convert even numbers of similar rocks into paired "pillars" or "vases," destroying the illusion of natural placement. For the 30-gallon tank in the previous examples, three to five main pieces of live rock will look best. Smaller pieces of live rock can be used to fill in spaces for decorative effects, or to provide a perch for a sessile invertebrate. Disc anemones come on pieces of rock that can be used in this way, as do fanworms.

You can make the aquarium look larger from front to back by placing an especially interesting or brightly colored piece of live rock near the front glass, and slightly left of the center. Build the main part of the reef behind this piece, leaving space between the reef and the back glass. (You'll need the space to fit in equipment, anyway.) In this rear space, place a pale-colored, wispy or fine-textured object, such as a piece of delicately branching dead coral or a clump of seaweed (real or artificial) or a single white fanworm. This arrangement distorts perspective and fools the eye into thinking that the space is larger than it is. Be sure to keep the rear object smaller than the one in front, to which the eye will be drawn first.

Conversely, if your intention is to give the feeling of peeking into an enclosed space to observe the life forms inside, place larger, more boldly colored pieces of live rock toward the back of the tank to form the main part of the reef. Leave the area in front open, with a pale, medium-textured substrate. In the front corners of the tank, plant seaweeds, or place a lacey-looking cluster of fanworms. It helps to elevate these objects so their tops are about two-thirds of the way up from the bottom. In this way, they will frame the central area of the tank. The eye will mostly see the bright colors in back, and in effect bring the reef forward. This and the frame at the front give the impression of a window into a secluded corner of a natural reef.

Unpacking the rock and placing it in the aquarium gives you numerous opportunities to be creative. Perhaps you'd like to build a cave. You can use plastic cable ties and/or underwater epoxy cement, both sold at aquarium shops and hardware stores, to hold rocks in position. Make sure the structure is stable. Place larger pieces near the bottom and smaller ones on top to avoid creating a top-heavy reef that may tumble down disastrously if someone slams a door nearby. Start a few inches back from the front of the tank and build a reef that slopes upward and back. Try to maintain an open structure through which water can easily move, rather than stacking the rocks like brickwork.

Live Sand, Refugia, and "Magic Mud"

The ocean teems with microscopic and nearly microscopic life. If the organism is free-swimming, we say it is a form of plankton. *Plankton* is a collective term for any free-swimming or free-floating fish larva, invertebrate, or algae smaller than a few millimeters in length. If the organism lives attached to a solid surface, or crawls on or among the particles of the substrate, we call it a *benthic organism*. Both plankton and benthic organisms are important components of the ecosystem, providing food for many types of larger creatures and carrying out the important function of reducing larger debris to smaller and smaller pieces easily decomposed by fungi and bacteria. It was not until minireef aquariums had been around for a few years that hobbyists began to recognize the value of the planktonic and benthic components of their captive reefs.

Together, live sand and live rock create not only the natural look of a genuine reef, but they also facilitate the development of natural biochemical cycles in the minireef ecosystem. Placing a live sand layer at the bottom of a minireef aquarium has become such a popular technique that live sand is now collected from the sea or cultured in large-scale aquariums and packaged for sale in plastic bags. One of the primary advantages of using these products is the speed with which the nitrogen cycle becomes established in the aquarium, due to the large amount of beneficial bacteria added with the live sand.

Besides being a source of beneficial bacteria, live rock and live sand both harbor small, benthic invertebrates, mostly crustaceans, that appear as if by magic after the aquarium has been set up a month or two. Copepods and amphipods (types of crustaceans distinguished by anatomical details unimportant here) are the main components of the suite of organisms that can be seen crawling around and rummaging about on rocks and in the substrate, feeding on algae and debris. Only a millimeter or two in length, copepods look like little specks of lint, albeit lint capable of mobility. Amphipods are a bit larger, about half a centimeter, and are clearly shrimplike in appearance. Some aquarists refer to them as *gravel shrimp* because they are often seen grubbing for food among the particles of substrate. Both copepods and amphipods are relished by many types of minireef-compatible fish, such as dragonets and basslets. It did not take long for someone to notice that their tank was producing a crop of homegrown fish food, and to make an effort to encourage the growth of these organisms. One factor limiting their population density, however, was the constant foraging by fish. To solve this problem, the aquarium was outfitted with a separate chamber that came to be known as a *refugium* providing an opportunity for the reproduction of desirable microinvertebrates unhindered by predation.

Sediment that accumulates in the refugium tank has been called *magic mud* by some hobbyists. Magic mud harbors abundant microfauna that contribute to aquarium waste management. For this reason, you should not be too scrupulous in trying to remove every speck of debris from your tank. Fine debris causes problems only when it inhibits water flow through some component of the filtration system, or when it is obviously providing a growing medium for slime algae or sulfide-producing bacteria. These conditions will be quickly noticed if you check on your tank every day. The simple remedy is to siphon out the pile of offending material. Leave the rest of the refugium and the main display tank alone. When you give your minireef the "hurricane treatment" described in chapter 8, expect an unusually large amount of magic mud to gather in your refugium. Check about a week after the hurricane to see if any piles of it need to be siphoned out.

Live rock, live sand, and magic mud all supply the aquarium with beneficial organisms that help with waste management and in maintaining a healthy, natural environment. Using a refugium can multiply these benefits because it gives organisms a chance to multiply away from predatory fishes. Together, these important components help form an aquarium ecosystem much like that found in the sea.

Creating a "Stage" for Coral "Performance"

On the wild reef, corals adapt their structure to local conditions of water movement, substrate, and light availability. On the turbulent outer reef the open, branching forms of small-polyped corals predominate. In quiet lagoons, large-polyped corals tend to outnumber the branched ones. On muddy bottoms, corals may be shaped like inverted cones, point down in the mud. On hard substrates, individual coral colonies are firmly attached. On sandy bottoms dwell corals that are able to move around to position themselves for catching prey. It's worth paying attention to these proclivities in placing corals in your minireef. Appropriate placement gives the aquarium a natural appearance and gives the coral the best chances for adapting successfully to captivity.

Place branching corals, such as *Pocillopora* and *Acropora*, near the top of the reef structure. Here, they will receive maximum illumination. Provide plenty of water movement by means of auxiliary powerheads directed near, not at, the coral. Corals can be secured to the rock in a variety of ways, depending on how large the coral is and how precariously you want it perched on the rock. Cements for gluing rocks and corals together that set underwater are sold in aquarium shops and online. Glue joints may need to be reinforced. One way to do this is to drill a hole in both rock and coral with a masonry bit and insert a length of rigid plastic pipe tightly into each hole before applying the cement. For small pieces, use a plastic cocktail toothpick instead of the plastic pipe. Don't worry about having the coral or live rock out of the water. Hold them securely in a towel dampened with seawater, and drill away. They are so soft that the bit will cut quickly. You may want to practice on some pieces of dead coral and coral rock to get the feel before trying this on a valuable specimen.

Large-polyped corals that are shaped like an inverted cone, such as *Euphyllia* and *Trachyphyllia*, should ideally be placed on the sand where they can sink in as they normally do. Sometimes these corals grow attached by the tip of the cone to a rock. You can simulate this

Decorating Tips

- Branching corals should go near the top of the tank.
- Corals shaped like an inverted cone should be placed on a sandy substrate, or mounted securely to a rock.
- Corals that can move should always be placed on the bottom of the tank.

positioning by drilling and scraping out a small concavity for the coral to sit in. Corals positioned like this may attach themselves and grow onto the rock.

Corals that are able to move about on their own, such as *Heliofungia*, need to be placed on an unobstructed area of soft sand or fine, shelly gravel under brilliant illumination. If placed on top of a reef structure, they invariably try to relocate themselves and topple to the floor of the tank. Usually they are damaged by the fall and seldom recover. The need for proper placement and a fairly large area in which to roam may explain why these corals are considered difficult to maintain in a minireef.

A minireef housing several specimens of corals is like a stage on which the various players, the corals, act out their ecological roles. Proper placement with regard to the substrate, vertical location on the reef structure, and light exposure will help your troupe to win accolades from everyone who sees the show.

What You Now Know . . .

- Setting up a quarantine tank is an important, though optional, first step.
- Setting up an aquarium of any size is a simple, step-by-step process.
- It is wise to allow the aquarium to run for at least 24 hours before stocking it with live organisms.
- Water conditions should be carefully checked before stocking the aquarium.
- Many materials are available for decorating a fish-only aquarium.
- Make sure anything you place in your tank is safe to use in saltwater.
- Live rock, live sand, and magic mud are all natural components that provide beneficial bacteria, waste management, and food organisms for the aquarium.
- Corals in the aquarium should be placed according to their individual preferences for best results.

Chapter 8

Keeping Your Aquarium Healthy

What's Inside . . .

- Learn how to avoid maintenance headaches.
- Learn what and how to feed your fish.
- Learn how to select appropriately from the variety of available aquarium foods.
- Learn to interpret water test results in terms of maintenance needs.
- Learn the benefits of an aquarium "hurricane."

Maintaining your saltwater aquarium properly is the key to long-term success. One important kind of maintenance is feeding the fish. All fish need a varied diet of wholesome foods to remain healthy.

Avoiding Maintenance Headaches

Properly acclimating and carefully handling all new arrivals provide good examples of ways to avoid problems with saltwater aquariums. Here are some more suggestions for sidestepping common problems. It is always easier to avoid trouble than to deal with it when it crops up.

Problem to Avoid: The water is cloudy after I do a water change.

Solution: This is usually due to one of two things: (1) fine debris stirred up during maintenance is suspended in the water, or (2) the synthetic seawater has not been mixed long enough prior to use. Fine debris will settle out in a day or two, but you can clean it up instantly with a canister filter available at your aquarium dealer. This filter is basically a large jar full of media with a pump to recirculate water from the tank through the filter media and back to the tank. Filters designed to use diatomaceous earth as the filter medium will remove very fine particles from the water in a matter of hours, leaving the tank crystal clear. Some aquarists call this "polishing the water" because the tank really sparkles. If the tank contains filter-feeding invertebrates, don't use this technique more than once a month or you'll deplete the aquarium of potential food for these specimens.

Cloudiness in freshly made synthetic seawater results from chemical components that take a while to dissolve in fresh water. Using a saltwater mixing container as described in chapter 2 will remedy this problem. If you don't want to set up a mixing container, make sure freshly prepared synthetic seawater sits at least overnight before you use it. If there is insoluble sediment at the bottom of the container after this long, use most of the water and discard the sediment. Always remember to double-check the salinity of new seawater before you use it.

Problem to Avoid: Algae is about to overrun the aquarium.

Solution: Excessive algae growth is almost always due to the accumulation of phosphate in the water. You can verify this by carrying out a phosphate test. To avoid phosphate accumulation, purify your tap water as described in chapter 3. Using a phosphate test kit, check a sample of your synthetic seawater. If you use any additives, fill a bucket with purified water and add the appropriate amount of the additive. Check the water in the bucket for phosphate. If you find phosphate in any of these products, try switching brands. If you neglect water changes, phosphate will build up in the tank, even if your water and additives have no detectable phosphate present. Excessive algae often grows in aquariums that are not regularly maintained. If you don't want to purify your tap water or bother with phosphate testing, you can make the algae at least *look* better by increasing the amount of light available. This will result in a lush, green carpet of filamentous algae that will be cropped by herbivorous fishes, such as dwarf angels and tangs.

Problem to Avoid: The water has a yellowish cast.

Solution: Yellow water indicates that dissolved organic compounds are accumulating. Do a partial water change first. Then either increase the size of your protein skimmer, or do more frequent small water changes in the future. If the water becomes yellow a few days after a partial water change, you definitely need more skimming. You may also be overfeeding the fish, so cut back about 20 percent on their food and see if that helps clear up the water.

Problem to Avoid: The pump is noisy.

Solution: A noisy pump either has air trapped in the volute (pump head), or needs the impeller replaced. Air entrapment usually means that a pinhole leak has developed in the plumbing between the tank and the pump, causing air to be sucked in by the force of the water movement. Shut off the pump and wait a few minutes. Water will ooze from the leak and you can make appropriate repairs. Of course, deal with this immediately upon discovery. If the power goes off while you're away, that pinhole leak will eventually drain the tank.

A noisy impeller should be replaced promptly. Because the impeller magnet wears unevenly, with use it becomes slightly off-center and wobbles, creating a squeaking or rattling sound. This indicates it is past time to replace the impeller. When you purchase the pump, check the manufacturer's directions for a recommendation on regular impeller replacement. If none is given, remove the housing and check for wear about every 6 months. While you have the pump apart, clean the housing with a toothbrush if you find debris or mineral accumulation.

Problem to Avoid: Fish are listless and some have hollow bellies.

Solution: Your fish are starving! Either they are not getting the right kind of food, or food is being offered in insufficient quantity. Double-check recommendations for feeding the species you have and make appropriate changes. Herbivorous fish are most susceptible to starvation, because their preferred food, seaweed, is not a concentrated source of nourishment. Vegetarian fish have to eat almost constantly.

Problem to Avoid: My fish are all eating well, but one of them is losing weight anyway.

Solution: If only some fish are wasting despite getting plenty of the right foods, they may have suffered internal damage during collection and transport. Collecting fish with chemicals may lead to intestinal abnormalities that prevent food absorption. Another cause of wasting may be internal parasites. In all of these situations, the fish may feed greedily, because they are starving despite having access to ample food. Some aquarists have reported that internally damaged fish may show unusually bright or intensified coloration, feed ravenously, then turn pale or off-color, decline, and die. If any of these things happens to you, remember that it's not your fault. The damage was probably done long before you obtained the fish. Unfortunately, unless the fish heals spontaneously (a rare occurrence) there is little you can do to reverse the damage. Fish that become debilitated should be euthanized.

Feeding Fish

Making sure your fish receive a healthy, balanced diet is another way to avoid problems. Fish need food of the proper kind, in the right amount, and on an appropriate schedule. For example, in a mature minireef, there will be an abundance of small organisms, microcrustaceans, and algae that serve as food for both planktivorous fish and filter-feeding invertebrates. "Home grown" foods, that is, those that are produced within the aquarium itself or its refugium, provide the best nourishment, but they cannot be relied on exclusively. The fish will need to be fed. The amount and nutritional quality of food that should be offered varies from one species to another. You can find out about species-specific feeding needs in chapter 4 or other references. The majority of fish will do just fine if you use dry and frozen foods made for saltwater use. Just remember to vary the diet. Don't fall into the habit of feeding one food exclusively. Make sure you feed herbivorous fish, such as most tangs, a diet that includes lots of seaweeds and algae. (Check package labels for the ingredients.) Big predators, such as lionfish, only need to eat a couple of times a week. Fish that feed only on tiny invertebrates, such as anthias, or those that continuously crop algae, such as the yellow tang, need to be fed three or four times a day. The majority of saltwater fish should be fed twice daily.

Fish-Feeding Tips

Remember these tips when feeding your fish:

- Feed your fish a balanced, varied diet.
- Don't let uneaten food decay in the tank.
- Establish and stick to a regular feeding schedule.
- Feed only as much as will be consumed within 10 minutes.

Uneaten food is a major source of pollution, which must be kept to a minimum. The food supply should be adjusted so that the fish consume as much as possible and very little sinks to the bottom to decay. Deciding how much to give at a feeding will take some experimentation on your part. Never mind that the fishes always seem hungry when you approach the tank. The fact that they are willing to eat does not mean that they should be fed. Establish a regular feeding schedule and stick to it. A good rule of thumb is to feed only as much as will be consumed within 10 minutes.

Feed as wide a variety of foods as possible. From the various fish foods mentioned in the following section, and any others that your dealer stocks, feed your fish as many different kinds as they will accept. I have observed two types of disease syndrome in saltwater fish that appear to be associated with an unvaried diet. These are described in chapter 9, along with HLLE, another malady commonly thought to be associated with dietary deficiency. Fish need a balanced diet for all of the same reasons that you do. Fresh, living foods are preferable to prepared foods. Prepared foods are a second choice, but you will need to feed these products at least part of the time, unless you have a much more relaxed schedule than I do! Above all, make sure the bulk of your saltwater fish food comes from saltwater organisms, as opposed to terrestrial or freshwater sources.

Live Foods

Adult brine shrimp, newly hatched brine shrimp, amphipods, grass shrimp, blackworms, guppies, and bait fish are commonly available. You can also raise brine shrimp, amphipods, and guppies if you have the space and time. Any of these live foods may be given to fishes that will eat them. Do not make the mistake of feeding your saltwater fish exclusively on blackworms, guppies, or goldfish, because these freshwater foods will not provide all the nutrition saltwater fish require. Use them to provide variety in your fish's diet. Live foods can also be used to acclimate finicky fish to the aquarium before weaning them to nonliving foods.

- **Blackworms** are freshwater annelids about 2 inches long. They look like little, thin earthworms. They keep very well in a shallow container of freshwater in the refrigerator. To keep the worms healthy, the water must be carefully poured off and replaced with fresh water daily. Tap water is fine for this purpose.

- **Bait fish** sold for aquarium food are usually goldfish. They will keep best outside in a large, well-areated tank or small pond. Some hobbyists use a child's plastic wading pool for storing feeder goldfish. Aeration should be provided by a recirculating pump or an air diffuser connected to an air pump. Either type of equipment is available from your aquarium dealer. Use these foods only occasionally, as they offer incomplete nutrition if fed exclusively.
- **Brine shrimp,** *Artemia salina,* naturally live in highly saline environments. Either as live adult shrimp or as resting cysts, brine shrimp are available year-round to aquarists. Newly hatched brine shrimp, called *nauplii*, are an old-fashioned staple food for all types of aquariums. The resting cysts, or "eggs," are widely available from aquarium shops. Your dealer can also provide you with everything needed to hatch them. This can be done in an empty quart mayonnaise jar, and is one of the best techniques for obtaining live food for small fish. Raising the nauplii to adult size creates more of a hassle. You'll need at least 100 gallons of aerated seawater and a continuous supply of algae for the shrimp to feed on. Many hobbyists find this too much trouble and instead buy adult brine shrimp from their dealer to give to the fish as a treat now and then.
- **Amphipods** are the little white crustaceans about ⅛ inch long that scurry over the rocks and among the substrate in mature saltwater aquariums. You can encourage their growth in your tank by installing a refugium, which provides the amphipods a chance to reproduce abundantly without exposing them to predation from the fish in the main tank. See chapter 7 for information on refugia. Amphipods can also be cultured in a

Hatching and Raising Brine Shrimp

To hatch brine shrimp, place about 2 tablespoons of dry seawater mix in a clean quart jar and fill with RO water. (RO water is tap water that has been purified by reverse osmosis. See page 39.) Drop in a small air diffuser connected with a length of tubing to an air pump. Turn on the pump and adjust the air flow to provide vigorous aeration, but not so much that water splatters out of the jar. Add about ¼ teaspoon of cysts. You can cover the jar with a piece of plastic wrap to keep spray inside. Poke a few holes in the plastic wrap with a pin to allow air to escape. The cysts will hatch in 24 to 48 hours, depending on the temperature. The warmer the room, the faster they will hatch. When you are ready to harvest your crop, you can take advantage of the fact that the nauplii are attracted to light. Turn off the aeration and place a flashlight next to the jar. This will lure the nauplii, causing them to collect at a spot from which they may be siphoned out. Strain the water containing the nauplii through a fine mesh net, and feed your aquarium.

To rear adult brine shrimp, a large shallow container holding at least 100 gallons, such as a child's wading pool, can be filled with old aquarium seawater. Add a pinch of houseplant fertilizer to supply nitrate and phosphate. Allow this to sit in a brightly lit area until the water turns green, indicating a thriving population of algae. Now you can add freshly hatched nauplii. They will feed on the algae and grow to adult size (about ½ inch) in approximately 3 weeks.

separate small tank set up in the garage. Install a recirculating filter, such as the type that hangs on the back of the tank. Fill the tank with old seawater. Use a heater to maintain a temperature of 75 degrees F. Install bright lighting, such as a 4-foot fluorescent shop light from a do-it-yourself store, over the amphipod farm. Turn everything on and wait until the tank has a good growth of algae, then add some amphipods from another aquarium. Leave them alone for a month, and then harvest them as needed to feed to your fish.

- **Grass shrimp** are collected by the millions in the marshes of the southeastern coast of the United States. Most of them are used for fishing bait, but plenty are sold to aquarium dealers for resale as fish food. They live quite well crowded into a small tank with 50 percent seawater and a system set up as described for amphipods. Dealers usually sell them by the dozen.
- **Guppies,** or more precisely "feeder guppies," are the culls from fancy guppy breeders and their offspring. They generally look like wild guppies and are seldom over an inch and a half in length. If you have room for a large, heated aquarium with abundant plants (real or artificial) you can easily raise hundreds of guppies from a few purchased pairs. They breed like crazy and the young find shelter from their cannibalistic parents among the plants. Most hobbyists just buy them by the dozen and use a 10 gallon holding tank with aeration. Kept this way, the guppies do just fine until they become dinner for your saltwater aquarium. Dump the water from the guppy tank and replace it a day or two before you buy more guppies.
- **Feeder goldfish** are sold as fisherman's bait, and are the culls from fancy goldfish breeding. Most shops sell them by the dozen for feeding predatory aquarium fish, both freshwater and saltwater. They need a somewhat larger holding tank than guppies. I suggest 30 to 50 gallons or more. Otherwise, the setup is the same. Alternatively, a small outdoor pond can hold a large number of small goldfish year-round. You can build a simple pond out of pressure-treated lumber and line it with plastic sheeting. A small pump from a do-it-yourself store creates a charming fountain and provides aeration for the goldfish. Other than you lurking around with a net when dinnertime approaches for the saltwater fish, goldfish find outdoor ponds a perfect home.

Fresh Foods

Few aquarium shops stock fresh foods, because they have a short shelf life. So don't go to the aquarium store for fresh food for your fish. Your grocery store stocks an abundance of foods that can be used in the aquarium. Fresh fish fillets, shrimp, clams, scallops, mussels, and squid (calamari) can all be chopped into pieces of a size appropriate for feeding aquarium fishes. Ocean fish, such as snapper, tuna, mahi-mahi, halibut, sole, cod, and grouper, are better choices than are freshwater fish, such as trout and catfish. The produce department stocks a host of vegetables that are good for herbivorous marine fish. Romaine and other types of lettuce, spinach, parsley, peas, broccoli, and zucchini have all been used with success. If the fish are finicky about eating land veggies initially, immerse them in boiling water for 1 minute, strain into a colander, and rinse with cold water. This will render the vegetable's texture more like that of seaweeds that herbivorous fishes are accustomed to eating. Use foods from terrestrial sources sparingly, as a supplement to, and not as a replacement for, ocean-derived foods. Many grocery stores stock seaweed products, both fresh and dried. Any of these is a better choice than vegetables for herbivorous fish. Look for seaweed in the Asian section of the store. Feed fresh seaweed by the date shown on the label, and store it refrigerated. Nori, the dark green sheets used for wrapping sushi, is dried seaweed and an excellent fish food. It keeps for months in a plastic bag in the refrigerator.

Frozen Foods

Available frozen foods include products made from one kind of food, such as brine shrimp, squid, mysid shrimp, or lancefish. In addition, many preparations containing a variety of ingredients and additives are sold in aquarium shops. Often, the product contains a specific diet for a certain type of fish, such as "herbivore diet" or "small fish diet." One manufacturer even makes one with sponges, an important constituent in the diet of some angelfish. Frozen foods often come in cube packs, which is very convenient. Just pop out as many cubes as you need and return the pack to the freezer. Frozen foods provide the best substitute for fresh foods. They are available in enormous variety. Best of all, frozen foods are always available, whereas fresh or live foods may not be. Keep a variety of frozen foods on hand and feed them to your fishes regularly. After thawing, frozen foods may be fed in quantities comparable to live and fresh food feedings. To thaw, simply place a portion of the food in a small bowl and add a little tap water. Let stand at room temperature for a few minutes.

Freeze-Dried Foods

Most freeze-dried aquarium foods contain crustaceans, such as krill or brine shrimp. Packed with concentrated nutrition and convenient, freeze-dried products should not be your fish's staple diet. Such foods are mostly protein and are deficient in other nutrients. Use them as a supplement to provide variety, not the exclusive source of nutrition.

Dehydrated Flake Foods

Although some nutritional content is lost during the dehydration process, dried foods still contain plenty of good things for your saltwater pets. Moreover, dried foods are cheap, convenient, and certain to be stocked by any aquarium shop. Choose flake foods specifically produced for saltwater fish. Despite the cost savings realized when flake foods are bought in quantity, it is best to purchase only a small amount at a time. After they are opened flake foods may lose food value or develop mold. Storing them in a cool, dry place will maximize their shelf life. I suggest replacing dried flake foods every 6 months.

Handling Aquarium Foods

Aquarium foods should be treated like foods for human consumption. For example, store frozen foods solidly frozen, thaw out only what you need, and do not refreeze completely thawed food. All foods should be purchased in small quantities that will be used within a reasonable period of time. Even foods not sold frozen should be stored in the freezer or refrigerator for maximum retention of nutritional value. Keep all foods tightly sealed. Air can break down valuable vitamins and moisture intrusion can lead to spoilage. Spoiled foods can be recognized by a foul odor; mold growth usually produces a "musty" smell. Discard spoiled or moldy foods immediately.

Many aquarists are concerned about transmitting disease to their fishes by feeding them fresh or frozen seafood. This is unlikely. Disease outbreaks in the aquarium more often can be traced to poor water quality than to tainted food. Any condition that stresses the fish leaves them more susceptible to infection. Feed your fish all the fresh seafood you want and don't worry about it making them sick. In fact, proper feeding is one way to *prevent* disease.

Establishing a Feeding Regimen

A proper feeding regimen for your minireef is easy to establish. First, learn all you can about the natural diet of the fish. Try to mimic it as closely as possible. As previously mentioned, feed as wide a variety of foods as possible. Don't be afraid to experiment. Try different brands and types of foods available. Each time you buy fish food, try one that you have not used recently. Make sure, of course, that it is recommended for the type of fish you have. Experiment with seafood and greens from the grocery store. In general, feed your fish once or twice daily. See chapter 4 for specific feeding recommendations for several saltwater fish species. While some fish specialize, most eat a variety of foods. On the reef all the food is fresh, and there are always a huge number of choices on the menu.

Some fish respond to the movement of living food and will accept nothing else when they are first placed in the aquarium. Some lionfish species provide examples of this behavior. With patience, it is possible to entice these fish to accept nonliving food. After the fish has been feeding well for several days on guppies or goldfish, reduce the amount of live food. Take one of those bamboo skewers you can buy at the grocery store for making kebobs on the grill and impale a piece of fish or shrimp near the tip. Using this bamboo handle, dangle the offering near the fish you are trying to feed. Move the food enticingly, trying to mimic the jerky swimming of a fish in trouble. Don't thrash around so vigorously that you intimidate your fish, of course. It may take a few tries before your predator gets the idea. Most eventually do, and then live happily ever after on various kinds of dead seafood.

Planktivorous fish present a special case. They spend the day snatching tiny invertebrates, collectively known as *plankton*, from the surrounding water. Different species of fish take different sizes of microprey. Some grab nearly anything up to a half an inch or so in length, while others eat thousands of tiny brine shrimp nauplii at a single meal. The former types are among the most easily fed saltwater fish, and include such familiar ones as anemonefishes. In the latter category are anthias, jawfishes, and many small gobies. These fish can be fed on a regular diet of fresh or frozen food chopped into sufficiently small pieces. Once a week or so, hatch out a jar of brine shrimp and feed them to your planktivores. Feed them brine shrimp more often, if you have the time and inclination.

Feeding Invertebrates

Fish feed pretty much like dogs: they grab the food tossed (or that swims) in their direction and swallow it. Feeding them is straightforward. Invertebrates, on the other hand, provide some special challenges. For one thing, they exhibit a variety of capture methods, from hunting to straining the surrounding water for particulate food items. Menus must be tailored to the feeding methods of the critters you are maintaining in your aquarium. This information is given for the invertebrates described in chapter 5. You can find information about other species from books or online.

Filter Feeders

A common feeding method among aquarium varieties of invertebrates is known as *filter feeding*. Filter feeders strain the surrounding water for particles of food. Usually, a particular animal specializes in particles of a certain size and has a feeding apparatus designed appropriately. Fanworms provide a good example. The fan is actually the worm's radioles, which function as both gills and food-gathering net. The feathery radioles entrap food particles and secrete mucus in which the food becomes embedded, preventing its simply washing back into the sea. Along the midrib of the radioles, tiny hairs beat back and forth to create a current that directs the mucus-coated food to the mouth, located at the center of the fan. Fanworms specialize in dust-sized particles and usually subsist quite well in a mature tank without specialized feeding. They'll respond well to small amounts of fish or shrimp juice, and they appear to capture brine shrimp nauplii, also.

Other types of filter-feeding invertebrates include sponges, which remove extremely small particles, such as bacterial cells, from the water. In fact, most of the sessile organisms encrusting live rock are filter feeders. Virtually all corals and other coelenterates are capable of feeding this way. The nonphotosynthetic corals require feeding with brine shrimp and other products several times a day. Most of these corals are short lived in the hands of a novice aquarist, and I don't recommend them.

Besides live brine shrimp, there are many options for filter feeders. Various liquefied foods are sold for the purpose. You can also add the juice that collects when you chop seafood for feeding the fish. Seafood can be pureed in a blender and strained through a fine net. The particles that pass through the net can be used as invertebrate food. When using any of the nonliving foods, care must be taken not to add an excessive amount, or you risk overloading the aquarium's capacity for waste removal. For this reason, and to avoid wasting the food, I suggest you use a medicine dropper or plastic syringe to squirt little "puffs" of food in the vicinity of the invertebrate you're feeding. It doesn't take much, maybe a teaspoon or two at a time. After all, these critters just sit in one place all day, so they have relatively small food requirements compared to an active, mobile creature.

Scavengers

Quite a few common invertebrates can be included in this group. Hermit crabs, shrimps, and brittlestars all scour the aquarium for bits of this and that, and seldom need to be deliberately fed. They perform a valuable service by cleaning up food missed by the other inhabitants of the tank.

Grazers

In this group can be found the critters placed into the tank primarily for algae control. Snails and small hermit crabs constitute the "lawn care" patrol. Sea urchins also feed on algae, but are not above munching a piece of shrimp unnoticed by the fish. Larger invertebrates that need a steady diet of algae can be fed fresh or dried seaweed or frozen foods containing a high proportion of green matter.

Predators

A few invertebrates are active hunters, and many are not above subduing a tank mate and killing it when no other food is available. Starfish, for example, normally feed off sessile invertebrates and bivalve mollusks. Predatory starfish can be distinguished from brittlestars because the latter have flexible, snaky arms, while the former are shaped like the stars on the American flag. The larger the starfish, the more likely it hunts for a living. Lobsters and crabs of all types, with the exception of anemone crabs, feed both by scavenging and predation. Large crustaceans of any kind are not to be trusted with small fish or delicate, sessile invertebrates. Similarly, large snails are usually predatory, unless they have been sold specifically for algae control. Any of these invertebrates can be kept in an otherwise fish-only aquarium, assuming the fish won't pose a threat to them. They are not good choices for a minireef.

Photosynthesizers

A great many of the desirable invertebrates for a minireef manufacture their own food with the help of symbiotic algae (see chapter 5). Nearly all of these, with the exception of giant clams and a few types of coral, will also feed on brine shrimp, uneaten fish food, and even fish feces that happen to fall on them. In this way, they obtain important nutrients not supplied by their symbiotic algae. As a rule, it is not necessary to deliberately feed photosynthetic invertebrates, as long as food is being added to the tank now and then for other inhabitants. None of these invertebrates will do well with inadequate lighting, remember. Anemones all have symbiotic algae, but all of them do best with a weekly feeding of a small bit of fresh shrimp or fish. A piece the size of a bean is adequate for a 4-inch diameter anemone, measured when fully expanded. Increase the size of the food in proportion to the diameter of the oral disk for larger specimens.

Specialized Feeders

Many types of invertebrates sold by aquarium dealers have specialized food requirements that cannot be easily met by everyone. If you are considering purchasing an unfamiliar specimen, make sure you understand its feeding requirements before you commit. Some mollusks, for example, require live corals as food. The beautiful harlequin shrimp feeds only on the tube feet of living starfish! With diligence, such critters can be accommodated, but make sure you are up to the task.

Water Changes

A water change is accomplished by removing some water from the aquarium and replacing it with freshly prepared seawater. As mentioned in chapter 2, you can use a hose to siphon water to a bucket, or include a built-in drain in the aquarium tank. As long as you remove some water and replace it, it does not matter how you go about it. Few maintenance procedures are more important, especially for a beginning saltwater aquarist, than carrying out a regular schedule of partial water changes. My recommendation is to remove 20 percent of the water each month, or 10 percent every other week, and replace it with prepared synthetic seawater. You can use at least some of the old water for cultivating aquarium foods, if that is your preference. Most people just dump it into a sink or flush it down the toilet.

Always remember to shut off all pumps, skimmers, and especially the heater before removing water from the tank. When the water level drops, leaving an operating pump high and dry will produce excessive wear on the impeller. Leaving a plugged-in heater high and dry is a major no-no. If the heater comes on when dry it will get hot enough to blister your skin, and may also crack, allowing water to come into contact with the wiring when it is once again submerged.

If you have convenient access to natural seawater, use it whenever possible. Some hobbyists elect to disinfect freshly collected seawater by adding chlorine, allowing the water to sit overnight, and then removing the chlorine with a commercial dechlorinator. Others simply allow the water to stand, covered, in a cool, dark place for a week or so. In some large coastal cities, seawater can be purchased from service companies who collect, disinfect, and deliver the water to your door. You can even have bottled seawater shipped to you, although many people find the cost prohibitive.

Whether you mix up your own seawater from dry salt or use the genuine article, the replacement seawater must be similar to the water in the tank in terms of its temperature, specific gravity, and pH before you add it. Otherwise, you'll cause a sudden, major fluctuation in tank conditions that may be stressful to the inhabitants.

Mixing Synthetic Seawater

If stored covered in a cool, dark place such as a garage, a basement, or a closet, natural or synthetic seawater keeps indefinitely. You can mix up a large batch to have available as needed. Slightly more than 2 cups of dry mix will make 5 gallons of seawater. Buy your salt mix in large quantities to save on its cost. It keeps indefinitely if stored in a tightly sealed container away from moisture. Dampness promotes caking, which makes the mix hard to measure and causes it to dissolve more slowly. Too much moisture can also cause chemical changes in the mixture, in which case it should not be used at all.

Salt mix will dissolve more quickly if you add the mix to a pail of water, rather than putting the mix in the bottom of the bucket and adding water. Agitating the mixture also speeds solution. If you use only a 5-gallon bucket for mixing, you can drop in a small air diffuser and bubble air into the bucket overnight. For larger amounts, consider making a mixing tank. See chapter 2.

Water Tests

The most important aspect of maintaining your saltwater aquarium is keeping water conditions within rather narrow limits. It's easier to do than it sounds. Make regular tests, then make adjustments. I like to say, "Test, then tweak."

Neglecting maintenance to the point that you can only bring the water conditions back in line by doing a massive water change virtually guarantees problems. This, nevertheless, is a common mistake. Regular testing and small corrections are the way to go. Buy good test kits, use them on a regular basis, and keep a written record of the results. Keeping a record lets you compare your results with previous tests, in order to refine your technique. You may learn, for example, that your aquarium evaporates about 10 ounces of water every week, consistently. Knowing that, you can just add 10 ounces of fresh water every Friday and dispense with testing until the next water change.

How to Test

Always follow the manufacturer's instructions when using test kits or instruments. Rinse out vials thoroughly with fresh water after each use, and store them upside down to drain. Rinse the vial with the water to be tested prior to each use. Use a cup or medicine dropper to remove water from the tank for testing. Do not dip the test vials into the water. *Take care never to spill test chemicals into the aquarium.* Do not store test chemicals for more than a year, and keep them out of children's reach.

Salinity

By determining the specific gravity of a water sample, the salinity can be calculated if the temperature is also known. To estimate salinity with a hydrometer:

1. Measure the specific gravity of your aquarium with a hydrometer and write down the observed reading.
2. Find the temperature column in Table 1 that is closest to the temperature of your tank.
3. From the temperature column in Table 1, note the conversion factor.
4. Add this to the specific gravity reading from step 1. *Note*: In Table 1, two leading zeroes are omitted from the conversion factors. Thus, for a specific gravity reading of 1.0260 at 75 degrees F, the density is 1.0282. (1.0260 + 0.0022).
5. Now look up the density in Table 2 and determine the corresponding salinity (use the value closest to the measured value).

Table 1: Conversion of Specific Gravity to Density by Temperature Correction

	Temperature (degrees F)					
Obeserved hydrometer reading	**68**	**70**	**72**	**73**	**75**	**77**
1.0170	10	12	15	17	20	22
1.0180	10	12	15	17	20	23
1.0190	10	12	15	18	20	23
1.0200	10	13	15	18	20	23
1.0210	10	13	15	18	21	23
1.0220	11	13	15	18	21	23
1.0230	11	13	16	18	21	24
1.0240	11	13	16	18	21	24
1.0250	11	13	16	18	21	24
1.0260	11	13	16	19	22	24
1.0270	11	14	16	19	22	24
1.0280	11	14	16	19	22	25
1.0290	11	14	16	19	22	

Table 2: Conversion of Density to Salinity

Density	Salinity	Density	Salinity
1.0180	25	1.0245	33
1.0185	25	1.0250	34
1.0190	26	1.0255	34
1.0195	27	1.0260	35
1.0200	27	1.0265	36
1.0205	28	1.0270	36
1.0210	29	1.0275	37
1.0215	29	1.0280	38
1.0220	30	1.0285	38
1.0225	30	1.0290	39
1.0230	31	1.0295	40
1.0235	32	1.0300	40
1.0240	32		

Nitrogen Compounds

Aquarium shops sell test kits for all the nitrogen compounds of interest: ammonia, nitrite, and nitrate. Regardless of the brand or particular compound being tested for, all these test kits involve adding chemical reagents to a sample of aquarium water and noting the color change that results. Different brands vary in both the reagents and the procedures, so make certain to follow the instructions that come with the kit. As described in the discussion of biological filtration in chapter 3, nitrate testing should always give close to the same result unless a major change, such as the addition or removal of a fish, has occurred. Many experienced hobbyists don't bother testing for nitrate unless they have altered something and want to know if the change has affected the tank. Beginners, though, should test at least once a month for nitrate and keep a record of the tests. After about a year, you should find that the monthly test yields pretty much the same number each time, which is what you want. Testing for ammonia and nitrite need not be done routinely, but always perform a test for both if you are having problems with fish or invertebrates. If you find either compound in the water, take action as described in the "How to Tweak" section in this chapter.

pH

Testing for pH simply involves placing a measured amount of aquarium water into a vial and adding the test chemical. Comparing the color to a color scale gives the pH.

Alkalinity

Testing for alkalinity involves taking a measured sample of seawater and adding acid to it while observing for a change in pH. Test kits provide a pH indicator that changes color at the appropriate point. The kit will also come with a standard acid solution that you add drop by drop, swirling the contents of the vial after each addition. Keep count of the drops; when the color changes abruptly, stop. The number of drops added can be converted to alkalinity by using the information given on the box, with each drop corresponding to a certain number of meq/L. Alkalinity may be expressed in several different ways, depending on which test kit you choose. Make sure you know in what units your test results are expressed. You may have to convert to meq/L. If so, see the information on page 25.

Calcium

You will need to monitor the calcium concentration of the aquarium if you have a minireef. Corals, soft corals, clams, snails, scallops, shrimps, crabs, starfish, sea urchins, and even some algae all need calcium for their skeletons. Adding a calcium supplement, in amounts determined by regularly testing the water, is important for these invertebrates. Calcium supplementation appears to have little benefit for fish, apart from its role in keeping the alkalinity at a normal level. The use of a calcium additive is a good example of a situation in which supplementation makes sense. (See my general comments about additions to the aquarium water on page 27.) Seawater normally contains about 400 ppm of calcium, but the aquarium will be just fine with a little more or a little less than this.

The calcium test is carried out in much the same way as the alkalinity test. You add reagent by drops to a water sample and keep count of the drops required to cause a color change. The chemicals and calculations are slightly different from the alkalinity test. Follow the specific instructions provided with the test kit you select.

Various brands of calcium additives can be found on the market. Follow the recommendations of your dealer, use the product as directed, and test the water to make sure the calcium level is where it's supposed to be. If you like the results, stick with that product. If not, try another. Carry out this sort of experimentation before adding anything especially delicate or demanding to the aquarium.

Phosphate

A phosphate concentration above the limit of detection for most test kits (about 0.05 to 0.10 ppm) will usually be noted in tanks that grow a lot of algae. The growth may range from a slimy film on the glass to green water. Algae itself generally is not harmful unless it is growing over and smothering a sessile invertebrate, but it can spoil the aesthetic appeal of the aquarium. Indeed, many fishes, such as tangs and angelfishes, like to nibble on green filamentous algae all day. You only need to test for phosphate if you are trying to limit algae growth for some reason. The kits are relatively expensive, and the test a bit tedious to perform correctly, thus I don't recommend routine phosphate testing for the average hobbyist.

Copper

Even the most scrupulously maintained aquarium is not immune to problems. Sooner or later, you will probably have to deal with a case of saltwater "ich" (*Cryptocaryon*) or "coral fish disease" (*Amyloodinium*) on your fish. Effective treatment for a fish infected with either of these microscopic parasites requires transferring it to a separate tank and adding a carefully measured dose of copper to the water. I will discuss in more detail the diagnosis and treatment of these two nuisances in chapter 9. You will purchase a copper test kit along with the copper treatment. As with other tests, you place seawater in a vial and add a chemical, then observe the color change. Copper tests are annoyingly difficult to read at the low levels required for medicating fish. You may need to get the advice of other family members to obtain a consensus on the reading. Hopefully, your maintenance program is so well managed that copper is needed only rarely.

How to Tweak

In this section, I explain what to do when a water test shows a deviation from normal. As a rule, this will involve making small alterations, "tweaks," to the water chemistry. You do this by doing a partial water change, by altering maintenance procedures, or by adding a supplement.

Nitrogen Compounds

Bacteria living in the live rock and live sand process nitrogen compounds and render them nontoxic to the aquarium inhabitants. As a result, ammonia or nitrite will not be present in the water as long as the bacteria are doing their job. Finding ammonia or nitrite during a routine test is always cause for concern. Determine the source of the problem immediately. Common possibilities are:

- The aquarium contains too many fish.
- Uneaten food or a dead animal is decaying in the aquarium.
- An antibiotic has been added to the aquarium, killing the nitrifying bacteria.
- There is a shortage of oxygen.

Responses to these problems are:

- Remove some fish.
- Find whatever is decaying and siphon it out.
- Remove the antibiotic with activated carbon filtration or by doing a large water change.
- Repair the pump, or add additional powerheads to increase the water movement (water movement improves the dissolved oxygen content of the aquarium).
- Lower the temperature by installing a chiller (cooler water holds more oxygen than warmer water does).

Thus, "tweaking" in the case of ammonia or nitrite involves determining the source of the problem that is affecting the nitrifying bacteria and taking steps to restore normal biological filtration. As long as the beneficial bacteria are performing normally, there should be no ammonia or nitrite present. Once you have dealt with the problem, do a 50 percent water change to reduce the ammonia or nitrite concentration immediately.

I have not provided suggestions for tweaking nitrate. In the case of this compound, the purpose of the test is to verify that all is normal. If the nitrate level has risen abruptly since the last test, reread the discussion in chapter 3 to determine if such a rise is to be expected. If you cannot figure out why the nitrate has increased, you may want to discuss your findings and the recent history of your aquarium with a dealer or other knowledgeable person. If you think the level of nitrate is too high, go ahead and change some water to lower it. You can never harm your tank by doing a partial water change.

pH

Consistently low pH may mean that carbon dioxide is accumulating. Check by removing a quart of water and aerating it vigorously overnight. Then check the pH of both the tank and the aerated water. If the pH of the aerated water is 0.2 units or more above that of the tank, there is too much carbon dioxide in the water. Increased water movement may be all that is needed to alleviate the problem. Keeping the aquarium at the correct pH can also be accomplished by adding a buffering agent to increase and stabilize the pH. A host of products are offered in aquarium shops for this purpose. Products that help both to buffer pH

Nitrate Anomaly Checklist

When your water tests indicate that nitrate is accumulating faster than normal, ask yourself the following questions to determine if there is a good reason for this anomaly.

- ☐ Did I carry out the test correctly? (It is always worth doing a confirming test before looking for other explanations. If the test result is correct, move on to the other considerations.)
- ☐ Have water changes been done on the proper schedule? (If not, do a water change sufficient to lower the nitrate level to the value you expect, then check again next month.)
- ☐ Has a new fish or invertebrate been added? (If so, the change in nitrate is expected, and you should consider this to be the new "normal" reading. If not, look further.)
- ☐ Have I used a new type of fish food? (If so, the result is essentially the same as in the case of adding new specimens. The new food is providing either more or less protein or is more easily decomposed than the old food.)
- ☐ Have I fed more of the regular fish food than normal? (Feeding too much will always increase nitrate. Do a water change and cut back on the feeding.)
- ☐ Has a fish or invertebrate died or been removed for another reason? (You would expect this to lower the nitrate level, not increase it.)
- ☐ Is everyone present and accounted for? (Small invertebrates, such as snails, can sometimes die in an out of the way spot. Decay will add nitrate.)
- ☐ Have I added anything out of the ordinary? (Medications, antibiotics in particular, may disrupt bacterial activity and alter the nitrogen balance of the aquarium.)

If you put a checkmark next to any of these questions, you may need to take appropriate action, such as changing water or removing a decaying corpse. If all your answers are "no" you may want to have a knowledgeable aquarist friend or your dealer help you figure out what's going on. It is important to remember that nitrate accumulation from adding specimens or additional food can be offset by also adding more live rock or increasing the size of the filter system.

and to maintain alkalinity may be the most useful. Seawater mix brands vary in the degree to which they maintain the correct pH when mixed. Always check each new batch of seawater before using it. If you find consistent problems, try a different brand. The use of aragonite sand as part of the substrate can also aid in pH stabilization. As the sand slowly dissolves, ions are released, helping to maintain alkalinity and calcium levels. When the alkalinity of the aquarium is at natural seawater level or above, the pH tends to remain within a suitably narrow range. Test pH weekly and use one of the buffering additives if you need it. Make sure to follow the directions on the package.

Alkalinity

Using a chemical additive such as limewater, adding aragonite sand to the substrate, or adding calcified water from a calcium reactor will all increase the alkalinity. There is seldom a need to *lower* alkalinity, which happens naturally. See the discussion of calcium maintenance in the next section for additional information.

Calcium

Several techniques exist for keeping the calcium content of the aquarium close to that of natural seawater, 400 mg/L:

- A simple approach is to add limewater to the aquarium. Limewater is a saturated solution of lime in water. It is prepared by adding dry calcium oxide to distilled water, allowing the mixture to settle, and decanting. Use about 2 teaspoons of lime per gallon of water. Some undissolved powder should always remain at the bottom of the container. Calcium oxide is sold in supermarkets for making lime pickles, or you can purchase it at an aquarium shop. Use limewater to replace all evaporated water. Limewater is alkaline. Take care that additions do not drive the pH above 8.6 for more than a few hours at a time. An hour after adding a dose, check the pH. You can quickly determine how much limewater to add on a routine basis after a few weeks of testing and keeping records. After that, just add the correct amount on a regular basis, and check the calcium concentration only once a month. Make up only enough limewater for a week's supply. After that, atmospheric carbon dioxide will cause much of the lime to precipitate out of solution as insoluble calcium carbonate.
- In aquariums with a deep substrate layer of aragonite sand, the pH will be very low in the anoxic regions of the substrate. The low pH causes aragonite to dissolve and return both calcium and carbonate ions to the water. Depending on the makeup of the community of organisms in the aquarium, pH/alkalinity/calcium balance may be maintained through this process alone, and no limewater or other additives will be required. Other aquariums may need additional help in the form of limewater additions as described above, or through enhancement of the aragonite dissolution process by means of a calcium reactor. This is simply a device that allows acidified distilled water to be passed over a layer of aragonite, which results in the enrichment of the water with calcium and carbonate ions. This water, which would be considered extremely "hard" by freshwater aquarists, is then added to the aquarium to replenish evaporation. This technique avoids the drawbacks inherent in the use of limewater, but requires more work. You can purchase a calcium reactor or make one yourself. It is basically a plastic pipe with screen at one end to keep the aragonite from falling out. Water is added at the top of the reactor, flows through the aragonite, and is collected below. Using distilled water to which a small amount of vinegar (about a tablespoon per gallon) has been added is most effective in dissolving the aragonite.

The Importance of pH

It is important to remember that the relationship between alkalinity and calcium concentration is reciprocal. Increase one, and the other decreases. In the early days in the life of your aquarium, you may have to experiment, with repeated testing, to determine the best way to keep pH, alkalinity, and calcium within their proper ranges. Of greatest importance to the inhabitants of the aquarium is the pH, influencing as it does not only the respiration of fishes, but also the deposition of calcium carbonate by several varieties of invertebrates. If the pH is correct, the specimens can get along with less than the natural amount of dissolved calcium. Therefore, if calcium reactors, limewater, and so forth are beyond your interest or abilities, focus on maintaining the correct pH.

Phosphate

If you find that you have excessive phosphate, there is no satisfactory way to merely tweak things back into line. You need to reduce the inputs of phosphate. Most often, this means purifying your tap water as described in chapter 2. Other possible sources are salt mix and tank additives. Try switching brands of salt mix, and stop using the additives for a while and note the effect.

Copper

Copper is used only to treat parasitic diseases. To be effective, it is important to maintain the copper level in your treatment tank.

Equipment Maintenance

Everything wears out, of course, but you can prolong the life of your aquarium equipment by properly maintaining it. Doing equipment maintenance at the same time as your monthly water change makes sense.

Follow these steps when performing routine maintenance on your equipment:

1. Turn off the tank lights and unplug the fixture. If you use metal halide lighting, the lamps will need to cool down before you can move the fixture, or you risk damaging them. Besides, a dark tank will make the whole operation less stressful for the fish.
2. Check the light fixture for any signs of salt accumulation or corrosion. Remove any that you find with a cloth dampened in freshwater. If corrosion is developing, try to determine why, and take steps to prevent further damage. Aquarium lighting is designed to

resist corrosion and to protect electrical connections from saltwater, so corrosion is a sign of improper installation or a break in the water barrier. Any damage you discover to the electrical parts of the lighting system should be repaired immediately by a skilled person. Such damage may pose an electrical or fire hazard. Problems such as this are rare with good-quality lighting equipment.

3. With a damp cloth, carefully clean dust and salt spray from the lamps themselves, as any accumulation will reduce the light output. You may need to remove the lamps from the fixture in order to do this effectively, depending on the fixture design. Many fixtures also have a plastic sheet that protects the lamps. The side of the plastic nearest the water surface invariably becomes spotted from droplets of seawater. Again, carefully clean the plastic with a damp cloth, ensuring that the maximum light output reaches the aquarium.
4. Shut down the filter pump and protein skimmer.
5. Wipe clean the outer surfaces of all the plumbing fittings and hoses. You'll be surprised at how much dust they can accumulate.
6. Clean dust from any portion of the pump intended to ventilate the pump housing. Dust clogging the vents reduces the cooling effect and makes the pump wear out faster. Pump designs will differ from brand to brand. Follow the manufacturer's directions for cleaning and maintenance of the pump. If it's time to replace the impeller, do so now.
7. Disassemble the protein skimmer and clean it in the sink, in accordance with the manufacturer's recommendations. Usually, the skimmer collection cup and the tube through which foam rises toward the cup will accumulate scum on their inner surfaces

When to Perform Protein Skimmer Maintenance

Only a process of trial and error will permit you to set a schedule for skimmer maintenance, since every tank is different. Your skimmer may get thoroughly dirty in a week's time, while mine may take 2 weeks to lose efficiency because of accumulated gook. Try to develop a schedule that results in a relatively constant amount of foam being collected per unit of time. If you keep track of the volume each time you empty the collection cup, you will note that a sparkling clean skimmer produces mostly thick, dark green foam, while a yucky skimmer collects a lot of diluted foam and water. You want to strive for a happy medium between these two extremes during the course of a month. Because skimmer designs vary, and because the amount of organic matter in the water also varies from one aquarium to another, it is impossible to give exact guidelines for properly adjusting the skimmer. You'll get the hang of it after a month or two. Skimmers that use air diffusers may need these replaced every month or so, as they will become clogged with mineral deposits. Similarly, air supply lines can develop mineral deposits where air and water come into contact. These deposits will eventually close off the line. They can be easily removed by soaking in a weak solution of vinegar and water, scraping with a toothpick, and rinsing in freshwater before reconnecting.

that interferes with efficient skimming. After a good cleaning to remove the scum, you'll find that foam "climbs" up the tube more readily, and you may need to adjust the skimmer to prevent overflow.

8. Always remember to unplug the heater before removing any water from the tank. Submersible heaters are usually trouble-free, but it doesn't hurt to check for any damage as a regular part of your maintenance routine.

The "Hurricane Effect"

Every now and then a hurricane or typhoon strikes near a reef. Wind-driven wave surges break off tons of coral fragments. The hurricane also stirs up debris, making the water turbid. Despite the apparent devastation, a hurricane actually benefits the reef ecosystem by flushing out accumulated sediments and pruning the coral. Coral fragments that happen to land in a suitable spot often resume growth as if nothing happened, creating a potential site for a new patch of reef to develop.

You probably won't want to be breaking off coral fragments in the process, but creating a "hurricane" in your saltwater aquarium now and then is not a bad idea. Sediment tends to accumulate on any horizontal surface in the aquarium, just like dust gathers on your furniture. Periodically removing it not only helps keep the aquarium looking tidy, but also exposes the area under the sediment to light, providing algae and sessile invertebrates a clean spot on which to grow.

Start by gently manipulating the top inch or two of the substrate layer with your fingers. This will stir up a lot of debris. If there are algae mats growing on the surface of the substrate, break them up with your fingers. Much of the sediment and algae will settle on the rocks and corals, but don't worry about that at this point.

Disconnect one of your powerheads. Holding it in your hand underwater, direct the outflow from the powerhead toward your live rock while someone else plugs the cord back in. Play the water jet over the surfaces of the rocks and corals, blasting debris into suspension where it can be picked up by the filter system. While the "hurricane" rages, you can also temporarily run a canister filter to "polish" the water by trapping most of the suspended sediment inside the filter. Try to sweep as much sediment as possible toward the front of the tank. With only a little practice, you will learn to operate the powerhead like a leaf blower to move piles of debris. When this step is completed to your satisfaction, turn off all pumps and allow suspended debris to settle out. Wait an hour or more. Overnight is fine. Then, use a length of hose to siphon as much of the sediment as possible off the bottom of the tank. Collect it in a bucket and discard. Top off the aquarium with freshly prepared seawater. *Voilà*! Hurricane complete, minireef freshly scrubbed. Doing this once or twice a year works wonders for keeping the aquarium looking healthy and sparkling.

Record Keeping

Having written records makes spotting trends a cinch. By looking back over your notes, you can often detect and correct problems in time to avoid serious consequences. I like to use a loose-leaf binder to hold both aquarium records and things like equipment manuals or instructions for test kits. I drop the binder in a large plastic bag and store it under the aquarium. The bag keeps out water damage, and the binder is there whenever I need it. Keeping everything organized and handy makes it easier to stay on top of maintenance and testing. If you have to scour the house for your notes and equipment, you are less likely to do what's required at the proper time. In time, your record book will become an irreplaceable history of the aquarium and its inhabitants. Because each aquarium is unique, there is no good substitute for a complete, conscientiously kept record book.

Record the following information about your aquarium in the log:

- Date
- Tests performed and results
- Anything added and amount
- Temperature
- Specific gravity and calculated salinity
- Amount of water changed
- Species and size of fish or invertebrates added
- Incidents of death or disease, treatments and results
- Any comments or observations you think pertinent

In appendix A I've provided a log sheet you can use. Use a digital camera to record the appearance of the aquarium and incorporate the pictures into your log. You might want to have step-by-step pictures showing the aquarium in various stages of construction. Each time you add a new fish or invertebrate you create another photo opportunity. Don't overlook using the camera to record problems. You can even e-mail a picture of a sick fish to someone helping you with the diagnosis.

Digital technology also makes possible continuous monitoring and recording of some important aquarium parameters, along with control of lighting and other equipment. Temperature, salinity, and pH are relatively easy and inexpensive to monitor in this way. Unfortunately, other chemical tests, such as for ammonia or nitrite, are difficult and costly to automate, but having the other tests automated saves time for carrying out manual testing. Aquarium monitoring and control devices will usually interface with your PC to permit display of information in various forms, such as a graph of pH versus time. You can find sources for such equipment on the Internet or in hobby magazines.

Family Aquarium Maintenance Routine

Aquarium chores can be easier and more fun to do if you set up a routine and have different family members share the work. Younger children can check the thermometer and report the tank temperature each day. Even a very small child can feed the fish with a little adult supervision. Water testing, because of the chemicals involved, should be reserved for older kids or adults. Changing water is mostly a lift-and-carry chore, so anyone physically able can easily do it. Only older children and adults should mix seawater and check it for pH and salinity before use. Everyone can take part in observing and recording interesting behavior exhibited by the fish, or the rate at which a soft coral spreads across the rocks.

Aquarium Maintenance: When, What, and Whom

Daily:

Task	Person Responsible
Feed the fish	
Check and record temperature	
Check for evaporation and top up tank	
Check and record salinity	
Check and empty skimmer cup	

Weekly:

Task	Person Responsible
Feed brine shrimp or another live food treat to tank	
Reset brine shrimp hatchery, if used	
Test and record pH	
Test and record nitrate	
Test and record alkalinity	
Add pH/alkalinity boosting additive	
Test and record calcium concentration	
Add limewater or other calcium additive	
Clean algae off front tank glass	
Clean dust and salt accumulation from cover glass or lighting lenses	

Monthly:

Task	Person Responsible
Change 20 percent of tank water	
Disassemble and clean protein skimmer, replace air diffusers if used	

continued

Aquarium Maintenance (continued)

Quarterly:

Task	Person Responsible
Inspect all equipment for wear or damage	
Disassemble and clean filter components	
Siphon debris from refugium or other areas of accumulation, if needed	
Check fish foods for freshness and replace as needed	
Check hardness of RO product water, replace membrane as needed	
Inspect RO particle prefilter, replace cartridge if excessively dirty	

Semiannually:

Task	Person Responsible
Hurricane descends upon captive coral reef!	
Check powerhead impellers for wear, replace as needed	
Check RO unit for chlorine in waste water, replace carbon filter if needed	

Annually:

Task	Person Responsible
Replace all fluorescent lamps	

As Needed or per Manufacturer's Recommendations:

Task	Person Responsible
Replace metal halide and/or LED lamps	
Replace pump seals	

Should We Hire an Aquarium Maintenance Service?

By now you surely realize that an aquarium can be a lot of work—relatively easy, routine work, but still work. With most of us multitasking these days, you may find the time available for aquarium maintenance limited. If this proves to be the case, you are better off to hire a maintenance service than to neglect caring for the aquarium. Problems with saltwater tanks tend be cumulative, and only regular maintenance, especially carrying out routine water changes, can prevent this. Many independent aquarium dealers offer maintenance plans. I suggest asking three different maintenance firms for a bid on keeping your tank looking great for a year. Generally, you pay a flat monthly rate, based on the size of the aquarium, but arrangements can vary widely. Sometimes the quoted rate only includes the labor, and the first bill arrives with a surprise additional charge for materials used, such as salt mix.

Getting a Maintenance Quote

Get these specific details in writing before you commit.

- How often will maintenance be done?
- Is the rate per month or per visit?
- Are materials included or billed separately?

Questions to Ask the Maintenance Service

- Do you have examples of supplies and costs? You'll want to compare this with retail pricing.
- Does the maintenance service operate independently, or is it associated with a shop? Often, the latter situation is better, since independent maintenance service operators have to buy materials and equipment from dealers. Many aquarium wholesalers will not sell to individual maintenance services because they usually cannot meet minimum order requirements. For you, that means the maintenance service must mark up the materials, and you end up paying more. Shops that provide maintenance also have a vested interest in providing top-quality specimens and equipment to maintenance customers, since doing otherwise only creates hassles for the maintenance staff, not to mention customer service problems for the manager.
- Is the maintenance service bonded and insured? Always evaluate any potential maintenance service with the thought in mind that you will be allowing strangers access to your house, perhaps when you are away. The best services are bonded and insured, which protects you against various kinds of mishaps. Consult an attorney if you are unsure about any potential contract in this regard. For example, if the maintenance worker is injured in your home, who's responsible?
- Will the maintenance service replace fish or invertebrates that die while the aquarium is in their care? Some do, most do not. Usually, this depends on whether you own the tank outright or lease it from the service. Leased tanks are usually a turnkey deal. You are paying for the total display and its care, and any losses are replaced by the maintenance crew. If you own the tank, the fish keeper is much like a lawn service, providing basic labor only. Fish, other critters, and supplies are your responsibility. Only you can decide which approach is better. Either way, hiring a maintenance service may make it possible for you to have a larger, healthier, and better-cared-for aquarium than would be the case if you go it alone.

What You Now Know . . .

- Setting up a quarantine tank is a smart move.
- The procedure for setting up a saltwater aquarium consists of a series of logical steps.
- Setting up a large aquarium involves the same basic steps as for a smaller one but requires more planning because mistakes may be difficult to rectify.
- During the first few weeks, your aquarium will be somewhat unstable. Take care to monitor it closely during this period.
- Accommodating an anemone or corals requires upgrading the lighting.

Chapter 9

Keeping Your Fish and Invertebrates Healthy

What's Inside . . .

- Learn why problems happen with aquarium fish and invertebrates.
- Learn when to medicate a sick fish.
- Learn about common ailments and what to do about them.
- Learn how to avoid diet-related problems.

Fish can survive severe wounds. I've even seen one swimming on the reef with about a third of its body missing. Something bit off the tail and most of the rear flanks, but apparently missed the vital organs. Fish can jump out of the tank, lie on the carpet covered in lint, become almost crispy from drying out, and then recover completely after being returned to the aquarium. So how come fish are susceptible to disease in the aquarium, and why do they often fail to recover? In my view, hobbyists do not recognize the early warning signs of common diseases. Further, when a problem is detected, hobbyists are unprepared to take immediate action. Delaying treatment vastly increases the likelihood that the disease will prove lethal. More than 90 percent of aquarium deaths could probably have been avoided.

Why Problems Happen

Sometimes chance events are responsible for aquarium troubles. A power outage, for example, can wreak havoc if it extends beyond a few hours' duration. Most problems, however, develop because the aquarium owner has not taken proper precautions. It is important to remember that problems are most likely to occur within 2 weeks after the fish is purchased, and established fish may exhibit problems shortly after some major stress has occurred in the display aquarium.

Fish Precautions Checklist

Omitting any of these steps will increase the chance of a disease outbreak in your saltwater fish.

- ☐ Make wise selections at the pet store, as discussed in chapter 2.
- ☐ As recommended in chapter 2, choose fish that fit into your aquarium design, instead of buying on impulse.
- ☐ Avoid fish that do not appear in perfect health in the dealer's tank. See chapter 2 for symptoms to look for.
- ☐ Stay away from the troublesome species mentioned in chapter 4.
- ☐ Make sure you have the proper food in regular supply if you choose a fish with special needs in this regard. Check the species accounts in chapter 4 for feeding suggestions.
- ☐ Without exception, new fish must be placed in a quarantine tank, as mentioned in chapter 7, for 2 weeks prior to introducing them into an established display aquarium. Assume that all new fish require rest, freedom from harassment, appropriate food, and possibly medication before they are ready for the display tank.

When Should I Medicate the Fish?

Two microorganisms, one a free-swimming protozoan and the other a form of algae, are responsible for almost all of the disease problems with which saltwater aquarium hobbyists must cope. Either one can be easily treated with copper medication, but novice hobbyists may fail to notice the telltale signs of this disease until it is too late. Don't make this common mistake! Hours are important. *Amyloodinium*, the rogue algae, attacks the gills, robbing the fish of the ability to efficiently extract oxygen from the water. For reef fishes accustomed to water supersaturated with oxygen, this is extremely stressful. Debilitated by stress, the fish may next be attacked by *Cryptocaryon*, the protozoan parasite. Inexperienced hobbyists often notice nothing out of the ordinary until little white dots, the reproductive stage of *Cryptocaryon*, appear on the fish. Only at that point do they begin treatment. By then, the gills have been so eroded by *Amyloodinium* that recovery is impossible. So the treatment fails.

I have observed cases in which the fish recovered without treatment. In none of these instances did the fish ever show the rapid, shallow breathing, suggesting that the gills remained intact. Other than carrying the white spots, and occasionally scratching themselves on the rocks, these fish exhibited no symptoms. On the other hand, fish that develop the gasping behavior invariably die if untreated.

Copper Treatment

Adding copper ions to the aquarium water is the only effective treatment for *Amyloodinium* and/or *Cryptocaryon*. The treatment must be carried out in a separate hospital tank if the display tank contains invertebrates (copper is toxic to invertebrates). Your quarantine tank can double as a hospital tank, which is another good reason for having one. See chapter 7 for

Invertebrates Precautions Checklist

Omitting any of these steps will increase the chance of a problem developing with your invertebrate specimens.

- ☐ Make wise selections at the pet store, as chapter 2 recommends.
- ☐ Choose invertebrates that fit into your aquarium design, instead of buying on impulse (see chapter 2).
- ☐ Avoid invertebrates that do not appear in perfect health in the dealer's tank. (Check out the species descriptions in chapter 5 for information on the normal appearance of some common varieties.)
- ☐ Stay away from the troublesome species mentioned in chapter 5.
- ☐ Make sure you have the proper food in regular supply if you choose an invertebrate with special needs in this regard. Chapter 5 gives feeding recommendations for the species discussed.
- ☐ Be sure to have adequate light for photosynthetic species. Suggestions for lighting equipment can be found in chapter 2.
- ☐ Never purchase an invertebrate that is obviously damaged. This applies particularly to anemones.

information on setting up a spare quarantine/hospital tank. A 10 percent solution of copper sulfate is added to the water at the rate of one drop per gallon. This will result in a copper concentration of 0.02 to 0.03 ppm. The concentration of copper should be adjusted to the midpoint of this range, 0.025 ppm. You do this by testing, adding another drop or two of solution, and testing again until the correct point is reached. Maintain the copper concentration in the hospital tank for 2 weeks beyond the disappearance of all symptoms. The fish should look healthy and feed normally. Many copper medications are available commercially. Different brands may have different dosing recommendations. My suggestion is to add the dose suggested on the label, and then keep testing and tweaking to make sure the correct copper level is kept constant.

Some hobbyists maintain fish-only aquariums with a constant therapeutic copper level, on the mistaken assumption that this will prevent disease outbreaks. This is the wrong approach for two reasons. First, if it is necessary to keep copper in the water all the time to keep the fish from getting sick, the basic aquarium design is flawed. Second, long exposure to copper may render the fish more susceptible to disease, not less so, because copper suppresses the immune system.

Other Problems Requiring Medication

The problems described in this section are fortunately rare, but they require appropriate treatment if they do crop up in your aquarium. It is always best to administer treatment in a separate quarantine/hospital tank.

Warning Signs of *Amyloodinium* and *Cryptocaryon*

Any fish that exhibits the following warning signs should be treated at once.

- Rapid, shallow fanning of the gill covers
- Stays in an area of high water movement near the surface
- Behaves lethargically
- Appears to be struggling to swim
- Displays tiny white dots on the fins or body surface
- Scrapes against tank decorations as if trying to dislodge something from the skin

Brooklynella

Brooklynella so commonly affects imported wild clownfish that it is often called "clownfish disease." Clownfish infected with *Brooklynella* become listless and refuse to eat. They may show gasping behavior as with *Amyloodinium*. Characteristically, they produce so much mucus that they appear to be sluffing off layers of skin. Commercial preparations containing formalin and malachite green are an effective treatment for *Brooklynella*; copper is ineffective. Clownfish should be treated immediately upon discovery of the problem, which usually manifests itself within a day or two after the fish arrive in the retail shop. Hatchery-produced clownfish are seldom affected by *Brooklynella*.

Ichthyophonus

Ichthyophonus is a fungus infection that sometimes strikes marine fish. It affects internal organs and may be evident only when the fish's behavior becomes unusual. Fish may refuse to eat and develop abdominal swellings. This problem is incurable, but can be diagnosed by a veterinarian if you feel you need to know the cause of a specimen's loss.

Other Parasites

Saltwater fish get all sorts of flukes, worms, and crustacean parasites both internally and externally. These problems are rare, although a reading of the hobbyist literature might lead you to suppose otherwise. A hobbyist is seldom able to treat these foes effectively. Professional help will usually be required to determine not only the identity of the parasite, but also an appropriate treatment. Internal parasites are, for all practical purposes, untreatable. Fish debilitated by parasites should be euthanized.

One common external worm parasite is easily treatable. It's known as the *black spot disease* of tangs. The parasite is a flatworm that burrows under the fish's skin. The fish looks as though it had been dusted with ground pepper. Yellow tangs often develop this problem; their coloration makes an infestation especially obvious. A dip in a bucket of seawater containing a commercially available solution of picric acid is an effective remedy. Most of the time, the dealer treats infected fish before they are put on display, because fish showing the black spots will be avoided by customers. Nevertheless, the problem can develop in the aquarium. Catching the tangs in order to medicate them is the biggest challenge.

Bacterial Infections

Treating a bacterial disease in a saltwater fish requires identification of the causative bacteria, antibiotic sensitivity testing, and appropriate dosage with antibiotics in a timely manner. Because of these complicated procedures, attempts by hobbyists to treat bacterial infections usually fail. Antibiotic preparations available in aquarium shops are likely to be inappropriate for the disease they purport to treat. They may be too stale to be effective. They are often supplied in a form inadequate for proper administration. Worst of all, the dosage recommendations given on the label are usually insufficient to effectively treat the disease. For example, manufacturers recommend that the medication merely be added to the water. Doing so won't achieve a high enough dose inside the fish to do any good in most cases. Improper use of antibiotics by hobbyists should also be discouraged because you may select antibiotic-resistant strains of bacteria. Subtherapeutic dosage and lack of targeted administration offers the perfect scenario for developing resistance. If you have ruled out the common problems mentioned previously, it is possible that a bacterial infection has attacked your fish. Sometimes, but not always, fish respond to bacterial disease with skin inflammation, open lesions, and swelling of the body. You'll want to consult a veterinarian in such cases. The vet can determine for certain what is causing the problem and recommend treatment. The infected fish should immediately be isolated in a quarantine/hospital tank, pending the vet's diagnosis.

Injuries

Fish wounded in a territorial battle or one that is injured after jumping out of the tank, may need some first aid. If the wound is small, and not near the gills, merely painting the damaged area with a swab dipped in a mixture of one part ordinary mercurochrome and one part aquarium water usually prevents infection. Minor damage heals in a week or two. More extensive injuries may require using a broad spectrum antibiotic, such as nitrofurazone or its chemical relatives. This antibiotic is added to the water at a dosage of 50 mg per gallon every other day for a week. Check with a veterinarian before attempting this treatment.

Diet-Related Problems

Three commonly recognized conditions are probably diet-related, although no one knows for certain. One has a name; the others do not.

- Head and lateral line erosion, abbreviated HLLE, appears to be caused by an insufficiency of some important food component, possibly vitamin C. It most often develops in fish that eat a large amount of vegetable matter, such as tangs, angelfishes, and damselfishes. Areas around the face and gill covers lose coloration and take on an eroded appearance. The fish looks and acts debilitated, although it may feed and swim normally. Eventually, the problem spreads along the lateral line, giving the whole fish a decidedly wretched look.

HLLE can be prevented, and in mild cases reversed, by feeding a diet rich in natural seaweeds. Vitamin supplements added to the food have also been recommended. If you plan on keeping any of the fish susceptible to this problem, make sure you avoid trouble by feeding them correctly.

- Another problem develops mostly in lionfish or other large predators that eat other fish. A steady diet of goldfish creates a nutritional deficiency, possibly of essential fatty acids found in saltwater fish oils. The symptoms are an inability to swallow, and in extreme cases, to open the mouth at all. There is no cure. Prevention, by feeding goldfish only now and then and saltwater fish most of the time, is the only solution to this problem.
- Similarly, fish that feed on crustaceans will develop mouth and jaw dysfunctions if they are fed exclusively on freeze-dried krill. Once again, the problem seems to be irreversible once the fish is noticeably affected. Feed fresh seafood in as wide a variety as you can obtain, and save the krill for occasions when there is nothing else in the house and the weather is too miserable to go out shopping for fish food.

Lymphocystis

Lymphocystis is fortunately a not too common problem in either fresh- or saltwater fish. It is usually not debilitating except in extreme circumstances. The problem is manifested in the appearance of white or grayish, cauliflowerlike growths on the fish's body and fins. Often an injury becomes the site for development of the lesions. Thought to be the result of a viral infection, lesions may grow in size and can impede normal behavior. For example, a large lesion on a pectoral fin can prevent the fish from swimming properly. On the lips, the lesions interfere with feeding. Surgery is an effective, but risky therapy. This is another problem best avoided rather than solved. Angelfish and butterflyfish appear to be especially susceptible. Infected fish should be isolated and the tank they were in emptied and thoroughly disinfected with bleach solution. If you keep other fish in any tank exposed to the virus, you run the risk of infecting them as well. There have been reports that lymphocystis can be successfully treated with antiviral drugs available only by prescription, so any attempt at treatment will require a professional consultation.

Invertebrate Parasites and Diseases

Thankfully, few parasite and disease problems plague invertebrates. Of course, invertebrates are subject to an array of problems in the ocean. Just listing all the parasites and pathogens would fill another book. But for some reason not too much goes wrong this way in the aquarium. About the only commonplace problems are parasitic snails, predatory flatworms, and some unusual, incurable coral diseases.

Parasitic snails in the family Pyramidellidae often colonize on giant clams, feeding on the mantle and weakening the clam. Usually, the parasites are brought in on the clams themselves, which are raised in seawater systems fed by the ocean. As mentioned previously in the discussion of giant clams, the best way to rid a tank of these pests is to place a neon wrasse in it. Two species are available, *Pseudocheilinus tetrataenia*, the four-lined neon wrasse, and *P. hexataenia*, the six-lined version. Besides performing a valuable service, these little wrasses are colorful, harmless to other fish, and small in size.

The flatworm pest is *Convolutriloba*. It feeds on various kinds of corals and soft corals and can reproduce to plague proportions if left unchecked. It is readily identified by the distinctive three-pointed tail. Reddish-brown in color, each worm is about ¼ inch in length. If discovered, remove the coral that the worms are feeding on immediately, as they often enter the aquarium on the coral itself. A small butterflyfish can be added to the aquarium to feed on the flatworms, or the coral can be dipped momentarily in fresh water. Use distilled water to which enough alkalinity supplement has been added to raise the pH to that of the aquarium. Make sure the water is close to the same temperature as the tank.

Two diseases of corals are wreaking havoc on some reefs, and they occasionally appear in aquarium corals. They are called *white band* and *black band disease*. Either one is distinguished by the characteristically colored ring of destruction progressively creeping across the coral head, eventually destroying it. Black band disease is poorly understood, but some scientists think the corals are being stressed by increased ocean temperatures due to global warming. This hypothesis argues for maintaining stony corals at the cooler end of the acceptable temperature range. White band disease is an infection, probably caused by a variety of agents. In aquarium corals, its appearance may result after an injury. Injured tissue may be siphoned away, and the affected specimen isolated, but either of these conditions is seldom curable.

Special Considerations for Reef Tanks

The inability to add any kind of medication to a minireef poses a special set of problems. First, if one fish has symptoms, all the fish in the aquarium should be removed and treated. *Amyloodinium* and *Cryptocaryon* both possess a free-swimming stage that spreads from one fish to another. Since it takes a few days for symptoms to appear after the parasite has attached to the fish's gills, you cannot know if asymptomatic fish are infected. For this reason alone, a separate tank that serves as a hospital is indispensable, and it should be of approximately the same capacity as the display tank.

Catching fish from a well-decorated and long-established minireef can be a real challenge. Too many hiding places exist among the pieces of rock. If you try chasing the fish down with a net, you run the risk of injuring delicate invertebrates by bumping them, snagging them with the net, or knocking them off their perch on the live rock. Various kinds of fish traps appeared on the market shortly after this problem became apparent to reef enthusiasts. Like trapping any sort of animal, fish hunting can be a frustrating effort. Fish are naturally wary of anything unusual placed in the tank, and it may take a while for them to throw caution to the wind and enter the trap to get at the bait. By the time this happens, the disease may have progressed dangerously. Another obstacle may be that sick fish often refuse to eat. Any bait, therefore, will be ineffective. Your best bet is to turn off the tank lights, wait an hour or so, and then stealthily go after your quarry with a net. If you are right-handed, you should hold the net stationary with your left hand and use your right to steer the fish toward it. It can also be helpful to drain some water out of the tank into a bucket, reducing the swimming room. You can also remove particularly delicate specimens to the bucket while you are working in the tank.

Minireef keepers who desire to include fish in the aquarium should limit themselves to a few carefully selected individuals. The fish should be quarantined; this cannot be over-emphasized. Make sure the minireef has matured for several weeks before the fish arrive. Take every precaution to maintain good water quality and to provide an appropriate diet. If you follow these rules, you can have fish in a minireef with minimum risk of having to remove them for treatment.

Frequently Asked Questions

Scan these questions to find answers to some common health problems. Knowing these answers now can help make you better prepared for future problems or to prevent them.

Soon after I brought a new fish home, there was an outbreak of parasites in my aquarium. Did the new fish bring disease into the tank?

Since you did not quarantine the new arrival before placing it in the display tank, there is no way to know if the fish was diseased to begin with. The organisms that cause parasitic infestations are always present in water that has held fish, so you may indeed have introduced a new strain to which your existing fish have not developed natural resistance. This is always a problem when combining fish from widely different habitats in the same tank. On the other hand, new arrivals may develop an active infestation due to the stress of accommodating to their new circumstances. There may be territorial aggression from the established fishes. The new fish is already weakened from the stresses of capture and shipment, even the short trip from the dealer's tank to your home. Just as a new fish can bring in new pathogens and parasites, so too can a new fish quickly develop problems from pathogenic organisms in the new aquarium that the fish has never encountered before. Once a problem takes hold in the disadvantaged new arrival, disease can easily spread to the other inhabitants of the tank.

I medicated my aquarium according to the directions on the package, but several fish died anyway. Did the medication harm my fish?

If you followed the package directions, the chances that you added too much or too little medication are slim. More likely, you simply did not notice the disease condition in time to save all the fish. Especially in the case of *Amyloodinium*, several days may pass with the fish exhibiting only rapid opercular movements. By the time other symptoms appear, much damage has been done to the fish's gills. Always examine each fish carefully each time you feed them. Any one that seems to be gasping for air should be cause for concern.

I need to medicate a fish that is in a tank with numerous invertebrates, but I don't have a hospital tank. What should I do?

Since you cannot medicate with the invertebrates present, the only option is to either move the fish or move the invertebrates. Effective treatment usually requires about 2 weeks. It is often easier in such cases to move the invertebrates, since they require less in the way of accommodations than fish do. Lacking a separate tank, you can use a plastic trash can outfitted with an air diffuser and heater as a temporary home for your invertebrates. The best arrangement, however, is to have a waiting hospital tank to which the fish can be removed for treatment.

I've heard about problems associated with copper building up in the aquarium. Is this really a concern?

Once again, when the display tank instead of a hospital tank is used for copper treatment, problems crop up. Yes, copper medications are readily absorbed by the dead corals, shells, coral rock, and sand (anything composed primarily of calcium carbonate) used to decorate the tank. At a normally high pH, the copper compounds remain insoluble and pose no harm. Should the pH fall too low, however, copper will dissolve out and its concentration in the water may become many times the therapeutic level. Not only will this be lethal to invertebrates, but enough copper can be present to harm the fish as well. If a hospital tank is used, this problem is avoided by using only plastic objects for hiding places for the patient. Copper is removed or eliminated after the treatment is complete simply by discarding the medicated water from the tank.

So using my main tank for a hospital is not a problem unless I let the pH fall too low?

Technically, yes, but why take this chance unnecessarily? Also, absorption of the copper by calcium carbonate decorations will alter the copper concentration of the water, making it far more difficult to maintain a constant, therapeutic level. This may result in the treatment being ineffective, since the copper has to be in the water, not sequestered chemically in the rocks, in order to kill parasites.

My dealer recommended antibiotics for treating my fish, not copper. Do I need a hospital tank in this case, too?

Absolutely. The effects of adding antibiotics to a display aquarium are unpredictable. Some invertebrates may be adversely affected. Another major risk is damage to the beneficial bacteria that are crucial for waste processing. Reread the salient parts of this chapter concerning antibiotic treatment. They are not effective against the common fish parasites responsible for the vast majority of home hobbyists' problems.

I have a hospital tank that I also use for quarantining new fish. Should I routinely treat new arrivals with copper? How about antibiotics or other medications?

The best approach is not to medicate unless there is a compelling reason. If the new fish is free of overt signs of problems, I recommend against any treatment. Often, simply a period of rest and respite from stressful conditions is all that new fish requires to settle down and adjust to aquarium life. That said, always observe new fish very carefully for signs of disease and treat immediately if you suspect a problem. One reason a quarantine tank is so valuable is that it permits close daily inspection of the fish housed in it. In a big display tank, a new fish may hide under the rocks, making a daily checkup impossible without goading the fish from its hidey-hole, needlessly adding to its stress.

What You Now Know . . .

- The most common fish diseases are caused by two similar parasites and can be effectively treated with copper.
- For maximum effectiveness, all treatments for fish disease must be carried out in a separate tank.
- Saltwater fish unfortunately sometimes develop problems for which no cure is possible.
- Invertebrates are subject to fewer parasite problems than fish, and those they do have are easily dealt with.
- Medicating fish in your display tank is risky for several reasons.

Chapter 10

Your Aquarium as Part of the Family

What's Inside . . .

- Learn how to care for your aquarium on a daily basis.
- Learn what to do about your aquarium when you vacation.
- Learn how to relocate your aquarium.

Daily Care

The devil, as they say, is in the details. Perhaps nothing characterizes the outstandingly successful saltwater aquarist so much as daily attention to the little things going on in the tank.

On Vacation

I have heard far too many horror stories about disaster striking the aquarium while the family is away on vacation. If you plan on an extended stay, always arrange for a competent person to be your tank sitter. Ideally, this will be a friend or relative who is also an experienced saltwater aquarist. A second choice would be a trusted acquaintance who is good at following the detailed directions you will prepare for them. The third choice, and possibly the only one for many of us, is to hire a professional. Most aquarium dealers and maintenance services can arrange for temporary care.

Regardless of whom you choose, have a clear understanding of what is to be done and when. Provide written instructions, using the Tank Sitter Journal in appendix A as your guide. Customize the journal to meet your specific needs. Every aquarium is different, and an experienced caretaker will understand this.

Asking a friend for a favor, giving them a few vague guidelines—"Feed the fish every day and make sure the temperature stays right"—is a near guarantee of problems. Even with

Checklist of Daily Chores and Observations

If you find anything amiss, take prompt corrective action. I find it is better to check on the tank each evening when I arrive home from work, since I have time to do whatever might be required in the way of maintenance. In the morning, a cursory check is all that's needed. Check the temperature, and make sure everything is working. Feed the fish if you keep varieties that need multiple daily feedings.

- ☐ Feed fish according to their individual needs.
- ☐ Feed invertebrates according to their individual needs.
- ☐ Observe fish for unusual behavior or signs of injury or disease.
- ☐ Observe invertebrates for damage or signs of disease.
- ☐ Check and record tank temperature.
- ☐ Check for evaporation and add distilled water, RO water, or tap water as needed.
- ☐ Check and record salinity.
- ☐ Check protein skimmer and empty the collection cup as needed.
- ☐ Check filter elements for debris accumulation, obstructions, or clogging.
- ☐ Wipe salt spray, fingerprints, and dust from outer surfaces of aquarium and cabinet.
- ☐ Sit in front of the tank for a while and enjoy the color and movement.

professional care, however, the tank may not receive the same careful daily attention that you are able to give. Therefore, be prepared for a thorough inspection, and possibly a water change, on your return.

Before going on vacation, try to schedule your regular monthly tank maintenance. That way, the aquarium will be in the best possible condition before your departure. By the same token, avoid major overhauls and new introductions of animals or equipment just prior to your vacation. Most problems develop shortly after such changes occur, and you need to be around to deal with any that arise.

Relocating

If you have plans to move more than once in the next 2 years, I suggest you reconsider having a saltwater tank until you are in a more permanent location. After the initial setup about a year is required for the aquarium's miniature ecosystem to mature fully and begin to take on a desirable, natural look. Tearing everything down to move means that you will be starting from scratch again—almost. After a move, expect 6 months to elapse before the aquarium looks as it did before relocation. This will be true, by the way, whether you are moving the tank across the room or across the country. In the latter case, the only difference is the extra precautions you will need to take because of the extended time the fish and invertebrates will spend in transit. At some point, of course, you may have no choice but to relocate an established tank. Use these steps to make sure everything goes smoothly and is minimally traumatic for the aquarium.

1. **Locate and check out an aquarium dealer in the new town.** Perhaps your former dealer can make a recommendation, or you can ask around in one of the online chat rooms or post a notice on a hobbyist bulletin board. Once you've located one or more likely candidates, visit them when you are in town house-hunting. It may be possible to arrange for this dealer to receive and care for your fish and invertebrates while you are getting resettled. This will make the move far less traumatic for both you and the fish, because you can take your time getting the tank reestablished before the fish go back in. Even if the dealer is unable to provide fish boarding, you are still going to need supplies and fish food.
2. **Check to see if the dealer offers prepared seawater.** You're going to need enough to refill your tank. Having it ready and waiting will save time and trouble when you are most harried by the move.
3. **Make sure you can properly pack all the living components of the aquarium so they will survive transport.**

   Start by determining how many boxes you will need for all the critters. Fish and invertebrates are shipped to dealers in Styrofoam "fish boxes" about 20 inches square and 10 inches deep, enclosed in an outer carton of corrugated cardboard. Most dealers can supply you with these for a small charge, especially if you ask well in advance.

   If possible, purchase a "box liner" for each box. This is a square-bottomed plastic bag made to fit the Styrofoam box. Your dealer can also provide you with plastic shipping bags in assorted sizes. You'll need at least two bags of appropriate size for each fish, along with a handful of rubber bands. For larger invertebrates, such as individual corals, anemones, or shrimp, bag individually as for fish. Smaller critters, such as algae-eating snails, hermit crabs, and brittlestars can travel three to six to a bag. In all cases, the roomier the shipping bag, the better.

   It is better to place fish and invertebrates in freshly made saltwater if they will be in the bags more than 24 hours. A couple of days before you plan to pack up the tank, prepare a supply of seawater, making sure it is the same specific gravity, pH, and temperature as that in the aquarium. Otherwise, use water from the aquarium.
4. **Shut down all the equipment.**
5. **Dismantle everything.** This is a great time to thoroughly clean the filter pipes, protein skimmer, or other equipment.
6. **Pack up your equipment.** Clear plastic storage boxes work well for transporting aquarium equipment. They are impervious to water, won't leak in the trunk of the car, and allow you to find components easily when you set up the aquarium again.
7. **Remove any large, sessile invertebrates, such as corals or giant clams that have been placed on the live rock.** If you find the creature has attached itself, remove rock and all to a bag of seawater. Don't try to pry the organism off the rock, or you risk damaging it.

8. **Pack each such specimen in enough saltwater to cover, trap air in the bag, and close it with a rubber band.** Trapping air in the shipping bag provides a supply of oxygen. Doing this correctly takes practice. If you are right handed, hold the bag in your left hand, grasping it by the edge of the opening. In one smooth motion, quickly grab the top of the bag, gathering it shut and trapping air inside. Holding the bag now in the right hand, gently rotate it with your left to twist the top tightly closed. You should now have a twisted handful of plastic bag about 4 inches long in your right hand. Without letting the air escape, slip a rubber band over the twisted part. Bend the top of the bag double. Give the rubber band a full turn, so that one end is looped around the neck of the bag and the other is in your hand. Wrap it around the folded top, encircling several times to ensure a secure seal. When done properly, you can grasp the free end of the top of the bag and pull sharply to open it. The band will pop loose, but remain over the top of the bag instead of flying across the room or into your eye. This technique is best learned by watching someone demonstrate it, but with a little practice, you should be bagging like a pro.
9. **Once the bag is tightly sealed, enclose it in another bag of the same size, and similarly seal the top with a rubber band.** Double-bagging provides an extra measure of security against leakage. If you are shipping excessively spiny things, such as a branching coral or a lionfish, after double-bagging the animal, wrap the package in several sheets of newspaper and enclose the whole thing in a third, larger bag.
10. **Remove and pack the live rock.** Check each piece carefully for attached invertebrates, such as snails. Remove them for separate packing. Similarly, check to make sure a fish or shrimp is not hiding in a crevice in the rock. If so, it must be carefully coaxed out and given a shipping bag of its own. Live rock can be transported by wrapping it in newspaper or cheesecloth that has been saturated with seawater. This keeps the rock wet as well as providing some protection from damage caused by pieces jostling against each other. Pack the wrapped rock in a Styrofoam-lined box, using newspaper or packing peanuts between the pieces to keep them from shifting.
11. **Let the water settle.** When all the rock has been packed, the water left in the tank will be turbid from stirred-up debris. Let it settle a while before you begin catching the fish.
12. **One by one, catch the fish and mobile invertebrates and place them in their individual shipping bags.** You want each bag to contain enough saltwater to cover the animal. When the bag is of the correct size, the water will occupy about one-third of its volume and entrapped air two-thirds. When in doubt, choose a larger bag. As each bag is sealed, place it in a Styrofoam container. Position them so they won't roll around. If necessary, pack newspaper or foam peanuts around the bags.
13. **Take special precautions for fish that may bite through a plastic bag, for example, triggerfishes.** For these, take a plastic kitchen storage container large enough to hold the fish comfortably and drill it full of holes with a quarter-inch drill bit. After catching the fish, place it inside the container, which you have submerged in water in a shipping bag. Snap the lid on the container, secure the lid with a large rubber band, and seal the whole thing in the shipping bag, trapping air as previously described. This same treatment works well for moving extremely delicate invertebrates, such as fragile branching corals, which can even be suspended inside the food container with a strand or two of nylon fishing line. Fish that are easily panicked, such as jawfish, dartfish, and torpedo gobies,

can also be placed in a ventilated plastic food container before bagging. For this purpose, choose a container that is opaque or dark in color, to provide the fish an added sense of security. When all the critters have been caught and bagged and placed in their boxes, close the box liners with rubber bands, and place the lids on the boxes. Wipe any spilled water off the outside of the boxes and slip them into their cardboard cartons. Seal the cartons with packing tape and label each one as to its contents. If you are shipping the boxes by common carrier rather than hauling them yourself, be sure to cover up or remove any extraneous writing or old shipping labels. Clearly mark "TOP" and place arrows pointing up on all four sides. Hopefully, this will prevent the carrier from shipping them upside down, but don't count on it.

14. **Remove the sand bed and place it in manageable portions into plastic bags with a little water.** Pack these in Styrofoam, as well.
15. **Make note of the time.** Your livestock should not remain in the bags for more than 24 hours from the time you pack them. If the trip to the new location will take longer than 24 hours (including the time needed to set up the tank and get it ready for fish again) make prior arrangements with your dealer to fill the bags with pure oxygen. Pack everything as just described and take the boxes to the dealer. Open each bag and press out the entrapped air. Fill the bags with oxygen from the dealer's supply and reseal each one. If you have many bags and little time, you may want to arrange to have a small tank of oxygen at home when you pack up. Check with a home medical supply company for an oxygen tank, and make sure to follow all recommended safety precautions when working with it.
16. **Drain the remaining water from the tank, completely disassemble the components, and pack everything for transport.**

Ideally, your fish and invertebrates will arrive at their new home with a brand-new tank set up and waiting for them. It will have been running for a couple of weeks, and all you have to do is unpack the shipping containers and place everything in the tank. The old tank you gave to your nephew or sold on eBay. Alas, in this less than perfect world, you will probably need to reuse the old tank and equipment. In that case, plan to stay up most of the evening to get everything set back up and running properly.

Start by mixing a batch of new seawater, giving it the maximum time possible to dissolve before it is needed. (Having this done a day or two before you arrive is a big help, if you can swing it. If you can buy seawater already prepared, go for it.)

Repeat the process you followed to set up the aquarium the first time. Remember to check that the support is level in both directions, and that adequate electricity and water are close to the tank location. Once the equipment is in place, start stocking the tank. Place the live sand in the tank first, followed by the live rock. Neither one needs to be acclimated. Just unpack and add to the tank. As you go, add saltwater to keep everything covered. Finally, place the plastic bags in the tank and acclimate everything as described in chapter 7. When the fish and invertebrates have all been released,

start the filtration system. Make any needed adjustments to the pump, protein skimmer, or heater. Add water to fill the tank to the top. When you are satisfied that all is well, leave the lights off and allow the aquarium to sit undisturbed for the next 24 hours. The next day, perform all routine water tests and log the results. I suggest testing for ammonia, nitrite, and pH every other day for the next week. If nothing amiss shows up in that time, you're home free. Correct any problems according to the guidelines suggested in chapter 7. Turn on the lights and set the timer. Begin your usual maintenance routine. Watch carefully for signs of disease in the fish, and for the latent appearance of damage on corals and other sessile invertebrates. Sometimes, injuries sustained during transport do not manifest themselves as tissue damage until a few days have passed. If nothing out of line turns up after 2 weeks, you can relax. The aquarium should be back to normal after a month, and in 6 months should be well-established once again.

What You Now Know . . .

- Daily care for the aquarium includes checking water conditions, feeding the animals, and simply observing the tank for anything unusual.
- When you are going to be away from home for awhile, it is best to arrange for someone to care for your aquarium.
- Relocating an aquarium involves considerable work, but it will go smoothly if you follow the recommendations in this chapter.

Appendix A

Useful Resources

How to Use This Appendix

I have repeatedly emphasized the importance of record keeping to the long-term success of your home aquarium. Jotting down important facts about your tank takes only a few minutes but can save you hours of trouble later. I've provided some forms you can photocopy that will simplify starting a record book.

Equipment and Maintenance Record

Make sure you save the technical data on your equipment. You may need this for warranty service, and you'll definitely want to remember required maintenance dates.

Item	Brand	Model	Date Installed	Date Serviced	Comments

Specimen Acquisition Record

I like to create a separate sheet for each individual fish or invertebrate specimen that I purchase. Include all the info you have about this individual, so you won't need to look it up later if a problem arises or something interesting happens.

General Information
Common Name
Scientific Name
Date Acquired
Length at Acquisition (mm)
Dealer
Dealer Address
Dealer Phone
Preferred Foods

Special Requirements

Observation Journal

Date	Observations Made

Tank Sitter Journal

Provide your tank sitter with your contact information, complete care instructions, and instructions for how to fill in the logs and perform water tests routinely.

Contact Information	Telephone Number
Cell Phone	
Emergency Contact Info	
Hotel Phone	

Hotel Name	Dates There

Reminders and Special Instructions:

Feeding Record

(Place checkmark in Fish Fed and Invertebrates Fed columns after they've been fed.)

Date	Fish Fed	Food Used	Invertebrates Fed	Food Used

Maintenance Record

Date	Maintenance Performed

Water Tests

Date	pH	Nitrate	Alkalinity	Calcium	Other (specify)

Fish Hospital Record

Don't go to all the effort to set up a hospital tank and isolate a sick fish unless you are willing to follow a treatment schedule. Maintaining the proper dosage of medication is essential for effective treatment.

Date

Species

Diagnosis

Treatment Journal

Date	Action Taken	Result

Saltwater Aquarium Log

Start one of these for each tank you own on the day you set it up. Accurate records of your water tests let you spot trends and take action before deviations from optimum conditions become dangerously large. Keeping your theme in mind will help in making future purchases for the tank.

Tank Info

Tank Number
Tank Size
Date Set Up

Theme for this tank:

Water Tests

Date	pH	Alkalinity	Specific Gravity	Temp. (°F)	Nitrate	Other Tests Performed and Results

Water Changes

Date	Water Change Performed

Appendix B

Saltwater Fish and Invertebrates Sold for Home Aquariums

This is of necessity only a partial list of genera. The total number of species in the aquarium trade is in the hundreds. Those mentioned here are the most common and widely available ones. Every genus mentioned in this book is included in the list, along with some other common ones that you are likely to encounter in shops and in the literature. I have included some regularly imported varieties that may present significant challenges in aquarium care, and are therefore not recommended for the novice.

Acanthurus—a type genus of the Acanthuridae family, commonly known as tangs or surgeonfish, marine fishes that are usually herbivorous grazers.

Acropora—a large genus of branching corals that are typically found in brightly lit waters with high oxygen concentration and heavy turbulence; several species are popular with aquarists owing to the ease with which they can be propagated.

Actinodiscus—a genus of corallimorphs or disc anemones, often cultivated by aquarium hobbyists; numerous forms and colors exist and the organisms are easy to propagate.

Actinopyga—a common genus of sea cucumbers found in shallow waters in the tropical Atlantic and Caribbean, popular with aquarists because of their habit of burrowing into the substrate.

Adamsia—a genus of sea anemones often found living on the mollusk shell occupied by a hermit crab.

Alcyonium—a typical soft coral without an axial skeleton, popular with aquarists.

Alpheus—a genus of snapping shrimps, including *Alpheus armatus*, found in association with the anemone *Bartholomea annulata* in the tropical Atlantic.

Alveopora—a genus of stony corals in the Poritidae family, generally considered difficult to maintain in the aquarium.

Amblycirrhites—a genus of hawkfishes found in both the Atlantic and Pacific regions.

Amblygobius—Indo-Pacific gobies that typically shelter in the burrow abandoned by another animal, although the most popular aquarium species, *A. rainfordi*, is found near coral heads.

Amphiprion—one of two genera of pomacentrid fishes that associated with sea anemones; also called clownfishes, they are popular with marine aquarium hobbyists.

Amplexidiscus—a genus containing a single species of corallimorph, commonly referred to as the "giant mushroom polyp"; it is capable of feeding on small fishes that become trapped in its stubby tentacles.

Anampses—a genus of small tropical wrasses, family Labridae, that feed on benthic invertebrates and are generally difficult to maintain in aquariums.

Anthelia—a genus of colonial soft corals with feathery tentacles that are popular with marine aquarists because some species pulse rhythmically.

Anthias—a genus of marine fishes in the sea bass family, Serranidae, that form large schools and feed on plankton in open waters.

Aplysia—a genus of opisthobranch mollusks, commonly called "sea hares."

Apogon—a type genus of the family Apogonidae, or cardinalfishes, these schooling tropical marine fishes are largely nocturnal; popular aquarium species are found near coral reefs.

Apolemichthys—a small genus of reef-dwelling marine angelfishes.

Astraea—a genus of tropical marine gastropods often imported for algae control in the aquarium.

Astrangia—a genus of star corals, stony corals usually forming small colonies and encrusting rocks, so named for the appearance of the skeletal cups from which the polyps protrude.

Astropecten—an Indo-Pacific sea star with large, distinctive spines at the edges of the arms; it feeds at night on small bivalve mollusks.

Balistapus—triggerfish, family Balistidae, including the large, aggressive undulated trigger, *B. undulatus*.

Balistes—triggerfish, family Balistidae, including the Atlantic queen trigger, *B. vetula*.

Balistoides—triggerfish, family Balistidae, including the clown trigger, *B. conspicillum*.

Bartholomea—the genus that includes the sea anemone commonly known as the curlicue anemone, owing to the spiral arrangement of stinging cells around its tentacles.

Blastomussa—a genus of stony corals with large polyps and interesting coloration that make them popular with minireef enthusiasts.

Blennius—a type genus of the Blennidae family, small tropical marine fishes that are often imported for minireef aquariums.

Briereum—a genus of soft corals that lack skeletal elements and which encrust solid substrates, popular with minireef enthusiasts due to their rapid growth rate.

Calcinus—a genus of hermit crabs popular with hobbyists because of their small size and bright coloration, usually added to the marine aquarium for algae control.

Calliactis—an anemone of the Atlantic and Gulf coasts of the United States that is often found attached to the mollusk shell inhabited by a hermit crab.

Calloplesiops—comet groupers, sea basses with nocturnal habits and flowing fins; has been propagated successfully in the aquarium.

Catalaphyllia—a single species, *C. jardinieri*, is called "elegance coral" by minireef enthusiasts; its range is restricted to the Coral Sea near Indonesia.

Caulastrea—trumpet coral, a stony coral of easy culture in marine reef aquariums.

Caulerpa—macroscopic green marine algae often cultivated in hobbyist aquariums, and characteristically possessing an upright, leafy portion arising from a runner that grows over or through a substrate; worldwide in distribution.

Centropyge—dwarf marine angelfishes, with approximately fifteen species imported for the aquarium trade; moderately easy to keep, requiring a diet rich in vegetable matter, these fish often spawn in hobbyist tanks but to date have not been successfully reared to maturity.

Chaetodon—a type genus of the butterflyfish family, Chaetodontidae, a marine group found only in association with coral reefs; a few species make good aquarium specimens, although the majority do not adapt well to captive conditions.

Chelmon—a popular marine species, the copperband butterflyfish, *C. rostratus*, feeds on small invertebrates with its elongated snout, while its orange-and-white banded pattern helps it blend into the branching corals among which it feeds.

Chromis—marine pomacentrid fishes that typically live in large shoals and feed on planktonic organisms plucked from the water column; several species are regularly imported and may be successfully maintained in a suitable aquarium.

Chrysiptera—the popular orange-tailed blue damselfish, *C. cyanea*, is but one species in this pomacentrid genus.

Cirrhilabrus—social wrasses, family Labridae, marine fishes that are usually found in small shoals consisting of a single, dominant male and several juvenile males and females; numerous, brilliantly colored species are popular with advanced hobbyists.

Cirrhipectes—Indo-Pacific blennies, family Blennidae, characterized by a row of cirri on the nape, often found on surf-swept ridges among algae or branching corals; herbivorous species are suitable for minireef aquariums.

Cladiella—an alcyonarian type of soft coral frequently maintained by minireef enthusiasts.

Clavularia—several species of encrusting, stoloniferan soft corals that are readily propagated in a minireef aquarium.

Clibanarius—marine hermit crabs of the tropical Atlantic and Caribbean, the most popular species is the tiny blue-leg hermit, *C. tricolor*, kept in marine tanks for algae control.

Condylactis—a tropical sea anemone from the Atlantic and Caribbean region, typically found in grass beds or near coral reefs, and regularly imported for the aquarium.

Conus—a genus of tropical gastropod mollusks capable of delivering a poisonous sting.

Corallina—one of many genera of red marine algae having a calcified skeleton.

Coris—tropical wrasses, family Labridae, that are popular with marine aquarium hobbyists due to the gaudy coloration of the adult males; many species are imported.

Cryptocentrus—watchman gobies, marine fishes often found in association with certain species of alpheid shrimps.

Ctenochaetus—bristletooth surgeonfishes, family Acanthuridae, imported primarily from Hawaii and valued for their propensity to consume filamentous algae.

Cymopolia—calcified tropical marine green alga with a skeletal structure resembling a string of beads, and bearing tufts of green, photosynthetic filaments at the ends of the strands.

Cynarina—a solitary stony coral that lies on sandy or muddy substrates and adapts well to the minireef aquarium.

Dardanus—tropical marine hermit crabs imported from Hawaii and the Indo-Pacific, and maintained primarily for their beautifully colored appendages; *D. megistos*, the Halloween hermit, has bright orange and black stripes, for example.

Dascyllus—several widely available damselfishes are placed in this genus from the Indo-Pacific region.

Dendrochirus—dwarf lionfishes, family Scorpaenidae, seldom over 6 inches in length; they feed mostly on crustaceans.

Dendronephthya—spectacularly colored soft corals that are challenging to maintain in the aquarium because they feed primarily on unicellular marine algae.

Diodon—porcupinefishes, family Diodontidae, with spiny skins and the ability to ingest water or air to inflate themselves, making them difficult for a predator to swallow.

Discosoma—a genus of false corals often imported for minireef aquariums.

Dolabrifera—sea cats; opisthobranch gastropods with an internal shell, included in marine aquariums for algae control.

Echinaster—a common sea star of the tropical Atlantic and West Indies often imported for the marine aquarium; predatory on bivalve mollusks and other sessile invertebrates.

Echinometra—rock-dwelling sea urchins sometimes imported for algae control in the aquarium.

Entacmaea—bubble-tipped anemone, a host for many species of clownfishes and the one most readily maintained under aquarium conditions.

Erythropodium—a soft coral with large, flowing polyps and a reddish-colored, rubbery skeleton that grows over solid surfaces.

Escenius—Indo-Pacific blennies, the most commonly imported species of which is *E. bicolor*, the orange and black bicolor blenny.

Euphyllia—a genus of stony corals, four species of which are popular with minireef enthusiasts because of their unusual tentacle shapes and ease of care.

Favia—a stony coral with individual corallites arranged like the cells of a honeycomb.

Favites—a stony coral similar to, and frequently confused with, *Favia*.

Forcipiger—long-snouted members of the butterflyfish family popular as aquarium subjects because of their hardiness.

Fromia—small sea stars popular with minireef enthusiasts because of their bright coloration and nonpredatory habits.

Galaxea—a stony coral characterized by massive, usually dome-shaped colonies with individual corallites forming raised bumps on the surface.

Gobiodon—coral gobies, tropical fishes from the Indo-Pacific region that live among the branches of various hard and soft corals and are amenable to hatchery production.

Gobiosoma—sharp-nosed gobies, fishes from the tropical Atlantic and Caribbean, including the neon goby, *G. oceanops*, and other popular aquarium species; several can be commercially produced through aquaculture.

Gobius—a type genus of the goby family, Gobiidae, characteristically with the pelvic fins fused to form a sucker-like appendage for holding on to solid surfaces.

Goniastrea—a stony coral, family Faviidae, with large, hexagonal corallites forming a hemispherical colony.

Goniopora—a genus of poritid stony corals, often imported but seldom successfully adapted to aquarium care.

Gramma—small sea basses of the tropical Atlantic and Caribbean frequently kept in aquariums because of their bright coloration, non-aggressive temperament, and hardiness.

Halichoeres—marine wrasses, many species of which are adaptable to aquarium care.

Halimeda—macrophytic green marine algae with a calcified skeleton consisting of flattened or plated disks attached to one another at the edges.

Heliofungia—plate coral, a stony coral with a rounded, biscuit-shaped skeleton and long tentacles often tipped in pink; it is a bottom-dwelling species capable of slow movement across the substrate and is sometimes confused with a sea anemone; difficult to maintain unless provided with bright illumination and appropriate water conditions.

Heniochus—pennant butterflyfishes, found in the Indo-Pacific and unlike other members of their family living in schools and feeding on planktonic organisms in midwater.

Herpolitha—slipper coral, a bottom-dwelling, mobile stony coral with an elongated skeleton rounded on either end.

Heteractis—a genus of tropical anemones of the Indo-Pacific, at least three of which are host to anemonefishes, and which are often kept in aquariums although they are difficult to maintain successfully.

Hippocampus—seahorses, comprised of some thirty species distributed worldwide in shallow seas.

Hippopus—a genus of giant clams, regularly produced by aquaculture and maintained in minireef aquariums.

Holocanthus—large marine angelfishes of the tropical Atlantic and Caribbean.

Hydnophora—horn coral, a stony coral, usually bright green, that is popular with reef aquarists because of the ease with which it may be propagated.

Isaurus—Indo-Pacific colonial anthozoans of the order Zoantharia, often maintained in marine aquariums.

Labroides—cleaner wrasses, family Labridae, found in the Indo-Pacific and often imported for the aquarium because of their habit of removing parasites from other fishes; they do not adapt well to captivity.

Lebrunia—the antler anemone, an anthozoan of Florida and the Caribbean characterized by two types of tentacles, one resembling the antlers of a deer; sometimes imported for the aquarium; although beautiful, it can deliver a painful sting.

Leinardella—large marine wrasses, the only species frequently imported is *L. fasciata*, the harlequin tusk fish, boldly striped in red and white, with blue teeth.

Lemnalia—a thinly branched, arborescent soft coral without visible skeletal elements, commonly called "spaghetti coral."

Leptogorgia—sea whips, gorgonian anthozoans often found in areas of lowered salinity, and sometimes maintained successfully in marine aquariums, they are more common in temperate than tropical waters.

Limia—file shells, bivalve marine mollusks often maintained in aquariums because of the bright red mantle; they require large amounts of planktonic food organisms.

Linckia—sea stars, typically with smooth, rounded arms, often kept in marine aquariums for their bright blue, lavender, and purple coloration, though somewhat challenging to maintain successfully.

Liopropoma—miniature sea basses, family Serranidae, generally found only in deep water; though expensive, they are sought after by aquarists because of their bright coloration and hardiness.

Litophyton—soft corals popular with marine reef hobbyists because of the ease with which they may be propagated.

Lobophyllia—a stony coral with large polyps that is adapted to living on the sea bottom in shallow water, it is often included in marine reef aquariums.

Lobophytum—a soft coral with lobed branches, knowns as "devil's hand" or "leather finger coral" in the aquarium trade.

Lutjanus—snappers, marine fishes of family Lutjanidae; harvested for table fare, smaller specimens are often kept in large aquariums.

Lybia—a genus of marine crabs of aquarium interest because of their habit of carrying small sea anemones in the chelae which are used as mops to collect particulate food and may also be brandished in defense.

Lysmata—marine shrimps frequently collected for the aquarium and popular with hobbyists because of their red coloration, sociability, and cleaning behavior.

Lytechinus—a sea urchin found in sea grass beds that often carries bits of debris in an effort at camouflage.

Macrodactyla—Indo-Pacific sea anemone often collected and exhibited as a host for clownfishes, it is generally hardy in the aquarium.

Macropharyngodon—marine wrasses, family Labridae, often collected because of their bright coloration, but seldom successfully adapted to the aquarium because of their specialized feeding habits.

Meiacanthus—fanged blennies, family Blennidae, of the Indo-Pacific, several species are imported for aquariums.

Millepora—fire coral, hydrozoans that produce a calcified skeleton superficially similar to that of scleractinians, contact with the living tissues of which can produce a painful, burning sensation accompanied by inflammation and swelling; found in all seas.

Montipora—a small-polyped, branching stony coral that is easily propagated in the aquarium by means of cuttings.

Mopsella—colorful gorgonian soft corals, often found in deep water, that are regularly imported and adapt well to the marine aquarium if provided with sufficient food.

Muraena—moray eels, family Muraenidae, nocturanal marine fishes with an elongate body and strong dentition, they prey on other fishes and large invertebrates; easily maintained in a large aquarium.

Murex—a genus of snails, worldwide in distribution, often predators of other mollusks, that are sometimes kept in marine aquariums because of their attractively ornamented shells.

Naso—large acanthurid fishes of the Indo-Pacific, in which males often develop a protuberance from the center of the forehead; suitable only for large aquariums, but regularly imported.

Nemateleotris—fire gobies, family Gobidae, popular with marine aquarium enthusiasts becauuase of their bright coloration and propensity to hover motionless in midwater; they feed on a variety of planktonic organisms.

Nemenzophyllia—a stony coral in which the individual polyps are disc-like, about an inch in diameter, and arrayed along the top edge of a wall-like skeletal structure, often displayed in minireef aquariums.

Neocirrhites—one of several genera of hawkfishes, family Cirrhitidae, including the popular flame hawkfish, *N. armatus*.

Novaculichthyes—dragon wrasses, family Labridae, imported for the marine aquarium as juveniles with striking green, white, and black coloration, adults reach about a foot in length.

Odontosyllus—one of several general of stomatopod crustaceans commonly known as "mantis shrimp" becauase their raptorial appendages resemble those of the praying mantis insect.

Ophioblennius—an Atlantic genus in the family Blennidae, the most commonly imported species of which is *O. atlanticus*, the red-lipped blenny.

Ophioderma—a common genus of serpent stars collected in the Atlantic.

Opisthognathus—a type genus of the jawfishes, family Opisthognathidae, of which the only common aquarium species is the yellow-headed jawfish, *O. aurifrons*.

Oreaster—sea stars typified by the large, West Indian species *O. reticulata*, which is predatory on sessile invertebrates.

Ostracion—a type genus of the boxfish family, Ostraciidae, marine fishes in which the body is enclosed in a shell made of interlocking bony plates instead of scales.

Oxycirrhites—a genus of hawkfishes, family Cirrhitidae, the most popular member of which is the longnosed hawkfish, *O. typus*, from the Indo-Pacific.

Oxymonacanthus—the only commonly imported species of this genus, *O. longirostris*, the orange-spotted filefish, seldom adapts to the aquarium because it normally feeds only on coral polyps.

Paguristes—the scarlet hermit crab, *P. cadenanti*, is often imported from the tropical Atlantic for algae control in the marine aquarium.

Pagurus—hermit crabs, typified by the small species, *P. longicarpus*, from the temperate Atlantic, often added to marine aquariums as scavengers.

Palaemon—glass or rock shrimps, often sold for fresh- or brackish-water aquariums or as fish food.

Palythoa—zoanthids, colonial anthozoans of which several species are collected for the aquarium, consisting of several short polyps connected at the base by a sheet of tissue.

Pavona—lettuce corals, delicate stony corals in which the polyps protrude from a thin, leaf-like skeleton and that will reproduce themselves in the marine aquarium.

Penicillus—green seaweed known as "merman's shaving brush," arising from the substrate as a short stalk topped with a thick, round tuft of filaments.

Pentacta—*P. pygmaea*, the red-footed sea cucumber, is imported for the aquarium from the Gulf of Mexico; it feeds on microorganisms strained from the water.

Periclimenes—one of several shrimps that live in association with sea anemones in tropical environments worldwide, they are often imported and make good aquarium subjects.

Petrochirus—hermit crabs from the tropical Atlantic, often collected as small specimens, but becoming large and too aggressive for most aquariums.

Phymanthus—shallow-water sea anemones from tropical Florida and the West Indies, known as "flower anemone" in the aquarium trade.

Physogyra—stony corals with bubble-like tentacles on the polyps that are easily maintained in minireef aquariums.

Plagiotremus—scale- or flesh-nipping blennies that mimic harmless species in order to get within striking range of their prey, sometimes exhibited as aquarium curiosities.

Platax—batfishes, family Platacidae, tropical marine species of which only one is commonly successful as an aquarium pet, and it may outgrow a smaller tank.

Plectorhynchus—sweetlips, tropical marine fishes with bold coloration and unusual swimming movements that unfortunately seldom adapt to a diet of aquarium foods.

Plerogyra—bubble coral, a stony coral popular with minireef hobbyists because of its unusual bulbous tentacles.

Plexaura—gorgonian soft corals often imported for minireef aquariums.

Pocillopora—a large genus of small-polyped stony corals that can be readily propagated from cuttings.

Podochela—a spider crab found in the Gulf of Mexico and collected for the aquarium because it characteristically covers its carapace with living invertebrates and algae collected from its immediate surroundings.

Pomacanthus—large marine angelfishes of the family Pomacanthidae, in which the juveniles are colored much differently from the adults, they are popular but demanding aquarium subjects.

Porites—a type genus of the large stony coral family Poritidae; many species are known, most rather challenging to maintain in a marine reef aquarium.

Premnas—spine cheeked anemonefishes, including the single species, *P. biaculeatus* and its color varieties; all popular with marine aquarium enthusiasts.

Pseudanthias—small fishes, family Anthiidae, that form shoals dominated by a single, distinctively colored male, and feed on plankton in shallow water; numerous species are imported for marine aquariums.

Pseudochromis—dottybacks, family Pseudochromidae, of the Indo-Pacific region, that can be propagated in commercial quantities for the aquarium trade; there are several species.

Pseudopterogorgia—sea feathers, gorgonian soft corals with the branches arranged in a single plane, superficially resembling a bird's feather.

Ptereleotris—torpedo gobies, family Gobidae, sometimes imported for marine aquariums, although inclined to jump from the tank if disturbed.

Pterogorgia—sea feathers, gorgonian soft corals with the branches arranged in a single plane, superficially resembling a bird's feather.

Pterois—lionfishes, any of several species in family Scorpaenidae that reach an adult length greater than 6 inches, all have venomous dorsal and pectoral fin spines.

Pterosynchiropus—the mandarinfish, *P. splendidus*, frequently imported for the aquarium from Indo-Pacific reefs, requires tiny living foods in order to survive; family Callyonimidae.

Pygoplites—the regal angelfish, *P. diacanthus*, often imported for the aquarium, but seldom adaptable to captive conditions.

Pylopagurus—marine hermit crabs, including the trapdoor hermit, *P. operculatus*, from the tropical Atlantic, a colorful species with an enlarged, white chela that it uses to close the opening of the snail shell in which it lives.

Rhinomuraena—ribbon eels, Indo-Pacific fishes once regularly imported for the aquarium, but seldom successfully adapted to captive conditions.

Rhipocephalus—a green seaweed with a calcified structure resembling a pine cone emerging on a stick from a solid substrate.

Rhodactis—several species of Indo-Pacific disc anemones imported for minireef aquariums, including a bright blue form from Tonga, bearing highly branched tentacles on the oral disc.

Rhynchocinetes—camel shrimp, or dancing shrimp, Indo-Pacific crustaceans having a distinct hump in the carapace; when kept in groups, they maintain contact and coordinated movement with one another.

Ricordea—a false coral genus once regularly collected in Florida and the Caribbean but now largely protected by environmental regulation, it can be propagated, although slowly.

Sabella—polychaetes, several species of which have colorful radioles and are often exhibited in marine aquariums.

Sabellastarte—feather duster worms, including several species from both the Atlantic and the Indo-Pacific, characterized by unusually large radioles that are rapidly withdrawn into a protective tube when the animal is disturbed.

Sarcophyton—mushroom corals, several species of alcyonarians so named because of their resemblance to the edible fungus; widely maintained in minireefs and easily propagated from cuttings.

Seriatopora—a branching, small-polyped stony coral easily propagated from cuttings.

Serranocirrhitus—a solitary anthias, family Anthiidae, from deep waters in the Indo-Pacific that is often exhibited in reef aquariums and adapts readily to captivity.

Signigobius—signal gobies, family Gobidae, benthic species that mimic the appearance and movements of a crab; pairs are sometimes exhibited in minireef aquariums.

Sinularia—an alcyonarian soft coral often maintained in minireef aquariums.

Sphaeramia—a cardinalfish genus, family Apogonidae, of which the pajama cardinal, *S. orbicularis*, is regularly imported for marine aquariums.

Spirobranchus—Christmas tree worms, polychaete annelids of family Serpulidae exhibited in marine aquariums because of their brilliantly colored spiral radioles that are immediately withdrawn into a protective tube at the slightest disturbance.

Stenopus—barber shrimps, family Stenopodidae, including the commonly imported species *S. hispidus*, the banded coral shrimp, and several other species that exhibit cleaning behavior.

Stenorhynchus—the arrow crab, *S. seticornis*, is often collected in Florida for exhibition in home aquariums; it feeds on polychate worms and other small invertebrates.

Stichodactyla—carpet anemones, at least three species of which are known in the marine aquarium trade; all host anemonefishes and are difficult for many hobbyists to maintain successfully.

Strombus—conchs, *S. gigas*, are cultivated in the Caribbean for food and as algae eaters for the marine aquarium.

Stylophora—a small-polyped stony coral forming rounded colonies of finger branches; widely distributed in the Indo-Pacific and easily propagated in minireef aquariums.

Synalpheus—snapping or popping shrimps, family Alpheidae, able to make a loud pop by means of a specially modified chela.

Synanceia—the stonefish, a deadly scorpaenid.

Synchiropus—the target fish, family Callionymidae, or spotted mandarin, exhibited in minireef aquariums where it feeds only on tiny, living crustaceans.

Telmatactis—a tiny sea anemone often carried by the boxing crab *Lybia*.

Thalassoma—wrasses, family Labridae, including many aquarium species.

Trachyphyllia—open-brain coral, a large-polyped stony coral adapted for living in bottom sediments; widely maintained in minireef aquariums.

Tridacna—giant clams cultivated primarily for food but also, because of their bright colors and ease of maintenance in minireef tanks, for the aquarium market.

Tubastrea—a nonphotosynthetic stony coral sought after by enthusiasts because of its bright orange coloration.

Turbinaria—cup coral, a stony coral with a skeleton resembling a wine glass, the inside of which is studded with corallites.

Turbo—marine snails, family Turbinidae, in which the shell resembles a turban, and of which several species are used in marine aquariums for the control of filamentous and encrusting algae.

Udotea—green marine algae with a calcified skeletal structure giving it the shape of a fan emerging from the substrate.

Valenciennea—marine sleeper gobies, family Gobidae, that feed by taking substrate material into the mouth and extracting benthic microinvertebrates.

Xenia—a stonloniferan soft coral often maintained in minireef aquariums; in some species the polyps pulse rhythmically.

Zanclus—the Moorish idols, family Zanclidae, marine fishes related to acanthurids and often imported from Hawaii, although extremely difficult to maintain in a home aquarium.

Zebrasoma—acanthurids with elongate snouts suitable for picking filamentous algae from rocks, the genus includes many marine aquarium species, such as the yellow tang, *Z. flavescens*.

Zoanthus—the genus of zoanthids most commonly seen in the aquarium trade.

Appendix C

Glossary

Included here are all of the aquarium jargon and scientific terminology used in this book, along with additional terms you are sure to encounter in fish stores, aquarium publications, and at hobbyist gatherings.

acclimation—the process of slowly introducing a fish or other organism to new water conditions, usually following transport from one aquarium to the other.

acid—a chemical compound that dissociates in solution to yield hydrogen ions, or protons, and a negatively charged ion.

acontia—filaments extruded from pores at the base of the oral disc of certain sea anemones, though to be utilized for defensive purposes.

actinopharynx—the body opening of cnidarians that serves as both mouth and anus.

activated carbon—a filtering medium prepared by exposing organic materials such as bones or coconut shells to high temperatures and steam, this highly porous material absorbs dissolved organic compounds and large ions, such as iodide, from aquarium water.

Aiptasia—a genus of small sea anemones that often multiply to plague proportions in marine aquariums with bright light and heavy loads of organic matter and algae nutrients in the water.

air pump—a device for delivering air under low pressure to aquarium equipment connected to it by means of flexible tubing; older models employ a reciprocating piston, while most modern versions use a bellows operated by an electric vibrator, to achieve pressurization.

air stripping—a synonym for foam fractionation.

airlift—a device that utilizes the principle of displacement for pumping water; forcing air in near the bottom of a tube immersed in the aquarium causes water to be pushed out the top of the tube as the column of air rises.

airstone—any of several types of porous diffusers used to release tiny air bubbles into the aquarium; made of fused sand, glass spheres, plastics, or even lime-wood.

alcyonarian—a soft coral lacking an axial skeleton.

algae—any of a wide variety of photosynthetic organisms lacking a vascular system; may be unicellular, filamentous, or, in the case of seaweeds, large and complex in form.

algae-eater—one of several species of fish and invertebrates that feed on encrusting and filamentous algae, introduced into the aquarium primarily for control of such growths.

algal turf scrubber—aquarium water purification system designed at the Smithsonian Institution and employing various species of algae growing on plastic mats in specially designed tanks, to remove pollutants from the water.

alkalinity—a measure of the ability of a solution to absorb acid without a change in pH.

alpheid—a member of the snapping shrimp family, marine crustaceans with one appendage modified for the production of a sudden popping sound that is thought to deter predators; some members have the sound appendage modified for digging, have lost the ability to pop, and rely on partnership with certain fishes for protection.

AMDA—acronym for the American Marinelife Dealers Association, an organization that promotes wise environmental practices in the marine aquarium industry.

ammonium—the ionized form of ammonia (NH_4^+).

amphipod—small, laterally compressed crustaceans that are often transported into marine aquariums via live rock and then begin reproducing; they are harmless scavengers and are eaten by many types of marine fishes.

Amyloodinium—a parasitic dinoflagellate that infests the gills and epidermis of many species of marine fishes, often fatally; synonyms are "marine velvet" and "coral fish disease."

anaerobes—bacteria that do not require oxygen to carry out metabolism; facultative anaerobes can survive in the presence of oxygen, while to obligate anaerobes free oxygen is poisonous.

anal fin—an unpaired fin arising on the midline of the ventral surface of a fish, anterior to the tail and usually just posterior to the anus and urogenital openings.

anemone—a noncolonial anthozoan with tentacles in multiples of six, lacking a calcified skeletal structure and usually attached to a solid substrate by means of the pedal disc.

anemonefish—any of the pomacentrid fishes of the genera *Amphiprion* or *Premnas* that associate with sea anemones.

angelfish—a saltwater angelfish is any member of family Pomacanthidae, all colorful, including small species of *Centropyge* that generally adapt well to aquarium care, and larger species in the genus *Pomacanthus* that can be challenging to maintain in the aquarium.

anglerfish—predatory fishes in the family Antennaridae, which entice prey within striking distance by means of a "fishing pole" formed from the first dorsal fin spine.

annelid—any member of the animal phylum Annelida, the segmented worms.

anoxic—lacking free oxygen.

antenna—the elongated sensory appendage of a crustacean.

anterior—referring to the front end of the body of an animal.

anthozoan—literally "flower animal," any member of phylum Cnidaria, class Anthozoa, characterized by the predominance of the flowerlike polyp form in the life cycle.

antibiotic—a medication that kills or otherwise halts the reproduction of bacteria.

antihelminthic—any medication used in the treatment of parasitic infestations by worms.

aplysiid—any member of the mollusk family Aplysiidae, or "sea hares," characterized by a reduced internal shell; all are vegetarian grazers.

aquaculture—production of aquatic organisms for food, aquarium, or scientific purposes, generally as a commercial venture.

aquaculturist—one who practices aquaculture.

aquarist—anyone who designs or maintains an aquarium.

aquarium—(1) a tank, often fitted with life support equipment, specifically constructed for housing living aquatic organisms for exhibition, aquaculture or scientific study, of dimensions appropriate to enclosure within a building; (2) an exhibit of living organisms, in one or several separate containers, intended to give the impression of a window into an aquatic habitat.

aquascape—the physical design of the interior of an aquarium, including rocks or other objects selected and placed in such a manner as to convey to the viewer the aquarist's impression of an underwater scene.

aragonite—a form of calcium carbonate deposited as skeletal elements in marine invertebrates such as corals.

arborescent—"treelike," usually in reference to the body structure of certain colonial marine invertebrates such as gorgonian soft corals that branch and rebranch.

arm—among aquarium organisms, this term is properly applied only to the appendages of brittlestars or to the body divisions of sea stars.

Artemia—the genus to which brine shrimp, a popular food for both marine and freshwater aquariums, are assigned.

arthropod—any member of phylum Arthropoda, invertebrates characterized by jointed appendages and an external skeleton composed of chitin, including the terrestrial insects as well as a variety of marine and freshwater organisms.

axial skeleton—the stiffened, proteinaceous internal structure that provides rigidity to the bodies of soft corals known commonly as gorgonians.

bait fish—any of several species of small fish sold as bait for anglers.

ballast—electrician's term for the transformer that boosts house current to the voltage required for the operation of fluorescent or metal halide aquarium lighting systems.

basslet—any of several genera of marine fishes, generally less than 4 inches in length, in the family Grammidae.

benthic—bottom-dwelling organisms, or those that characteristically live upon a solid substrate, such as rocks or corals.

Berlin-style aquarium—one established according to methods developed in Germany, utilizing only live rock and protein skimming for accomplishing biological filtration, nitrate reduction, and organic matter removal.

bio-ball—a spherical plastic object, available in various designs, intended for colonization by nitrifying bacteria in a biological filtration system.

bio-wheel—a rotating pleated structure over which a stream of water is directed as part of a biological filtration system, and upon which nitrifying bacteria grow.

bioaccumulation—the concentration of a chemical substance, such as mercury, at successively higher levels in an ecological food web.

biodiversity—the condition of an ecosystem determined by the variety of species it supports.

biogenic—referring to any substance created as a result of the activities of living organisms, for example, petroleum or atmospheric oxygen.

biolimiting—said of any factor that prevents the growth of an organism if in short supply.

bioload—in an aquarium, the demand placed upon the life support system as a result of the metabolism of all the organisms present within the tank.

biomass—the total amount by weight of living organisms within a specified amount of space.

biotope—a specific portion of an ecosystem, defined by the physical conditions and types of organisms usually found, and generally limited in extent geographically; aquariums are frequently designed to represent a particular biotope.

black band disease—a poorly understood pathological condition observed in stony corals, both in aquariums and in the ocean.

blackworm—an aquatic annelid about 2 inches in length that is sold alive as fish food.

bleaching—with reference to stony corals, a condition in which the zooxanthellae are lost, rendering the coral white in color.

blenny—common name for any member of the family Blennidae.

boxfish—any member of the Ostraciidae, a family of marine fishes in which the body is enclosed in a series of interlocking bony plates that provide protection.

Brachionus—the marine rotifer most often cultured for feeding newly hatched fish larvae.

brine shrimp—common name for *Artemia salina*, a crustacean that is often used as food for both freshwater and marine aquarium inhabitants.

bristle—short, thick hairlike epidermal outgrowths, often pointed on the distal end, and sometimes hollow and venomous, found on certain marine annelids.

bristleworm—marine annelids with setae, or bristles, along the length of the body, generally considered an aquarium pest because some species feed on corals.

brittlestar—any member of the echinoderm class Ophiuroidea, in which there are multiple arms, usually five, extending radially from a central, disc-shaped body; the name derives from the ease with which some species are damaged by handling.

brood—a group of sibling offspring arising from a clutch of eggs of any species of fish or invertebrate.

brood pouch—a specialized invagination of the abdomen of the male seahorse, in which fertilized eggs develop and are nourished by a placenta-like structure.

Brooklynella—a protozoan parasite infesting the epidermis of marine fish, especially those in the genus *Amphiprion*, commonly known as "clownfish disease"; the condition is abetted by crowding and poor water conditions, but often responds to treatment with medications containing malachite green.

bryozoan—any member of the phylum Bryozoa, filter-feeding marine invertebrates with an encrusting growth form typically found on live rock; the few freshwater species are of no interest to aquarium hobbyists.

budding—a form of reproduction in certain corals and anemones, in which fully formed offspring result as an outgrowth of the body of the parent organism.

buffer—a solution of chemical compounds and water that resists a change in pH when either acid or alkali is added.

butterflyfish—any fish of the marine family Chaetodontidae, found exclusively in association with coral reefs; most are delicate and difficult to feed, but a few species make excellent aquarium subjects.

calcareous—having calcium carbonate incorporated into a body structure, usually as skeletal elements or a shell.

calcification—(1) the process by which calcium carbonate is incorporated into the body structure of a living organism; (2) the deposition of calcium carbonate as a mineral through chemical processes taking place in aquatic habitats.

calcium carbonate—$CaCO_3$, a crystalline solid, insoluble in water, that is incorporated into supportive or protective structures in a variety of animal and plant species.

calcium reactor—a device for increasing the content of calcium ions in the water of a marine aquarium that functions by passing acidified water over pieces of calcium carbonate, such as shell fragments.

calcium supplement—any chemical added to a marine aquarium to increase the calcium content of the water.

calyx—the cuplike structure of a colonial coral from which the individual polyp protrudes and into which it can usually be withdrawn.

canister filter—an aquarium filter in which the media are enclosed in a plastic can located external to the tank, with water entering and leaving the filter by means of hoses leading to the aquarium.

carapace—the outer integument of a crustacean.

carbon dioxide—CO_2, along with water, is the end product of food metabolism by the majority of living organisms; accumulation in aquarium water is to be avoided because of toxic effects on fish; absorbed by plants and eliminated by aeration and buffering.

carbonic acid—the compound that results when carbon dioxide dissolves in water.

cardinalfish—any of the marine fishes in family Apogonidae.

carnivore—an organism the primary diet of which is animals.

caudal fin—the tail fin of a fish, used primarily for locomotion in the majority of species.

caudal peduncle—the fleshy, posterior portion of a fish's body to which the caudal fin is attached.

cephalothorax—the anterior portion of the body of a crustacean, to which the feeding appendages and antennae are attached.

chelae—singular, chela; the often enlarged anterior appendages, or "pincers," of crustaceans.

chemical filtration—the removal of chemical compounds from aquarium water by foam fractionation or adsorption on various media.

chitin—a tough, proteinaceous material found abundantly in the external skeleton of crustaceans, it also occurs in such diverse organisms as fungi and mollusks.

chiton—any of numerous species of primitive mollusks in which the shell consists of a series of eight calcified plates, class Amphineura; most species attach themselves to a solid substrate and move about under cover of darkness to graze on algae.

chlorophyll—one of a group of green pigments that permit photosynthetic organisms to utilize the energy of sunlight for food production.

chloroplast—a subcellular structure found in photosynthetic organisms that contains chlorophyll.

chordate—a member of phlyum Chordata, characterized by the presence of a stiffening rod of cartilage, the notochord, develops at some point in the life cycle; in vertebrates the notochord is present in the embryo and is replaced by the vertebral column.

cirri—singular, cirrus; short, bristle-like projections from the epidermis of certain invertebrates and fishes; in blennies, the cirri are often referred to as "eyelashes."

clonal—referring to any mode of vegetative reproduction of a single individual, whereby all the offspring are genetically identical to, and thus are clones of, the parent.

clownfish—originally only *Amphiprion ocellaris*, but now any of the pomacentrid fishes that associate with sea anemones; also known as "anemonefishes."

clutch—a mass or cluster of eggs deposited by a fish or invertebrate, often but not always receiving protective care from one or both parents.

cnidarian—any member of phylum Cnidaria, invertebrates having a three-layered body lacking clearly defined organs, a single opening serving as both mouth and anus, and a ring of tentacles surrounding the opening that bear specialized stinging cells.

cnidoblast—the stinging cells of cnidarians, containing the nematocyst.

coelenterate—a synonym for cnidarian.

column—the stalk supporting the tentacular crown of a polyp, especially an anemone.

commensal—said of a relationship in which two species co-occur but neither one helps or harms the other.

commensalism—the symbiotic relationship between commensal organisms.

Convolutriloba—a flatworm pest, recognizable by its distinctive three-pointed posterior, that feeds on aquarium cnidarians.

copepod—tiny crustaceans found in a variety of aquatic habitats and often able to reproduce in the aquarium; free-living forms are eaten by a variety of fishes, a few are parasitic, but are seldom a problem in the aquarium.

copper—a chemical element required in trace amounts by many organisms, it is used in the treatment of protozoan parasite infestations of marine fishes and sometimes for control of undesirable algae or mollusks in freshwater aquariums.

coral—any of the colonial anthozoans, but most frequently applied to the order Scleractinia, or stony corals, in which a calcified skeleton is produced.

coral reef—an ecosystem associated with a massive underwater structure comprised of the skeletons of millions of stony corals.

coral rock—the fossil remains of coral reefs formed prior to the last Ice Age.

coral sand—granular aggregate of pulverized coral rock, shell fragments, and other minerals formed by erosion and deposited on the sea bottom.

corallimorpharian—any member of the anthozoan order Corallimorpharia, commonly known as false corals or disc anemones.

coralline—referring to any of the marine algae that possess a calcified skeleton.

cowery—common name for any marine gastropod of the family Cypraeidae, recognizable by a colorful, highly polished shell completely enveloped by the mantle.

crepuscular—said of any animal that is active primarily at dusk.

crinoid—a feather star, or member of the echinoderm class Crinoidea; sometimes imported, most are too delicate to adapt to aquarium life.

crushed coral—coral rock that has been milled to granules approximately ⅛ inch in diameter, and used as a substrate material in marine aquariums.

crustacean—any member of phylum Crustacea, marine or freshwater animals with jointed appendages, an external skeleton, and a body divided into the unsegmented cephalothorax and a segmented tail section.

crustose—"crustlike"; said of algae or colonial invertebrates that form a thin, hard layer on a solid substrate.

cryptic coloration—a pattern of pigmentation that allows the organism to blend into the background of its preferred habitat.

Cryptocaryon—a ciliated protozoan that infests the gills and epidermis of marine fishes, commonly known as "white spot" or "marine ich"; it is susceptible to copper treatment.

curing—allowing freshly harvested live rock to sit in an isolation tank for about 2 weeks until natural die-off has taken place and the rock can be placed in a display aquarium.

current—one-directional movement within a mass of water or air.

cyanoacrylate glue—a type of adhesive that adheres well to living tissue, it can be used to attach living coral colonies, for example, to a piece of rock.

cyanobacteria—photosynthetic prokaryotes commonly called "blue-green algae" that are often considered pests in both freshwater and marine aquariums.

cycling—establishing a population of beneficial nitrifying bacteria in an aquarium's biological filtration system, the name comes from the ecological term "nitrogen cycle."

damselfish—pomacentrid fishes that do not associate with anemones, they may be either solitary and territorial, or schooling forms; solitary types are often kept by beginning marine aquarium hobbyists because they are widely available, colorful, cheap and extremely hardy.

dartfish—any of the gobies in the genera *Nemateleotris*.

daylength—the period of time during which there is sufficient sunlight for photosynthesis to take place.

decapod—crustaceans having ten pairs of locomotory appendages.

degrees of hardness—divisions on an arbitrary scale for expressing the amount of dissolved carbonates of calcium and magnesium present in a sample of water.

denitrator—a device for removing nitrate ions from aquarium water.

denitrification—the process by which anaerobic bacteria convert nitrate ion into nitrogen gas.

denitrifier—any species of bacteria able to convert nitrate ion into nitrogen gas.

detritus—tiny fragments of slowly decomposing plant material that may accumulate in both marine and freshwater aquariums over time.

diatom—any of the unicellular algae, freshwater or marine, that produce a bivalved shell composed of silicon dioxide.

diatom filter—a device for clearing fine particulate matter from aquarium water, employing diatomaecous earth as the medium.

diatomaceous earth—mineral deposit comprised of the shells of billions of fossil diatoms, often mined for use as an abrasive and filtration medium.

dinoflagellate—any of the algae comprising phylum Pyrrhophycopyta, characteristically bearing two locomotory flagella, each lying in a groove around the body, one perpendicular to the other; certain species are important to aquarists as fish parasites (*Amyloodinium*) and as the zooxanthellae (*Gymnodinium*) of various cnidarians.

dorsal—anatomical reference to the back; in vertebrates, the spinal cord is in this position.

dorsal fin—the appendage, sometimes consisting of both spinous and a nonspinous sections, arising from the midline of the back of all fishes.

dorsal spines—the supporting elements of the dorsal fin.

dottyback—any of the small sea basses in the genus *Pseudochromis*.

dragonet—any of the marine fishes of family Callionymidae; the two most popular species are also known as mandarinfish.

Dutch-type aquarium—(1) an aquarium in which various species of freshwater aquatic plants, arranged in an artistic, naturalistic manner, are the primary aesthetic feature, rather than fish; (2) if marine, referring to a tank in which both invertebrates and fishes are maintained and filtration is accomplished by a wet/dry filtration system.

dwarf angel—any of the marine fishes of the genus *Centropyge*, mostly under 3 inches in length and feeding primarily on algae and small invertebrates.

echinoderm—literally "spiny skin"; any member of phylum Echinodermata, exclusively marine invertebrates with radially symmetrical bodies and a water vascular system found in no other animal group.

eco-labeling—a proposed system for categorization of species according to their relative adaptability to captive husbandry, designed with the goal of reducing the number of non-adaptable species collected for the aquarium trade.

ecosystem—all of the physical and biological components of a specific geographic area and the interactions among them, usually defined by a dominant feature, such as a coral reef or lake.

erythromycin—an antibiotic sometimes added to the marine aquarium for control of blue-green algae, it is extremely toxic to nitrifying bacteria and so should be used with caution.

euphausid—krill; shrimplike marine crustacean often sold in freeze-dried form as an aquarium food.

euthanasia—mercy killing, or the deliberate killing of an organism to spare it from pain or suffering.

external filter—any aquarium filter not located within the tank itself.

fanworm—any of the segmented worms of families Sabellidae and Serpulidae that possesses a feeding structure superficially resembling a fan, feather duster, or parasol, often imported for marine aquariums.

filamentous—having a threadlike structure, as with many freshwater and marine algae that grow in aquariums.

filter—any device for maintaining the quality of aquarium water by removal of particulate or chemical substances, the accumulation of which would be harmful to the organisms exhibited in the tank.

fireworm—one of several tropical polychaete annelids with venomous bristles capable of delivering a painful sting if the organism is carelessly handled.

flashing—a fish behavior characterized by rapid, glancing contact with a solid object in an effort to displace an external parasite or other irritation, so called because the light-colored underbelly of the fish is thus exposed to momentary view.

flatworm—any member of phylum Platyhelminthes, including the nonparasitic freshwater form, planaria, and numerous parasites of marine and freshwater fish and invertebrates.

fossorial—a relationship in which two species share the same living space, such as a burrow, constructed by one of them, or in which one species occupies such a space vacated by the builder.

fry—recently hatched fishes.

gastropod—a snail, or mollusk with a univalve shell and in which the developing larva undergoes twisting, or torsion, that results in the juxtapositioning of anterior and posterior ends of the alimentary tract.

Gelbstoff—literally "yellow matter" in German, a term coined to refer collectively to the organic compounds that produce yellowing of both fresh and marine aquarium waters.

genus—a group of closely related species.

GH—abbreviation for "general hardness" or the total amount of dissolved salts of calcium and magnesium present in a sample of water.

gill—the anatomical structure in some aquatic organisms that permits gas exchange across the walls of capillaries between the bloodstream and the surrounding water.

gill cover—the opercle, or flap, that protects the gills of fishes.

gorgonian—any of the eight-tentacled anthozoans that produces an axial skeleton covered by a usually colorful outer tissue layer that gives rise to the polyps.

ground fault circuit interrupter (GFCI)—an electrical device that compares the current flowing on one side of a circuit with that flowing on the opposite side, and which opens the circuit to prevent personal injury when a difference greater that a few milliamps is detected.

habitat—the geographic locality, together with its biological components, in which a species is typically found.

hawkfish—one of several marine fishes in the family Cirrhitidae that characteristically perch atop a coral head or other prominence to watch for prey; many are popular aquarium fishes.

head and lateral line erosion (HLLE)—a condition observed in some marine fishes, notably those in families Acanthuridae, Pomacanthidae and Pomacentridae, but not restricted to these, in which the scales and epidermis of the face and along the lateral line erode away, leaving depigmented areas that may become infected; while the exact cause is unknown, most studies suggest that the condition is associated with deficiencies of vitamin C or A or both.

herbivore—any organism the primary diet of which is living plant matter.

hermaphroditism—a condition in which a single individual possesses both male and female reproductive organs, either simultaneously or at different stages in its life cycle.

hermatypic—corals that contain symbiotic dinoflagellates known as "zooxanthellae."

hexacoral—a colonial anthozoan with tentacles in multiples of six.

holdfast—any structure produced by a sessile organism for the purpose of anchoring it to a solid substrate.

homeothermic—referring to an organism with the ability to maintain a constant internal body temperature.

hood—an enclosure housing light fixtures for aquarium illumination, usually incorporating a cover for the entire tank.

hydrogen ion—a hydrogen atom that has lost its electron, thus a proton, abbreviated H^+, the concentration of which determines the pH of a solution.

hydrogen peroxide—chemically H_2O_2, a compound sometimes added to aquarium water to increase the oxygen content, as it dissociates rapidly into water and free oxygen; also used as a disinfectant for treating wounds in fishes.

hydrometer—a device for measuring specific gravity.

ichthyologist—a biologist who specializes in the study of fishes.

ichthyology—the branch of biological science concerned with the morphology, physiology, taxonomy, and ecology of fishes.

Ichthyophonus—a microscopic fungus that sometimes infests captive marine fishes; it is incurable.

illuminance—a measure of the amount of light falling upon a given area.

impeller—a series of paddles arranged around a shaft or axle, the spinning of which pushes water through the volute of a pump.

Indo-Pacific—the region of the sea including both the Indian and Pacific Oceans, or referring to any species or feature of this region.

infauna—collectively the organisms inhabiting the interior of an object, such as a porous rock or wooden dock piling, or between the grains of an aggregate such as sand or gravel.

iodine—a chemical element, I, present in seawater at approximately 0.6 ppm, and essential for certain marine invertebrates, notably crustaceans and many corals.

ion—an atom or molecule with a net electrical charge resulting from the gain or loss of electrons.

irradiance—the amount of light energy falling on a given area.

Isochrysis—a unicellular marine alga often cultured as a food for certain other organisms, such as rotifers intended for feeding to fish larvae.

jawfish—any of the family Opisthognathidae, marine fishes with large mouths that typically burrow into the substrate; the most commonly seen aquarium species is *Opisthognathus aurifrons*, from the tropical Atlantic and Caribbean.

kalkwasser—literally "chalk water," a German term for limewater, a solution of calcium hydroxide added to marine reef aquariums as a source of calcium ions.

KH—"German hardness," a scale of measurement of alkalinity or carbonate hardness, which may be converted to milliequivalents per liter by multiplying by 2.8.

krill—any euphausid crustacean, but often *Euphausia superba*, harvested from the sea and sold in freeze-dried form as a food for aquarium fish.

lancefish—any of several small marine species harvested and sold, usually frozen, for feeding predatory aquarium fish.

larva—an immature form of an invertebrate or fish that develops from the fertilized egg and changes into the adult form after a period of growth and development.

lateral line—a structure lying, typically, along the middle of either side of the body of bony fishes, together with interconnected structures in the head, that senses changes in water pressure, permitting the fish to control its swimming precisely.

light spectrum—electromagnetic radiation with a wavelength between 350 and 750 nanometers, including ultraviolet, visible, and infrared light; also a graphic representation of such radiation.

limestone—rock formed by deposition of calcium carbonate in marine sediments, it occurs in many forms worldwide and is often used for decoration in marine aquariums and those designed for African rift lake cichlids.

limewater—a saturated solution of calcium hydroxide often added to marine reef aquariums as a source of calcium ions.

lionfish—any fish of the genera *Dendrochirus* or *Pterois*, but often applied only to *P. volitans.*

lux—a unit of irradiance equivalent to one lumen per square meter.

lymphocystis—a condition in marine fishes produced by a virus and equivalent to a wart, characterized by the formation of a grayish-white, cauliflowerlike growth anywhere on the body but especially on the fins; treatable with antiviral drugs only.

MAC—Marine Aquarium Council, an international nonprofit organization established to create a certification system for ornamental marine fishes captured via sustainable techniques and held and handled under best management practices.

macroalgae—algae of larger than microscopic size, but to aquarists any seaweed with a noninvasive growth habit exhibited in a marine aquarium.

mantle—the fleshy structure enclosing the body of a mollusk, it secretes the shell.

mariculture—captive propagation of marine organisms, usually on a commercial basis, by sexual or asexual methods.

marinelife—collective term for all species of organisms exhibited in aquariums devoted to oceanic habitats.

MASNA—Marine Aquarium Societies of North America, a confederation of hobbyist clubs focused on saltwater aquariums, it sanctions MACNA, the annual Marine Aquarium Conference of North America.

mechanical filtration—any method of water purification primarily intended to remove particulate matter.

metal halide lamp—a high-intensity device, operated by electricity, utilized as an aquarium light source when very bright light is needed, as with a miniature reef aquarium or freshwater plant tank.

microalgae—any small, though not necessarily microscopic, seaweed growing in a marine aquarium, particularly one unwanted by the aquarist.

microbiota—living organisms of a particular habitat that are too small to be seen with the unaided human eye.

microcrustacean—any tiny to microscopic species, such as a copepod, in freshwater or marine habitats.

microfauna—collectively the tiny to microscopic animals found in a specific habitat.

microinvertebrates—any tiny to microscopic animals of any phylum lacking a notochord at any stage of the life cycle.

micronutrients—food compounds required by an organism only in very small quantities.

microplankton—free-swimming, tiny to microscopic plants and animals that constitute an important source of food in freshwater and marine habitats.

milliequivalent—one thousandth of one chemical equivalent, or the amount of acid or alkali required to exactly neutralize a 0.001 molar solution of reagent.

mimicry—an adaptation in which one organism evolves to resemble another in order to gain some survival benefit.

minireef—an aquarium in which a variety of marine invertebrate species, particularly corals, is exhibited in a naturalistic setting.

mollusk—any member of phylum Mollusca, invertebrates such as clams, snails, chitons, and octopus, which share specific anatomical and developmental characteristics.

Monaco-style aquarium—a tank in which biological filtration and denitrification occur in a deep bed of sand placed on a plenum over the bottom of the aquarium.

mutualism—a symbiotic relationship in which two species typically live together each benefiting the other.

mysis shrimp—also called "opossum shrimp," any crustacean of the class Mysidacea, often harvested from the sea and frozen as a food for aquarium fish.

nauplius—the first instar, or larval stage, of a crustacean such as *Artemia salina.*

necrosis—deterioration of the tissues of a living organism as a result of disease or injury.

nematocyst—a subcellular structure found only in cnidarians, consisting of an often venomous piercing or ensnaring projectile and launching mechanism contained within a cnidoblast cell and ejected upon stimulation by external contact, employed for prey capture and defense.

night coloration—a pattern, often strikingly different from the one assumed during daylight, adopted by some fishes after sunset or during sleep.

nitrate—a weakly toxic anion, NO_3, the end product of the metabolism of ammonia by nitrifying bacteria, which must be periodically removed from aquarium water to prevent harm to the inhabitants.

nitrification—the complete oxidation of ammonia to nitrate by means of certain bacteria; the process of biological filtration as it occurs in the aquarium.

nitrifier—any of the bacteria capable of ammonia oxidation.

nitrifying bacteria—those prokaryotic organisms that collectively carry out nitrification, or biological filtration.

nitrite—a toxic anion, NO_2, intermediate in the process of ammonia oxidation carried out in the aquarium by certain bacteria.

Nitrobacter—a genus of bacteria once thought to be solely responsible for oxidation of nitrite to nitrate during biological filtration; recent research has shown that other genera are more likely involved.

nitrogen—the chemical element N, comprising most of the atmosphere and present in thousands of biologically important compounds.

nitrogen cycle—the natural process through which nitrogen incorporated into food molecules by photosynthetic organisms is consumed directly or indirectly by other organisms and subsequently excreted, acted upon by bacteria, and made available again for plant nutrition.

Nitrosomonas—a genus of bacteria once thought to be solely responsible for oxidation of ammonia to nitrite during biological filtration; recent research has shown that other genera are more likely involved.

nocturnal—active primarily during the hours of darkness.

nonphotosynthetic—unable to produce food from simple molecules, and thus relying on food produced by organisms with this ability.

nudibranch—any member of the molluscan order Nudibranchia, marine snails lacking a shell and with the gills exposed and often retractable; often attempted by aquarium hobbyists because of their brilliant coloration, they are difficult to maintain successfully due to their specialized dietary requirements.

nutrient—any molecule that serves as food for a living organism.

octocoral—any member of the anthozoan subclass Octocorallia, including soft corals and gorgonians, in which the tentacles are arranged in multiples of eight.

octopod—any species of octopus or argonaut, cephalopod mollusks with eight arms surrounding the mouth.

omnivore—an organism that feeds on both plant and animal matter.

opercle—the flap that covers the gills of fishes.

operculum—in snails, a calcified or proteinaceous plate used to cover the opening of the shell when the animal is withdrawn inside.

ophiuroid—any member of the echinoderm class Ophiuroidea, the serpent and brittle stars, characterized by a disc-shaped body from which radiate five flexible arms bearing tube feet; in some members the arms branch repeatedly, giving the impression of many more than five.

oral disc—the upper surface of an anemone, bearing the tentacles and with the mouth in the center.

organic matter—any substance produced by a living organism, but usually refers to nonliving remains, excreta, or the like.

osmoregulation—control of the water and electrolyte balance in the body of a living organism.

osmosis—the movement of water molecules across a semipermeable membrane from an area of higher solute concentration to an area of lower solute concentration.

osomotic pressure—the tendency of water to move across a semipermeable membrane, as a consequence of the difference between solute concentrations on either side.

ozone—the triatomic form of oxygen, O_3, with a characteristic odor, it is used in aquarium husbandry as a disinfectant and to add free oxygen ions to the water.

ozonization—the process of introducing triatomic oxygen directly into aquarium water.

ozonizer—a device for the production of ozone, usually by passing air across an electric spark discharge.

parasiticide—any substance used to kill parasites.

particle filter—any device designed for removal of tiny flecks of unwanted matter from aquarium water.

pathogenic—disease producing, as of bacteria.

pectoral fin—the most anterior of the paired fins of a fish, homologous to the arms of higher vertebrates.

pedal disc—the flattened base of the column of a sea anemone or other solitary polyp, by means of which the animal attaches itself to a solid surface.

peduncle—the fleshy lobe by which a fin is attached.

pelagic—living primarily in open water, rather than in association with a solid surface.

pelecypod—any bivalve mollusk, such as an oyster or clam.

pelvic fin—the most posterior paired fins of a fish, homologous to the legs of other vertebrates.

pH—the negative logarithm of the hydrogen ion concentration of a solution; pure water is at 7.0 on this scale, with acidity of the solution increasing below this point and alkalinity likewise increasing above this point; aquarium waters are usually in the range of 6.0 to 8.5, depending upon the environment being replicated.

phoresis—literally "carrying," used to describe the habit in some organisms of attaching objects to themselves for camouflage.

photoperiod—that portion of the day-night cycle during which light is of sufficient intensity for photosynthesis to take place.

photosynthesis—the process by which certain organisms capture light energy and store it in the form of food molecules, thus forming the basis for most of Earth's food webs.

photosynthesizer—any organism capable of photosynthesis.

phytoplankton—unicellular algae swimming or suspended in the water column, and important as the basis for aquatic food webs.

picric acid—a toxic chemical sometimes used in low concentrations as a parasiticidal dip for aquarium fishes.

pigmentation—having color, or the color pattern of an organism such as a fish.

plankter—any organism comprising the plankton.

planktivore—any organism feeding primarily on plankton.

plankton—unicellular and small multicellular organisms, both plant and animal, suspended or swimming in the water column, forming an important food source for numerous other organisms.

plenum—an area of water underneath a sand bed, created by supporting a sheet of porous material a few centimeters off the bottom of an aquarium tank and placing the sand bed on top.

polychaete—segmented marine worms in the annelid class Polychaeta bearing numerous bristles on the segments; there are some 15,000 species, several of which are exhibited in marine aquariums, and a few which are pests thereof.

polyp—the flowerlike form in the life cycle of most cnidarians, consisting of a column attached at the base to a substrate or, in colonial forms, to another portion of the colony, and topped with an oral disc consisting of the tissues surrounding the mouth and forming an encircling ring of tentacles.

power filter—any water purification device that operates by pumping water under pressure through a medium intended for removal of particulate or chemical contaminants.

powerhead—a small submersible water pump, so named because the first models were intended for installation at the top, or "head," of the airlift on an undergravel filter, replacing the air-supply system, and supposedly increasing filtration "power."

ppb—parts per billion, equivalent to micrograms per liter times specific gravity.

ppm—parts per million, equivalent to milligrams per liter times specific gravity.

ppt—parts per thousand, equivalent to grams per liter times specific gravity.

predatory—descriptive of any animal that actively seeks out other living animals and consumes them.

prefilter—any contrivance intended to protect filtration equipment from damage by preventing the intake of oversized objects, or to protect aquarium specimens from entrapment by filtration equipment, or both.

protandrous hermaphroditism—a condition of some species in which individuals begin life as males and later change to females as a result of maturation or environmental stimuli.

protein skimmer—any water purification device that removes dissolved organic and inorganic matter from water by their sequestration on the surfaces of air bubbles, and is so designed as to trap the viscous, greenish-brown foam produced in a receptacle from which it can be periodically discarded.

protogynous hermaphroditism—a condition of some species in which individuals begin life as females and later change to males as a result of maturation or environmental stimuli.

puffer—a fish of family Tetraodontidae, able to inflate itself by drawing water into a specialized chamber, thus deterring many predators.

Pyramidella—parasitic gastropods that sometimes infest giant clams and sea stars exhibited in aquariums.

quarantine tank—an aquarium intended for the temporary housing of any living specimen to assess its state of health before exhibition in a display tank, to prevent transmission of disease to specimens already therein.

rabbitfish—any member of family Siganidae, so named because of their herbivorous feeding habits.

radiole—in certain polychaete annelids, a structure employed both for gas exchange and in food capture, and which in aquarium species is often strikingly colored.

raptorial appendage—any extension of the body employed primarily for prey capture, but especially that of certain crustaceans.

reefkeeping—coined term for the hobby of maintaining coral reef organisms in aquariums.

refugia—areas deliberately provided in the design of an aquarium in which certain species can seek shelter from potential predators in the same tank.

reverse osmosis (RO) unit—a water purification device that forces tap water under pressure through a semipermeable membrane, allowing only pure water with reduced solute content to pass out as the product.

rotifer—any member of phylum Rotifera, tiny to microscopic animals of both freshwater and marine habitats; important as a food source for many aquatic organisms; at least one species, *Brachionus plicatilus*, is employed extensively as a first food for larval marine fishes.

run-in—to operate a new aquarium without fishes for a period of time to permit the growth of desirable microorganisms and to assess equipment performance.

sabellid—any polychaete annelid of family Sabellidae, commonly known as fanworms or feather duster worms.

salinity—a measurement of the total amount of dissolved salts in a sample of seawater, defined as the ratio of the conductivity of the seawater sample to the conductivity of a solution of 32.4356 grams of potassium chloride per kilogram of pure water at 15 degrees C and 1 atmosphere of barometric pressure (normal sea level barometric pressure); a salinity of 35 parts per thousand is considered "full strength" seawater.

sand—any aggregate material having grains smaller that 1⁄16 inch in diameter, but large enough to be individually discernible with the unaided eye.

scale—an outgrowth of the skin of most fishes, flattened and arranged in overlapping rows and variously modified depending on species.

schooling—fish behavior in which numerous individuals swim coordinately.

scleractinian—a stony coral, or member of the cnidarian order Scleractinia.

scorpionfish—any member of family Scorpaenidae, venomous marine fishes of uncertain taxonomic affiliation, but specifically the species in the genus *Scorpaena*.

sea cucumber—any of the echinoderm class Holothuroidea, so named because of the resemblance in shape of many species to the common vegetable.

sea star—a starfish, or any of the echinoderm class Asteroidea.

sea urchin—an echinoid, or any of the echinoderm class Echinoidea.

seaweed—any marine algae visible to the unaided eye, especially one having a structure superficially similar to a terrestrial plant.

sedentary—spending most or all of one's time in the same spot.

segment—a repeated body element.

serpulid—a polychaete in which the radioles are arranged in one or more spiral structures, and that secretes a protective, calcified tube around itself.

sessile—among animals, one which is attached to a substrate.

shell—any calcareous or siliceous integument enclosing the body of an animal, but especially that of a mollusk.

shoaling—fish behavior in which numerous individuals gather in large groups, but without swimming in a coordinated manner.

shrimp—any small crustacean, but especially a decapod of order Natantia.

siphon—suction created by the movement of water through a pipe in response to gravity, or to transfer water by means of such a pipe; also a duct through which water enters or leaves the body of a mollusk.

small-polyped stony (SPS) corals—those species in which the individual corallites are only a few millimeters in diameter, generally amenable to aquarium propagation by cutting up the colony into daughter colonies.

Smithsonian-style aquarium—an aquarium built according to the design worked out by Walter Adey of the Smithsonian Institution, in which the primary mode of filtration is an algal turf scrubber.

standpipe—a tube extending vertically from a drain, allowing the level of water in the container to rise or "stand" above the level at which the drain exits.

stoloniferan—soft corals in which the individual polyps are connected by horizontal threads of tissue resembling stolons, including several species maintained in minireef aquariums.

stonefish—a scorpaenid fish, *Synanceia*, bearing venomous spines that have caused human fatalities; it should never be exhibited in a home aquarium.

substrate—(1) the material placed on the bottom of an aquarium tank; (2) any surface to which a living organism attaches itself.

sump—a reservoir for water being transported by a pump.

surgeonfish—any of family Acanthuridae, so called because of a blade-like modified scale, often retractable into a sheath on the caudal peduncle, which can deliver a serious cut.

sweeper tentacle—an elogated appendage produced by some stony corals that stings other organisms that move or grow too near the coral colony.

taxonomic hierarchy—a logical series of successively larger groups into which a species may be placed according to its supposed evolutionary relationships with other species.

taxonomy—the science of classification of species according to their evolutionary history.

tentacles—the appendages of certain animals, especially cnidarians and cephalopod mollusks, generally elongated, more or less cylindrical and with a sensory or food capture function or both.

titrant—a reagent used to neutralize an acid or base with the goal of determining the equivalency of the latter, used in carrying out aquarium tests for alkalinity and calcium.

topping-up—adding water to an aquarium to compensate for evaporation.

total hardness—the combined mass of carbonates of calcium and magnesium per unit volume of water.

trace element—components of seawater present at a concentration of 1 part per billion or less.

trickle filter—an aquarium water purification device in which tank water flows slowly, or trickles, over any of a variety of media not submerged but held in a tray or chamber, with the intent of facilitating attachment and growth of nitrifying bacteria; synonym for "wet/dry" filter.

tridacnid—any of the mollusk family Tridacnidae, or giant clams that feed by harboring photosynthetic unicellular algae within their mantle tissues.

triggerfish—any marine species of family Balistidae, characterized by dorsal and anal fin spines bearing a locking mechanism, allowing the fish to wedge itself inextricably into a crevice or other space, as a mode of defense.

tubeworm—any aquatic species that dwells within an elongate, hollow burrow or refuge it constructs or secretes and into which, typically, it is capable of withdrawing to escape danger.

ventral fin—an alternative name for the pelvic fin, or most posterior paired appendage of fishes.

venturi—a device for injecting gas into a stream of water, consisting of a specially milled pipe that creates a pressure drop near an orifice, resulting in the intake of gas via the latter.

verrucae—small bumps or raised areas on the column of an anemone, useful for identification.

volute—the "head" of a water pump, with inlet and outlet openings, through which water is propelled by the movement of the impeller.

water changes—the removal and replacement of old aquarium water with new.

wavemaker—an electrical device that enables timed switching of power between two or more pumps, with the aim of creating changing currents.

wet/dry filter—any device for enhancing bacterial nitrification in which the medium the bacteria attaches to is not submerged, but rather moistened by water pumped over or through it.

white band disease—a pathogenic condition of stony corals in which an area of dying tissue is preceded by a distinctive, pale ring.

wrasse—any of the numerous species in the marine fish family Labridae, with elongate body and large canine teeth.

zoanthid—any of the sea mats of the anthozoan order Zoantharia, colonial polyps up to several inches in height, usually interconncted at the base by a sheet of tissue and lacking a skeleton, often exhibited in minireef aquariums.

zooplankton—nonphotosynthetic organisms suspended or swimming in the water column, often feeding on phytoplankton and in turn providing food for a variety of larger organisms.

zooxanthellae—dinoflagellate algae living in mutualistic symbiosis with certain invertebrates, including many species of cnidarians and mollusks kept in minireef aquariums; they are of critical importance in the physiology of reef-building stony corals.

Appendix D

Additional Saltwater Aquarium Resources

Loads of information is out there for saltwater aquarium hobbyists. Here are just some of the sources you can use to find detailed information about particular fish, invertebrates, or aquarium techniques.

Periodicals

Tropical Fish Hobbyist

Freshwater and Marine Aquarium

Aquarium

Aquarium USA (annual)

Organizations

American Marinelife Dealers Association
www.amdareef.com

Marine Aquarium Societies of North America
www.masna.org

Marine Aquarium Council
www.aquariumcouncil.org

Reef Protection International
www.reefprotect.org

Books

Adey, Walter H. and Karen Loveland. (1991) *Dynamic Aquaria*. Academic Press, New York.

Debelius, Helmut. (1989) *Fishes for the Invertebrate Aquarium*. Aquarium Systems, Mentor, OH.

Delbeek, J.Charles, and J. Sprung (1994) *The Reef Aquarium, Volume I*. Ricordea Publishing, Coconut Grove, FL.

Fautin, Daphne and Gerald Allen. (1986) *Field Guide to Anemonefishes and Their Host Sea Anemones*. Western Australian Museum, Perth.

Humann, Paul. (1990) *Reef Fish Identification*. New World Publications. Jacksonville, FL.

Kaplan, E.H. (1982) *A Field Guide to Coral Reefs of the Caribbean and Florida*. Houghton-Miflin Company, Boston, MA.

Knop, Daniel. (1996) *Giant Clams*. Dähne Verlag GmbH., Ettlingen, Germany.

Littler, Diane S., Mark M. Littler, Katina E. Bucher, and James N. Norris (1989) *Marine Plants of the Caribbean: a Field Guide from Florida to Brazil*. Smithsonian Institution Press, Washington, DC.

Magruder, William H. and Jeffrey W. Hunt. (1979) *Seaweeds of Hawaii*. Oriental Publishing Company, Honolulu, HI.

Moe, Martin A., Jr. (1989) *The Marine Aquarium Reference: Systems and Invertebrates*. Green Turtle Publications, Plantation, FL.

Myers, Robert F. (1989) *Micronesian Reef Fishes*. Coral Graphics, Guam.

Spotte, Stephen (1992) *Captive Seawater Fishes*. John Wiley & Sons, New York.

Sprung, Julian and J. Charles Delbeek (1997) *The Reef Aquarium, Volume 2*. Ricordea Publishing, Coconut Grove, FL.

Tullock, John (1997) *Natural Reef Aquariums*. TFH/Microcosm. Neptune, NJ

Veron, J.E.N. (1986) *Corals of Australia and the Indo-Pacific*. Angus and Robertson, North Ryde, NSW, Australia.

Index

C

D

E

F

J

K

L

O

P

Q

R

T

U

V

W

Y

Z